THE COMPLETE IDIOT'S GUIDE® TO

Pressure Cooking

by Carole Jacobs and Chef Patrice Johnson

ALPHA

A member of Penguin Group (USA) Inc.

ALPHA BOOKS

Published by the Penguin Group

Penguin Group (USA) Inc., 375 Hudson Street, New York, New York 10014, USA

Penguin Group (Canada), 90 Eglinton Avenue East, Suite 700, Toronto, Ontario M4P 2Y3, Canada (a division of Pearson Penguin Canada Inc.)

Penguin Books Ltd., 80 Strand, London WC2R 0RL, England

Penguin Ireland, 25 St. Stephen's Green, Dublin 2, Ireland (a division of Penguin Books Ltd.)

Penguin Group (Australia), 250 Camberwell Road, Camberwell, Victoria 3124, Australia (a division of Pearson Australia Group Pty. Ltd.)

Penguin Books India Pvt. Ltd., 11 Community Centre, Panchsheel Park, New Delhi—110 017, India

Penguin Group (NZ), 67 Apollo Drive, Rosedale, North Shore, Auckland 1311, New Zealand (a division of Pearson New Zealand Ltd.)

Penguin Books (South Africa) (Pty.) Ltd., 24 Sturdee Avenue, Rosebank, Johannesburg 2196, South Africa

Penguin Books Ltd., Registered Offices: 80 Strand, London WC2R 0RL, England

Copyright © 2011 by Carole Jacobs and Patrice Johnson

International Standard Book Number: 978-1-61564-073-7
Library of Congress Catalog Card Number: 2011902714

15   8 7 6 5 4

Interpretation of the printing code: The rightmost number of the first series of numbers is the year of the book's printing; the rightmost number of the second series of numbers is the number of the book's printing. For example, a printing code of 11-1 shows that the first printing occurred in 2011.

Printed in the United States of America

Note: This publication contains the opinions and ideas of its authors. It is intended to provide helpful and informative material on the subject matter covered. It is sold with the understanding that the authors and publisher are not engaged in rendering professional services in the book. If the reader requires personal assistance or advice, a competent professional should be consulted.

The authors and publisher specifically disclaim any responsibility for any liability, loss, or risk, personal or otherwise, which is incurred as a consequence, directly or indirectly, of the use and application of any of the contents of this book.

Most Alpha books are available at special quantity discounts for bulk purchases for sales promotions, premiums, fund-raising, or educational use. Special books, or book excerpts, can also be created to fit specific needs.

For details, write: Special Markets, Alpha Books, 375 Hudson Street, New York, NY 10014.

Publisher: *Marie Butler-Knight*

Associate Publisher: *Mike Sanders*

Executive Managing Editor: *Billy Fields*

Senior Acquisitions Editors: *Brook Farling, Paul Dinas*

Senior Development Editor: *Christy Wagner*

Senior Production Editor: *Kayla Dugger*

Copy Editor: *Christine Hackerd*

Cover Designer: *Rebecca Batchelor*

Book Designers: *William Thomas, Rebecca Batchelor*

Indexer: *Johnna VanHoose Dinse*

Layout: *Ayanna Lacey*

Senior Proofreader: *Laura Caddell*

Contents

Appendixes

Introduction

It's so easy and fast to make meals in a pressure cooker, we can't imagine why every-one doesn't use one! You simply fill it up with your ingredients, put on the lid, set it on the stove, and crank up the heat, and in 70 percent less time than you'd need to cook the same meal using conventional cooking methods, you're sitting down to a delicious, homemade meal.

This wasn't always the case, however. In the 1940s and 1950s, manufacturers pro-duced inexpensive, low-quality pressure cookers that were prone to rupture, explode, and send supper to the ceiling. Over time, cooks relegated their cookers to the back burner and turned their attention to more reliable modern appliances such as the microwave oven.

Fortunately, today's pressure cookers are equipped with a bevy of safety features that make them 100 percent safe, fool-proof, and able to cook practically any kind of food to perfection—from corn on the cob and roast beef to chocolate fudge and lemon cream pie. After decades of suffering a bad reputation, pressure cooking is finally enjoying a well-deserved Renaissance, with nearly 2 million cookers sold every year in the past 5 years.

If you've been afraid to buy a pressure cooker for fear it might destroy your meal—or maybe even your kitchen—this book will erase those fears and show you how to turn your pressure cooker into your very own personal chef.

For starters, pressure cooking is one of the fastest ways to get a meal on the table. If you're making pot roast, stews, or homemade spaghetti, a pressure cooker can collapse cooking time from several hours to several minutes. When you're crunched for time, a pressure cooker can mean the difference between eating nutritious, tasty meals and being forced to resort to that other kind of fast food, which is often high in fat and calories, low in nutrients and fiber, and devoid of taste.

Pressure cookers are also an economical way to cook, allowing you to feed the entire family for what you'd spend on one meal at a restaurant. Your pressure cooker excels at turning inexpensive cuts of meat into tender, juicy morsels, and at turning a hand-ful of inexpensive grains and vegetables into a savory soup, stew, or curry.

Unlike conventional cooking methods, which wash out valuable nutrients, pressure cookers preserve the flavors, colors, textures, and nutrients of foods, so you get more vitamins, minerals, and fiber for your food dollar. In addition, the high cooking tem-perature used with pressure cookers kills off most harmful bacteria and helps prevent food poisoning.

A pressure cooker is an extremely versatile kitchen appliance that allows you to prepare nearly any type of food in practically any way, including steaming, boiling, sautéing, puréeing, roasting, baking, braising, poaching, steam roasting, and stewing. With a pressure cooker, you won't have to invest in a steamer, an oven roaster, baking pans, sauté pans, sauce pans, skillets, dessert pans, slow cookers, or a microwave oven. Besides dollars spent on pots and pans, you'll also save on kitchen counter and cabinet space!

The pressure cooker makes cooking so easy, we predict you'll become a more confident and adventurous cook. You, too, can create homemade soups, stews, sauces, and stocks without being glued to the Food Channel or going to an expensive cooking class.

We love the pressure cooker, but we admit it's not a wonder machine. There are a few things it can't do, such as produce a fluffy omelet, a crispy pepperoni pizza, a savory gazpacho, or a fragrant loaf of yeast bread. But when you understand your pressure cooker's limitations as well as its full potential, you may wonder how you ever made a meal without one.

How This Book Is Organized

Part 1, Getting Started, teaches you everything you need to know before using a pressure cooker for the first time. We explain how a pressure cooker works, how they've evolved over the years, and why they're faster and more efficient than conventional cooking methods. We also show you the many different ways you can cook using your pressure cooker, the best foods for pressure cooking, along with some necessary accessories. Tips for cleaning, maintaining, and storing your pressure cooker so it lasts for years are also shared.

Part 2, Sensational Starters, shows you how to use your pressure cooker to make fast, easy, and delicious dishes that start off any day or meal right. You'll find recipes for dips, appetizers, finger foods, and salads, as well as egg-based dishes that work great for breakfast, brunch, or a light bite any time of day.

Part 3, Soup's On!, demonstrates how to use the pressure cooker to make fast and delicious homemade stocks, soups, and chowders from scratch. The recipes in Part 3 run the gamut, from vegetable soups and stocks, to meaty soups with foreign flair, to tasty poultry soups, to seafood-based soups.

Part 4, Sultry Stews and Curries, shows you how to create innovative stews and curries in record time using vegetables, meat, poultry, seafood, and a dash of seasonings and spices. From homey chicken stews that warm a cold winter's night, to sophisticated five-alarm curries that ignite everyone's taste buds, you'll find a stew or curry for every occasion.

Part 5, Everyday Entrées, demonstrates how to use your pressure cooker to create effortless entrées and one-pot wonders, with recipes for everything from Monday night suppers to special company dinners. You also learn how to make amazing main dishes that revolve around beef, poultry, pork, ham, and lamb.

Part 6, On the Side, teaches you how to make scrumptious side dishes that add interest and variety to a meal. You learn how to make amazing grains without the hassles of soaking, as well as sauces, toppings, and condiments that add fun and flavor to any dish.

Part 7, Sweet Surrender, reveals the secret sweet side of pressure cooking and shows you how to make delicate desserts and melt-in-your-mouth confections that give any meal a grand finale. From cheesecakes, custards, and puddings, to fruity desserts and fudge, these recipes are guaranteed to satisfy the most discriminating sweet tooth.

Extras

Throughout the book, we give you sidebars that provide extra information, helpful tips, and fascinating facts. Here's what to look for:

FOODIE FACT

Check out these sidebars for fascinating food facts, culinary trivia, and amusing quotes about food. You'll impress your friends and sound like a real foodie!

PRESSURE POINTER

Pressure Pointers are full of helpful tips and suggestions to make pressure cooking faster, easier, safer, and more fun.

STEAM SPEAK

Cooking has a language of its own, and if you don't know what something means, it could affect the final outcome of the recipe. Check out these sidebars for helpful definitions and explanations.

UNDER PRESSURE

It's always helpful to be warned of potential problems in advance. These sidebars provide a friendly heads-up about things to avoid for safer and more efficient pressure cooking.

Acknowledgments

We'd like to thank our agent, Robert DiForio, the great editorial team at Alpha, and our many family members and friends who offered their palates to taste-test the recipes in this book. We'd also like to thank our prospective pressure cookers—Carole's "Steamy Wonder" and Chef Patrice's "Little Hisser"—for churning out some of the most delicious food on the planet.

Trademarks

Getting Started

Today's pressure cookers are light-years removed from the cookers your granny used to use. Equipped with numerous safety features, they're safe, efficient, and virtually foolproof, delivering dinner in a third less time and using much less energy than conventional cooking methods. As well as saving you time and energy costs, modern-day pressure cookers preserve more of foods' nutrients, flavors, colors, and textures than traditional cooking methods. They're also an extremely economical way to cook, turning tough, inexpensive meats into fork-tender morsels, and creating sensational soups and stews from a handful of grains, beans, and pasta.

In Part 1, we take a quick look at how pressure cookers have evolved over the years to become safer, more efficient, and virtually goof-proof. We also review the basic principles and techniques of pressure cooking to give you a better understanding of how pressure cookers work. We show you beginner and advanced techniques for creating a wide variety of foods, tell you the best foods to cook in your pressure cooker, and provide a short list of foods not suitable for pressure cookers.

Once you discover how easy, fast, and foolproof pressure cooking is, you may find yourself using your pressure cooker on a daily basis to create everything from breakfast soufflés and savory soups to one-pot roasts and sinfully scrumptious desserts. *Bon appétit!*

Pressure Cooker Basics

In This Chapter

- Getting to know your pressure cooker
- Pressure cooker safety
- Cooking with pressure and steam
- What to cook … and what not to cook
- Pressure cooker accessories
- Keeping your pressure cooker clean and safe

Remember that delicious pot roast your grandmother used to make—the one that tasted like she slaved over a hot stove all day? Chances are pretty good she created it in mere minutes using her handy pressure cooker.

Even if you can't boil water, or if the only kitchen appliance you're comfortable using is your microwave oven, by the time you finish this book, you'll know how to use your pressure cooker to create awesome appetizers, scrumptious brunches, homemade soups and stews—even a four-course dinner. That's how easy pressure cooking really is!

Understanding your pressure cooker is essential to producing high-quality home-cooked foods. In this chapter, you learn how your pressure cooker works and what you can—and should not—do to maximize its versatility and efficiency.

The Anatomy of a Pressure Cooker

Unlike the one-size-fits-all pressure cookers of yesteryear, modern-day pressure cookers are made of aluminum or stainless steel and come in a variety of sizes, from $2\frac{1}{2}$ to 12 quarts. If you're cooking for just one or two, a small pressure cooker could be the perfect kitchen companion. On the other hand, if you have a large family or you entertain a lot, a large pressure cooker can make cooking for a crowd effortless. The 6-quart pressure cooker is the most popular pressure cooker for home use. Small enough to fit on any kitchen stove, it's big enough to feed a family of 6 with leftovers.

You can still buy inexpensive aluminum pressure cookers, but a stainless-steel pressure cooker is a much better investment for your money. Stronger and sturdier than aluminum pressure cookers, they're also equipped with a three-ply plate attached to the bottom of the pot that distributes heat more evenly and helps prevent burning and scorching.

FOODIE FACT

Cooking with pressure is nothing new. More than 300 years ago, people used cast-iron pots with tight-fitting lids to "pressure cook" their food over hot cinders. Alfred Vischer invented the first official home pressure cooker in 1938. His 4-quart cast-iron "Flex Speed Cooker" debuted at a New York City trade show and was an overnight sensation.

If you're mechanically challenged or klutzy around moving parts, you'll be happy to know that today's pressure cooker is the ultimate in simplicity, with no moving parts and only four major components: the pot and lid, the plastic handles, the rubber gasket, and the pressure regulator valve. Let's take a closer look at what each part does.

The Pot and Lid

The pot and lid are the two main parts of a pressure cooker. Unlike early pressure cookers, the pot and lid on modern-day pressure cookers self-lock into place and create an enclosed system in which heat builds steam and creates the pressure to cook food faster.

Today's pressure cookers have safety features that make it impossible for you to peek during the cooking process, which eliminates the risk of sending food rocketing to the ceiling. You also can't open the lid before the pressure has been released, which reduces the risk of getting nasty burns from escaping steam.

In short, modern-day pressure cookers are foolproof, even if users always aren't. You must lock the lid into place before the pressure cooker begins cooking and building pressure, and you won't be able to budge the lid until you've released all the pressure from the pressure cooker. If you were planning to spy on your pressure cooker while it was doing its thing, you've been foiled.

Safety Handles

Today's pressure cooker pots are equipped with two heat-resistant plastic handles and two matching handles on the cover that work together to make it safer than ever to use your pressure cooker. The handles make it easier to lift the pot, which weighs 7 or 8 pounds empty and 25 pounds or more when filled with liquids and food, plus they also line up and indicate that your pressure cooker is closed properly.

Some pressure cookers are equipped with high-tech handles that contain a locking mechanism that must be activated to lock the cover in place. Others have handles that self-lock when the cover is turned and locked into place.

The Rubber Gasket

The gasket is the rubber seal in the lid of the pressure cooker. The most important part of the pressure cooker, the gasket traps steam inside the pot, where it builds into pressure and creates steam that cooks the food inside. Without a gasket, you're not pressure cooking.

> **UNDER PRESSURE**
>
> Gaskets are not eternal. Over time, they age, dry out, and develop wrinkles and cracks. Those imperfections eventually destroy the airtight seal between the pot and lid and make it impossible for your pressure cooker to build pressure. To be sure your gasket is alive and well, check it after every use and replace it at least once a year. Never use a pressure cooker with a damaged gasket.

Pressure Regulator Valves

Pressure regulator valves are fixtures that let you control the amount of pressure inside the closed pot. There are two types of regulator valves, including the older, jiggle-top regulator valve and the modern stationary pressure regulator, which is built into the pressure cooker's lid.

The older, jiggle-top valve is a heavy, removable weight that fits on top of the steam-vent pipe in the center of the lid. When pressure reaches the desired level, steam is released through the vent and jiggles the weight.

Stationary valves are spring-operated rods that rise silently to indicate pressure as it builds up in the pressure cooker. On some models, you can adjust their dials to set the pressure. Some pressure cookers have dials as well as rods.

Safety First

When the European pressure cooker was finally introduced to the United States in the 1980s, Americans, initially skeptical, were eventually won over by the design improvements. In time, American manufacturers began producing high-quality pressure cookers that duplicated the European-style safety and efficiency features. In the early 1990s, the pressure cooker became the darling of celebrity chef cooking shows, and by 2000, more than 2 million pressure cookers were being sold in the United States every year. After three decades of being shunned and ridiculed, the pressure cooker was finally reborn in America.

Cooking with Pressure

The pressure cooker, as the name implies, uses pressure in the cooking process. A large, heavy lid locks into place on top of the pot and forms an airtight seal, trapping steam inside the pot. This causes pressure to build and forces the temperature to rise above the boiling point.

How It Works

The principle behind pressure cooking is very simple. All liquids containing water boil at 212°F, with the exception of oil and fat. When water boils, it creates steam, which is 38°F hotter than boiling water. The steam is the "fuel" that cooks the food inside your pressure cooker.

You can control the pressure inside the pressure cooker by lowering or increasing the heat on the stove. The more you increase the heat and pressure in a pressure cooker, the higher the temperature rises inside the pressure cooker, and the faster the food cooks.

When pressure cooking, the cooking countdown begins when the pressure cooker reaches the desired level of pressure, not when you put the pressure cooker on the stove or heat source. You set your timer when the pressure cooker reaches the desired pressure level. Because pressure cookers cook food up to three times faster than conventional cooking methods, if you start the countdown too early, you'll end up with mush or burnt food.

 FOODIE FACT

For every 1,000 feet above 2,000 feet you live, increase the cooking time and amount of liquid by 5 percent. For example, if you live at 4,000 feet, increase the cooking time and amount of liquid by 10 percent.

PSI Primer

PSI, or pounds per square inch, is how pressure is measured in pressure cooking. The higher the pressure, the hotter the food is cooking. Most modern-day pressure cookers have three PSI settings—high, medium, and low—each of which corresponds to a specific temperature or range of temperatures:

- High pressure, 15psi, is the most common setting for pressure cooking and is used to cook the vast majority of foods.

- Medium pressure, between 8psi and 10psi, is the equivalent of 234°F to 240°F. This setting is used for rice and steamed desserts such as custards, puddings, and flans.

- Low pressure, 5psi, is the equivalent of 228°F. This setting is used to pressure cook delicate foods such as seafood and tender-crisp produce.

Letting Off Steam

Once the food in your pressure cooker is cooked, you must allow the pressure to be released from the pressure cooker so the temperature and pressure inside the pot can drop and the food can stop cooking. You should release the pressure immediately after the designated cooking time listed in the recipe, using the release method specified in the recipe.

There are three ways to release pressure from your pressure cooker. Each recipe in this book calls for a specific release method, so be sure to note which method is called for before you release the steam from the pot.

The *natural release method* is the easiest, slowest, and most common way to release pressure. Simply remove the pressure cooker from the heat source and let the pressure inside the pot decrease naturally without removing the lid from the pressure cooker. Usually, this takes about 15 minutes. The natural release method is the best method to use for foods like pot roast and stock that you want to continue cooking for a few more minutes so they become more flavorful.

The *quick release method* is the best method for interrupted cooking, or when you're going to be stopping the cooking process frequently to add ingredients, because it allows the pressure cooker to return quickly to the required pressure. Many modern-day pressure cookers are equipped with a built-in quick release mechanism that lets you quick release the pressure without lowering the temperature of the food.

The *cold water release method* is the fastest way to stop the cooking process because it rapidly lowers both the pressure and temperature of the food. Use this method for foods with a short cooking time, or when you need to stop the cooking process very quickly, such as when you're making delicate seafood or tender-crisp vegetables.

With a little practice, you'll be able to release pressure without thinking twice. In the meantime, here are a few tips to keep in mind:

- Never open the lid of the pressure cooker while food is still cooking. The cooking temperature in pressure cookers is extremely hot and can give you a nasty burn.

- Always release pressure immediately after the designated cooking time stated in the recipe. If you wait too long, the food may become mushy or burnt.

- Never fill your pressure cooker more than half full of food or two-thirds full of liquid. Liquids boil harder and faster at higher temperatures, while foods tend to increase in volume.

- Be sure to use enough liquid in your pressure cooker so your pressure cooker can build pressure, or at least 1 or 2 cups, depending on your pressure cooker, and at least 3 cups if you're steaming foods in a steaming basket or on a rack.

Vital Accessories

While your pressure cooker is practically a Jack-of-all-trades, by investing in a few accessories, you can dramatically expand its usefulness and make a wider variety of recipes.

Most modern-day pressure cookers come with a stainless-steel or aluminum rack or trivet, a necessary accessory for pressure cooking. Racks have many different uses, but their general purpose is to raise food above the water or liquid in the pressure cooker so food can steam more efficiently. Racks also prevent food from burning and scorching the bottom of the pressure cooker. If your pressure cooker didn't come with one, you can buy a collapsible, 7-inch wire cake rack in a kitchen supply store, or improvise and use a collapsible stainless-steel steamer basket.

Another handy accessory is a steaming basket, which is about 7 inches in diameter and 2 or 3 inches long. Similar to a rack in that it keeps food out of contact with water or cooking liquid, you can use steaming baskets to steam large cuts of meat, such as roasts and chuck, as well as vegetables.

Insert pans are another must-have for pressure cookers. As their name implies, insert pans are pans, dishes, and ramekins you place on racks inside the pressure cooker so you can cook different foods at once or several individual-size servings of food. Insert pans range from Bundt pans, quiche pans, nonstick loaf pans, and nonstick spring form pans, to individual-size ramekins and custard dishes.

Another accessory you'll need if you use your pressure cooker regularly is a set of storage containers. Stock up on pint- and quart-size stacking freezer containers for freezing stock and leftovers. Remember that even a small, 6-quart pressure cooker makes enough food that you'll probably have leftovers. If you have a large pressure cooker, you can save time and money by making large batches of recipes and freezing the leftovers in meal-size containers.

Pressure cooking is an exact science where every second of cooking counts. To be sure your food doesn't overcook or undercook, invest in a digital timer that tracks the time down to seconds. You may also want to invest in a waterproof digital thermometer to test the temperature of foods inside the cooker.

Also, have nonstick cooking spray and nonstick parchment paper on hand to line pans so foods won't stick to them.

Finally, consider investing in a heat-safe glove that's fire-proof and insulated to protect you against high temperatures. Most brands fit either hand and cost $15 to $30.

Caring for Your Pressure Cooker

Give your pressure cooker lots of TLC, and it will reward you with years of reliable, foolproof service without the need for expensive repairs.

Cleaning Tips

Before using your pressure cooker for the first time, and after each use, wash it thoroughly in hot, soapy water, using a sponge or cloth for general cleaning. Dry it thoroughly before storing. Never put it in the dishwater.

The gasket is the most important player on your pressure cooker, so be sure to remove it from the lid after each use, and clean it manually in hot soapy water. Be careful not to stretch or twist it, and look for signs of wear such as small tears or cracks that may indicate you need a new gasket. If you're installing a new gasket, be sure you put it in the lid with the printed side face-up.

To remove burnt or scorched food from your pressure cooker, heat the pot, add 1 cup water until the water vaporizes, and immediately scrape the pan with a straight-edge spatula. Wash the pan in soapy water and dry it thoroughly. After cooking foods that froth or foam, remove the valve and clean according to the manufacturers' guidelines.

Maintenance Tips

Like any appliance, your pressure cooker will perform better and last longer if you maintain it after each use. Follow these tips to keep it in tip-top shape:

- Replace gaskets regularly. In addition to tell-tale cracks and tears, you can tell it's time to replace your gasket if your pressure cooker won't pressurize. Overheating and damage caused by hot fats and oils may also make gaskets wear out faster. To be safe, keep a supply of gaskets on hand so you have a spare when you need one.

- Be sure the valves on the lid are clean and that all the parts move freely. Clean the small overpressure valve with a small brush, and disassemble the pressure regulator valve units every month or so and wash by hand with a small brush in hot, soapy water. Let all parts air dry thoroughly before reassembling.

- Periodically tighten all screws on your pressure cooker to ensure they're snug.

Storage Tips

Always be sure your pressure cooker is clean and thoroughly dry before putting it away. Never store your pressure cooker with the lid on because odors will accumulate and the gasket will become compressed. Store the pressure cooker with the gasket loose on the lid, but removed from the groove.

To protect fragile parts of the pressure cooker during storage, invert the lid and put it on top of the pressure cooker to protect the valve or vent pipe. If you're going to be storing your pressure cooker for more than a few months, place the detachable pressure regulator and gasket inside the pressure cooker, and sprinkle with 2 table-spoons baking soda to absorb odors and moisture. Invert the lid and put it on top of the pressure cooker to protect the valve or vent pipe from damage. Wash the cooker, regulator, and gasket again before using.

Warranty Matters

A high-quality stainless-steel pressure cooker should last about 25 years if handled properly. Expect to pay anywhere from $40 to $100 for a 6-quart cooker. Be sure your pressure cooker comes with a warranty that covers it for at least 10 years. If you want, you can take out additional coverage to cover the other 15 years.

PRESSURE POINTER

Remember that replaceable parts of your pressure cooker, including gaskets, are not under warranty and should be replaced periodically. If possible, buy your pressure cooker from a qualified retailer who stocks replacement parts, and be sure the manufacturer of your pressure cooker has a customer service line you can call or a website you can log on to for information on replacement parts and repairs.

Finally, read the fine print carefully. Warranties differ greatly in terms of what they cover, and for how long. Be sure your pressure cooker's manufacturer hasn't set unrealistic restrictions that would make it difficult for you to get coverage in the event your machine needs repairs.

The Least You Need to Know

- Pressure cookers use a combination of pressure and intense heat from trapped steam to cook food 70 percent faster than conventional cooking methods, while preserving nutrients, flavors, and textures.

- Unlike early pressure cookers, which had a reputation for exploding and rupturing, modern-day pressure cookers are equipped with safety features and improved valves that make them 100 percent safe, efficient, and foolproof.

- Pressure cookers prepare food in many different ways and eliminate the need to buy separate pots and pans for boiling, braising, sautéing, steaming, baking, and deep-frying.

- A few inexpensive accessories, including racks, steaming baskets, and insert pans, will dramatically expand your pressure cooker's usefulness and the type of dishes you can make.

- With routine cleaning, maintenance, and proper storing, a high-quality stainless-steel pressure cooker can last 25 years.

Pressure Cooking Techniques

In This Chapter

- Finding the pressure cooker for you
- Getting started with your pressure cooker
- The importance of a trial run
- Beginner and advanced cooking tips
- Seasoning and your pressure cooker

Modern-day pressure cookers are very easy to use. Because they have very few moving parts, they rarely break or malfunction. In addition, new safety features prevent the pressure cooker from exploding, rupturing, and spewing steaming-hot food all over you and your kitchen.

That said, things can go wrong, especially if you're new to pressure cooking or if you're using an antiquated, hand-me-down pressure cooker. Pressure cooking certainly isn't rocket science, but if you've never used a pressure cooker before, this is no time for a blind date! Before you put that pressure cooker on the burner, be sure you understand how it operates and what each part does.

In this chapter, we give you pointers for choosing a pressure cooker, share some tips and techniques, and help you season your way to success!

Tips for Beginners

As with any kitchen appliance, you'll want to learn some basic guidelines for safe and efficient pressure cooking so you get off to a safe start.

Before preparing anything, read your recipe all the way through to be sure you understand all the steps and you have everything you need on hand.

Pressure cooking happens very quickly, so before you put the pot on the burner, be sure you have all the ingredients for the dish cleaned, trimmed, chopped, diced, sliced, and otherwise ready to go. Remember, every second counts in pressure cooking, and overcooking food just a little could turn it into baby food.

When in doubt, undercook rather than overcook foods. You can always cook undercooked food a few more minutes until it's done, but once food turns to mush, there's no turning back.

Choose the Right Pressure Cooker

Manufacturers are still making inexpensive first-generation aluminum jiggle-top pressure cookers, but second-generation stainless-steel pressure cookers are well worth the extra cost because they're easier to use, more energy-efficient, and equipped with advanced safety features.

For safety reasons, buy a pressure cooker that has a long handle as well as a short handle, not a pressure cooker with two short handles. With a long handle, you're less likely to touch the hot pressure cooker and burn yourself. A long handle also makes it easier to lock the lid into place and carry the pressure cooker from one burner to another or to the kitchen sink.

Avoid aluminum pressure cookers if possible. Although they're less expensive, they're lighter and more prone to damage and warping, which can prevent the pot and lid from forming an airtight seal. Because aluminum is thinner than stainless steel, food is also more likely to scorch and burn. Aluminum pressure cookers may impart a flavor and smell to food. Over time, aluminum pressure cookers may also develop pits and dents that can become a breeding ground for bacteria.

UNDER PRESSURE

Beware of faddish pressure cookers with extra "special" features that cost more but do nothing other than give you headaches. These include pressure cookers with nonstick interiors (over time, the interior erodes and flakes into food) and electric pressure cookers, which have fewer controls and safety features than regular pressure cookers. Also avoid pressure cookers that cook only at low pressure. Most recipes call for cooking at high pressure, so using a pressure cooker with low pressure will force you to spend a lot of time adapting ingredients and cooking times.

Before buying any pressure cooker, check out reviews conducted by independent testing organizations such as Underwriters Laboratories (ul.com) or Consumer Reports (consumerreports.org).

Beginning Cooking Methods

Most people never go beyond learning one or two basic pressure cooker techniques, such as steaming or boiling. There are actually many different ways to use the moist steam of pressure cookers to prepare a variety of foods. The more techniques you know how to use, the more foods you'll be able to make in your pressure cooker. Let's look at some beginner techniques you can use to create a wide array of scrumptious foods:

Steaming is the most popular way to use a pressure cooker. It's also one of the healthiest ways to prepare foods because no additional fat is required, and it also preserves nutrients and vitamins. Steaming is very fast and takes just a few minutes for most foods. Use steaming to create fluffy rice and other grains; delicate fish and seafood; tender-crisp vegetables; and steamed desserts like cheesecakes, custards, puddings, and flans.

Infusion cooking means using broths, marinades, and other liquids to infuse flavors into foods. When you use your pressure cooker to infuse flavors, the cooking liquids penetrate deep inside the foods and don't just float on the outside like they do with conventional cooking methods. Infusion cooking is a great way to infuse flavor into thin cuts of meat, poultry, fruit, polenta, and risotto.

You probably already know how to *boil* water in your pressure cooker. But don't stop at water! You can use your pressure cooker to boil inedible bones so they become delicious stocks and broths or turn tough cuts of meat into tender forkfuls.

Pressure cooker *stewing* is similar to infusion, but instead of using broths or marinades, you use water. Stewing is the perfect way to cook small pieces of meat, and it also makes tough cuts of meat extremely tender. You can also use the stewing method to make stewed vegetables and fruits.

PRESSURE POINTER

The pressure cooker is very forgiving, but you can't just haphazardly throw everything into the pot and expect it to come out appetizing. If you're making a dish with meat, partially thaw and brown or sauté it before placing it in the pressure cooker. Otherwise, you'll get a tasteless, bland, gray, mystery meat. To ensure vegetables cook evenly, cut them into uniform sizes. Otherwise, you could wind up with peas that crack dental fillings and carrots that have the consistency of purée.

You can also use your pressure cooker to *precook* large cuts of meat, poultry, ham, lamb, and pork that would otherwise take hours to cook by conventional methods. For instance, precook barbecued ribs or chicken wings in the pressure cooker and then pop them on the grill or under the broiler and baste them with barbecue sauce to give them a smoky flavor and those authentic grill stripes.

Your pressure cooker is also a master at *braising*, or cooking and tenderizing tough meat. Unlike stewing, where food is cut into small pieces, when you braise food, you cut it into serving-size portions and cook it in water, stock, wine, beer, or juice, with the liquid covering just half of the item being braised.

To *poach* is to cook food in a small amount of liquid, usually water (although seasoning may be added), so the food maintains its natural texture, delicate flavor, and tenderness. After the food is poached, you can reserve the liquid as a broth or reduce it so flavors intensify and serve it with the poached food. Use poaching for small or thin cuts of food that cook quickly.

Advanced Methods

After you've mastered the beginner techniques, you're ready to up the ante with advanced techniques that will really impress your family and friends! These tips take a little more practice to perfect, but once you see the culinary doors they open, you'll be glad you took the time to master them.

Officially called *interrupted cooking*, you use this two-step approach when you're making a dish with ingredients that take varying times to cook. In interrupted cooking, you start the ingredients that take the longest to cook in the pressure cooker first. When those ingredients are cooked, you remove the pot from the heat, use the quick release method to release the pressure, remove the lid, and add the ingredients that take less time to cook.

Interrupted cooking is a great technique to use when you're making two-step dishes like beef stew, where the beef takes 15 minutes to cook and the vegetables only require 5 minutes. If you're cooking foods with varying cooking times and you don't want to use the interrupted cooking method, you can cheat by cutting quick-cooking foods into larger pieces, cutting long-cooking foods into smaller pieces, and putting everything in the pot at once.

Pan-in-pot cooking is exactly what it sounds like—you put an insert pan into the pressure cooker and cook food in the pan separately. This is a great technique for making a one-pot meal, cooking a single serving of rice or pasta, or creating creamy desserts like cheesecake and custards. Because the insert pan sits on a rack above the water or cooking liquid, there's little risk of foods burning or scorching.

Tiered cooking is basically pan-in-pot cooking, but on steroids. Instead of using just one pan, you use two, three, or even more pans. And no, you don't have to be Martha Stewart to pull this off. All you need is a couple racks, a trivet with two or more tiers, and some practice. Use the bottom tier or rack to cook the longest-cooking foods, such as meats, and the upper racks or tiers for side dishes that take less time to cook. Once you get the hang of it, you'll be able to amaze your friends and family by making four-course meals in one pot!

PRESSURE POINTER

Clay, ceramic, and glass dishes are poor at conducting heat and should never be used in your pressure cooker. Use aluminum or stainless-steel insert pans instead. If you don't have the right type or size pan, you can wrap food in aluminum foil and seal it tightly to create a packet. Or get creative and turn a 1-pound coffee can, muffin tins, or empty aluminum food cans into impromptu cooking pans.

During *steam roasting and baking*, you place foods on a rack or steaming basket above water level and cook in steam. Because less moisture is lost during steam roasting and baking than during traditional roasting and baking, you get meats, vegetables, casseroles, breads, and cakes that are more tender, moist, and flavorful. Before steam roasting or baking meat, sear it in hot fat and brown on both sides so the juices stay inside the meat.

Seasoning Savvy

Pressure cooking tends to intensify flavors, so a little seasoning goes a long way. As a general rule when seasoning foods for pressure cooking, use about half the amount of seasonings you'd use for conventional cooking methods.

Fresh herbs tend to lose their flavor when cooked in the pressure cooker. To maximize their flavor, add them to the dish just before serving. And go easy on the salt and pepper before cooking. Better yet, wait until the food is cooked and then add salt and pepper to taste.

> **UNDER PRESSURE**
>
> If you add too much salt to the pressure cooker, you can undo most of the damage by adding a few sliced potatoes to the cooking liquid and remove them before serving. The potatoes will absorb a lot of the salt as it cooks. If you add too much pepper, there's really no effective way to cool the flames. You can either start over, or warn your family or friends that you're serving a three-alarm dinner!

Full-flavored oils, such as peanut oil, become more potent when cooked in a pressure cooker. To prevent a full-flavored oil from flavoring or altering the taste of a dish, use a bland or mild-flavored vegetable oil such as canola oil.

Always brown foods in the pressure cooker before you start cooking under pressure. Browning meats, poultry, and vegetables in the pressure cooker adds flavor and richness to the cooking liquid and is very easy to do. Just add a little canola oil to the pressure cooker, heat it until it's hot, and add the food to be browned. Be careful not to overbrown foods because pressure cookers also intensify the flavors of burnt foods!

The Least You Need to Know

- Stainless-steel pressure cookers, although more expensive than aluminum pressure cookers, are safer, more efficient, and well worth the extra cost.

- Most people with pressure cookers learn just a few techniques and never tap the full potential of their pressure cookers. The more techniques you know, the more recipes you can make and enjoy, so make the effort to master beginner as well as advanced techniques.

- Cooking begins when the food reaches pressure, not when you put the pressure cooker on the burner.

Sensational Starters

Whether you're planning a birthday dinner, hosting an office get-together, or looking for some super snacks, the starter recipes in Part 2 can set the tone for a delicious meal, stand alone as delicious and attractive finger foods, or serve as scrumptious breakfast or brunch dishes that wake up your taste buds and energize your morning.

From incredible dips and awesome appetizers to sensational salads and light bites revolving around eggs that start your day off right, your pressure cooker can make starters in a fraction of the time required by conventional cooking methods. Whether you're making a family friendly breakfast or sophisticated appetizers for a party, your pressure cooker has the starters covered.

Dippity Dos

In This Chapter

- Quick and easy dips
- Hearty bean dips
- Sensational seafood and veggie dips
- Dips go ethnic

If you thought your pressure cooker was just for making stews and soups, you're about to be surprised. In this chapter, we look at your pressure cooker's incredible versatility at mastering delectable dips that give any meal or party a festive start. These dip recipes showcase regional and international flavors, such as Italian Caponata, Spanish Olive Tapenade, Southwestern Garlic Hummus, and all-American Spinach Dip.

Dip's Best Friends

Dips made in your pressure cooker will come out rich, savory, and creamy-smooth, with colors, flavors, textures, and nutrients intact. Plus, your pressure cooker keeps dips piping hot without burning or scorching them. You can serve them from the pressure cooker and have one less dish to wash.

The dips in this chapter are rich and thick and call for sturdy dippers that won't break or get mushy. For the Southwestern dips, try corn chips or tortilla chips. Crackers, pita toast, pita bread, and mini-rounds of bread work great for caponata, tapenade, and pâté, while carrot, celery, and pepper sticks give bean and veggie dips extra crunch and flavor and up the nutrition ante.

Garlic Hummus

The mellow flavor of roasted garlic melds with the nuttiness of chickpeas in this zesty dip with a Middle Eastern flair.

Yield:	Prep time:	Cook time:	Serving size:
4 cups	15 minutes plus over-night refrigeration	30 minutes	¼ cup

2 cups dried chickpeas

9 cups water

4 heads roasted garlic

2 TB. freshly squeezed lemon juice (or bottled)

½ cup creamy peanut butter

2 tsp. kosher salt

½ tsp. freshly ground black pepper

1. Rinse chickpeas in a colander, and place in a large bowl. Cover beans with 6 cups water, and let soak overnight.

2. Drain beans, and discard soaking water. In a pressure cooker over high heat, combine beans and remaining 3 cups water.

3. Lock the lid in place. Bring to high pressure, and maintain for 30 minutes. Remove from heat, and reduce pressure using the cold water release method.

4. Let beans cool for 10 minutes. Transfer to a food processor fitted with a steel blade, or a blender, and purée for 2 or 3 minutes or until smooth. Stir in roasted garlic, lemon juice, peanut butter, kosher salt, and pepper.

5. Transfer hummus to a bowl, cover with plastic wrap, and refrigerate overnight to let flavors mingle. Serve with fresh vegetables or crackers.

UNDER PRESSURE

When soaking beans, never add salt to the water. It will toughen the bean skins and lengthen the cooking time, often to the point that the beans never cook. For best results, salt beans during their final cooking to improve their flavor.

Pinto Bean Dip

This dip combines *pinto beans*, green chiles, cilantro, and spicy cheeses for a fresh taste that takes you south of the border.

Yield:	Prep time:	Cook time:	Serving size:
4 cups	15 minutes	50 minutes	1 cup

3 cups canned pinto beans, rinsed	½ cup canned diced green chiles
1 tsp. kosher salt	2 cloves garlic, peeled and minced
½ tsp. freshly ground black pepper	1 tsp. fresh minced cilantro
3 TB. extra-virgin olive oil	½ cup grated Mexican cheese blend
3 cups water	

1. In a pressure cooker over high heat, combine pinto beans, kosher salt, pepper, extra-virgin olive oil, and water, ensuring beans are completely covered.

2. Lock the lid in place. Bring to high pressure, and maintain for 50 minutes. Remove from heat, and reduce pressure using the quick release method.

3. Transfer pinto beans to a bowl, and let cool for 10 minutes.

4. Place pinto beans in a food processor fitted with a steel blade, or in a blender, and purée for 2 or 3 minutes or until smooth.

5. Scrape mixture into a large bowl. Stir in green chiles, garlic, cilantro, and Mexican cheese blend.

6. Transfer dip to a slow cooker or fondue pot to keep warm. Serve immediately with tortilla chips.

STEAM SPEAK

Pinto beans are small, flavorful, reddish-brown beans popular in Spanish-speaking countries as well as the United States. In Mexico, they're called red Mexican beans. Pinto beans are available dried and canned year-round.

Fava Bean Dip

This light and healthy bean dip combines the nuttiness of fava beans with hints of onion, garlic, parsley, and paprika.

Yield:	Prep time:	Cook time:	Serving size:
2 cups	15 minutes plus over-night refrigeration	8 minutes	¼ cup

2 cups dried fava beans

3 cups water

4 cups chicken stock or canned chicken broth

1 large *Vidalia onion* or other sweet onion, chopped large

3 cloves garlic, minced

2 TB. minced fresh Italian parsley

5 TB. plus 2 tsp. extra-virgin olive oil

2 tsp. kosher salt

½ tsp. freshly ground black pepper

1 tsp. paprika

1. In a pressure cooker, combine fava beans and water, ensuring beans are completely covered with water. Soak overnight. Drain beans and discard soaking water, remove beans from the cooker, and peel off outer skin from beans.

2. In a pressure cooker over high heat, combine beans, chicken stock, onion, garlic, Italian parsley, and 5 tablespoons extra-virgin olive oil.

3. Lock the lid in place. Bring to high pressure, and maintain for 8 minutes. Remove from heat, and reduce pressure using the quick release method.

4. Remove onion, and drain mixture in a colander.

5. Return beans to the pressure cooker, and set over medium heat. Cook, uncovered and stirring constantly, for 5 minutes. Remove from heat and let beans cool. Transfer to a food processor fitted with a steel blade or a blender, and purée for 2 or 3 minutes or until beans are smooth.

6. Scrape into a serving bowl. Stir in kosher salt and pepper. Cover bowl with plastic wrap, and refrigerate overnight.

7. Transfer dip to a large, flat platter. Drizzle with remaining 2 teaspoons extra-virgin olive oil, and sprinkle with paprika. Serve with pita chips.

STEAM SPEAK

Vidalia onions are named after the town of Vidalia, Georgia, where they thrive. The region has the perfect combination of weather, water, and soil to produce some of the world's sweetest onions.

Black Bean and Mozzarella Dip

Black beans combine with mozzarella cheese, thyme, and picante sauce to create a savory dip that's hot and spicy.

Yield:	Prep time:	Cook time:	Serving size:
5 cups	15 minutes plus over-night soaking	20 minutes	1 cup

2 cups dried black beans	3 cloves garlic, minced
6 cups water	1 tsp. dried thyme
¾ cup grated mozzarella cheese	2 tsp. kosher salt
1 cup medium picante sauce	½ tsp. freshly ground black pepper
1 medium white or yellow onion, diced small	4 large green onions, white and green parts, chopped small

1. In a pressure cooker, combine black beans and 3 cups water, ensuring beans are completely covered with water. Soak overnight. Drain and discard soaking water. Cover beans with remaining 3 cups water.

2. Lock the lid in place, and set over medium heat. Bring to high pressure, and maintain for 25 minutes. Remove from heat, and reduce pressure using the quick release method.

3. Transfer beans to a colander, and rinse with cold water. Return beans to the pressure cooker, and reheat over low heat for 5 to 10 minutes. Stir in mozzarella cheese, and cook for 2 more minutes or until cheese is melted.

4. Stir in picante sauce, onion, garlic, thyme, kosher salt, and pepper.

5. Transfer dip to a fondue pot or place in a heated casserole to keep warm. Top with green onions, and serve immediately with tortilla chips.

PRESSURE POINTER

Cooked beans are more flavorful when they're made a day ahead of time, so consider making them the day before you plan on serving them. Store the beans tightly covered in their cooking liquid in the refrigerator, and use within 3 days.

Roasted Red Pepper Dip

Garlic and onion enliven this rich and spicy dip, which tastes like it was made with red peppers roasted on the grill.

Yield:	Prep time:	Cook time:	Serving size:
3 cups	15 minutes	10 minutes	1 cup

¼ cup extra-virgin olive oil

1 medium white or yellow sweet onion, diced small

4 cloves garlic, freshly minced

4 large red bell peppers, ribs and seeds removed, and cut into large cubes

2 TB. minced fresh Italian parsley

1 tsp. freshly ground black pepper

1 cup crumbled *feta cheese*

1. In a pressure cooker over medium heat, heat extra-virgin olive oil. Add onion, and cook for 3 to 5 minutes or until brown. Add garlic, and cook for about 30 seconds or until fragrant. Add bell peppers.

2. Lock the lid in place. Bring to high pressure, and maintain for 5 minutes. Remove from heat, and reduce pressure using the quick release method.

3. Let cool for 10 minutes. Transfer to a food processor fitted with a steel blade, or a blender, and purée for 2 or 3 minutes or until smooth. Add Italian parsley, pepper, and feta cheese.

4. Transfer to a serving bowl, cover with plastic wrap, and refrigerate for at least 4 hours to let flavors mingle. Serve with pita crisps or crackers.

STEAM SPEAK

One of the world's oldest cheeses, **feta cheese** has a rich, tangy flavor and creamy texture and ranges from semi-soft to semi-hard.

Spinach Dip

A pair of tasty cheeses gives this elegant spinach dip a rich and mellow flavor, while garlic and onion provide depth and zesty undertones.

Yield:	Prep time:	Cook time:	Serving size:
3 cups	10 minutes	2 minutes	¼ cup

2 TB. unsalted butter

1 large sweet onion, diced small

3 cloves garlic, minced

1 (24-oz.) pkg. frozen chopped spinach, thawed and squeezed dry

1 cup grated Parmesan cheese

2 cups grated Monterey Jack cheese

2 tsp. kosher salt

½ tsp. freshly ground black pepper

1. In a pressure cooker over medium heat, heat unsalted butter until melted. Add onion, and cook for 2 to 4 minutes or until soft. Add garlic, and cook for about 30 seconds or until fragrant. Stir in spinach.

2. Lock the lid in place. Bring to high pressure, and maintain for 2 minutes. Remove from heat, and reduce pressure using the quick release method.

3. Stir in Parmesan cheese, Monterey Jack cheese, kosher salt, and pepper. Reduce heat to low, and cook, uncovered and stirring frequently, for 30 seconds, or until cheese is melted.

4. Transfer mixture to a fondue pot or chafing dish to keep warm. Serve immediately with crackers.

FOODIE FACT

Spinach is packed with iron and vitamins A and C, but it also contains oxalic acid, which inhibits the body's absorption of calcium and iron and gives spinach its bitter flavor.

Caponata

This flavorful eggplant dip blends the rich flavors of balsamic vinegar, onion, and black olives for a fresh and tangy taste of Italy.

Yield:	Prep time:	Cook time:	Serving size:
3 cups	15 minutes	6 minutes plus 4 hours refrigeration	½ cup

¼ cup extra-virgin olive oil

½ cup dry white wine

2 TB. balsamic vinegar

1 large white onion, diced fine

3 ribs celery, diced small

1 large eggplant, peeled and diced small

3 cloves garlic, minced

2 TB. minced fresh Italian parsley

½ cup kalamata olives, pitted and chopped fine

1 tsp. kosher salt

1 tsp. freshly ground black pepper

1. In a pressure cooker over medium heat, combine extra-virgin olive oil, white wine, balsamic vinegar, onion, celery, eggplant, garlic, Italian parsley, and kalamata olives. Mix gently with a wooden spoon.

2. Lock the lid in place. Bring to high pressure, reduce heat to low, and maintain pressure for 6 minutes. Remove from heat, and reduce pressure using the quick release method.

3. Add kosher salt and pepper, and transfer *caponata* to a bowl and let cool. Cover with plastic wrap, and refrigerate for at least 4 hours to let flavors mingle.

4. Serve cold with fresh vegetables, crackers, or bagel chips.

STEAM SPEAK

Caponata is a popular Sicilian dish with many variations. The traditional version contains eggplant, tomatoes, olives, pine nuts, capers, anchovies, and vinegar cooked together in olive oil and served as a salad, side dish, or dip.

Olive Tapenade

This savory olive spread combines the fruity flavor of olives with the kick of onion and garlic and just a hint of lemon and parsley.

Yield:	Prep time:	Cook time:	Serving size:
2 cups	10 minutes	5 minutes	¼ cup

¼ cup extra-virgin olive oil	3 TB. freshly grated lemon zest
1 medium white onion, diced small	¼ cup freshly squeezed lemon juice
2 cloves garlic, minced	
1½ cups pitted kalamata olives	4 sprigs fresh parsley, minced
1½ cups pitted green olives	1 tsp. freshly ground black pepper

1. In a pressure cooker over medium heat, heat extra-virgin olive oil until hot. Add onion, and cook for 2 or 3 minutes or until soft. Add garlic, and cook for about 30 seconds or until fragrant. Add kalamata olives and green olives.

2. Lock the lid in place. Bring to high pressure, and maintain for 2 minutes. Remove from heat, and reduce pressure using the cold water release method.

3. Transfer olive mixture to a food processor fitted with a steel blade or a blender, and blend for 2 minutes or until very smooth. Stir in lemon zest, lemon juice, parsley, and pepper.

4. Scrape *tapenade* into a bowl, and serve at room temperature with baguettes. Or cover with plastic wrap and refrigerate for up to 2 days.

STEAM SPEAK

Originating in Provence, **tapenade** is a thick spread or paste with many variations. Traditional tapenade is made with ripe olives, capers, anchovies, lemon juice, and seasonings.

Liver Pâté

Ideal for parties, this elegant pâté has undertones of sage and thyme and just a kiss of Madeira wine.

Yield:	Prep time:	Cook time:	Serving size:
2 cups	15 minutes	20 minutes	1/8 cup

3 TB. unsalted butter or margarine	1/2 tsp. ground sage
1 large sweet onion, diced small	1/2 tsp. kosher salt
1 1/2 lb. chicken livers	1/4 tsp. freshly ground black pepper
1 TB. fresh thyme	3 TB. Madeira wine

1. In a pressure cooker over medium heat, heat unsalted butter until melted. Add onion, and cook for about 5 minutes or until soft. Do not brown.

2. Add chicken livers, and cook for about 3 minutes or until light brown.

3. Lock the lid in place, and increase heat to high. Bring to high pressure, and maintain for 4 minutes. Remove from heat, and reduce pressure using the quick release method.

4. Stir in thyme, sage, kosher salt, pepper, and Madeira wine.

5. Transfer mixture to a food processor fitted with a steel blade. Process for 1 or 2 minutes or until mixture is finely chopped but not completely puréed.

6. Scrape pâté into a small bowl, cover with plastic wrap, and refrigerate overnight. Remove pâté from the refrigerator and let stand at room temperature for 20 minutes before serving with toasted French baguette slices.

UNDER PRESSURE

Don't confuse *pâté,* French for "pie" and referring to preparations made with finely ground meat, with *pate,* which is French for "batter," "dough," or "pastry."

Savory Crab Cheesecake Dip

Worcestershire and hot sauces bring heat and spice to this rich and creamy dip with dill undertones.

Yield:	Prep time:	Cook time:	Serving size:
8 cups	15 minutes	25 minutes	1 cup

1 small white or yellow onion, diced small

1 (16-oz.) pkg. cream cheese, softened to room temperature

2 large eggs

½ cup sour cream

½ cup shredded medium cheddar cheese

1 tsp. dried dill weed

½ tsp. hot sauce

½ tsp. Worcestershire sauce

1 (18-oz.) can blue crabmeat, drained and squeezed dry

½ tsp. freshly ground black pepper

2 cups water

1. In a large bowl and using an electric mixer on medium speed, or in a food processor fitted with a metal blade, blend onion and cream cheese together for about 5 minutes or until very smooth.

2. Add eggs, sour cream, and cheddar cheese, and mix thoroughly. Add dill weed, hot sauce, and Worcestershire sauce. Fold in blue crabmeat and pepper.

3. Spray the bottom of a round 3-quart soufflé dish with nonstick cooking spray, place nonstick parchment paper in the pan, and spray the paper with nonstick cooking spray. Pour crab mixture into the dish, and cover tightly with a double layer of aluminum foil.

4. Insert a rack in the pressure cooker, and pour in water. Place soufflé dish on the rack. Lock the lid in place, and set the cooker over high heat. Bring to high pressure, and maintain for 10 minutes. Reduce heat to medium, and cook for another 15 minutes. Remove from heat, and reduce pressure using the cold water release method.

5. Using heat-safe gloves, remove the soufflé dish from the pressure cooker, and transfer to a cooling rack to cool for 5 minutes. Remove and discard the aluminum foil, and let dish cool to room temperature. Cover dish with a new sheet of aluminum foil, and refrigerate overnight.

6. Transfer dip from the soufflé dish to a serving platter, and serve with crackers.

Crab Artichoke Cheese Delight

Artichokes, cheddar cheese, and mayonnaise lend a creamy richness to this delicate crab dip with just a hint of sherry.

Yield:	Prep time:	Cook time:	Serving size:
4 cups	15 minutes	10 minutes	½ cup

1 small white onion, diced small

1 (16-oz.) pkg. *cream cheese,* softened to room temperature

½ TB. dry sherry

½ tsp. Worcestershire sauce

½ tsp. freshly ground black pepper

1 (18-oz.) can blue crabmeat, drained and squeezed dry

1 (15-oz.) can artichokes, drained and chopped small

½ cup mayonnaise

1 cup shredded medium cheddar cheese

2 cups water

1. In a large bowl and using an electric mixer on medium speed, blend onion and cream cheese together for about 5 minutes or until very smooth.

2. Add sherry, Worcestershire sauce, and pepper. Fold in crabmeat and artichokes, and stir in mayonnaise. Add ½ cup cheddar cheese.

3. Spray the bottom of a round 3-quart soufflé dish with nonstick cooking spray. Pour crab mixture into the dish, and cover tightly with a double layer of aluminum foil.

4. Insert a rack in the pressure cooker, pour in water, and place the soufflé dish on the rack. Lock the lid in place, and set over high heat. Bring to high pressure, reduce heat to medium, and maintain pressure for 10 minutes. Remove from heat, and reduce pressure using the cold water release method.

5. Using heat-safe gloves, remove the soufflé dish from the pressure cooker, and place on a warming tray. Remove aluminum foil, and sprinkle remaining ½ cup cheddar cheese on top of soufflé. Serve immediately with crackers.

STEAM SPEAK

Cream cheese is a sweet, soft, mild-tasting white cheese that's been around since 1650. Unlike other soft cheeses, it's not naturally matured and should be consumed fresh. Cream cheese originated in France, not Philadelphia.

Awesome Appetizers

Chapter **4**

In This Chapter

- Appetizers from around the globe
- Mad about meatballs
- Hot and spicy bites

Many cultures, from Chinese to Italian, have long recognized that sharing small servings of many different dishes with family or friends is a bonding experience that relaxes participants and prolongs an enjoyable dining experience. Because a pressure cooker lets you make exquisite, party-worthy appetizers quickly, you'll have time to enjoy the fruits of your labor with others instead of being stuck in the kitchen.

In this chapter, we show you how to use your pressure cooker to make a wide variety of appetizers, from fabulous finger foods and sassy bites that ignite any party to stand-out hors d'oeuvres that whet the palate for a scrumptious meal.

An Appetizer by Any Other Name

Many of the recipes in this chapter take their cue from ethnic appetizers, from Middle Eastern *mezze* and Spanish *tapas,* to Chinese *dim sum,* French *canapés* and *hors d'ouevres,* and even Italian *antipasto.* In Vietnam, small bites, or "drinking dishes," are called *do nhau,* or "little bites," which sounds similar to the all-American *doughnut.* In Thailand, appetizers are called *kanto.* In India, samosas and other fried finger foods are called *chat.*

Polenta Squares

Cornmeal, Parmesan cheese, and butter give this elegant cornbread its crunchy texture and rich, cheesy flavor.

Yield:	Prep time:	Cook time:	Serving size:
16 squares	15 minutes	10 minutes	2 squares

5 cups water

1 tsp. salt

2 cups yellow cornmeal

2 TB. unsalted butter

½ cup unsalted butter, softened
   and cut into small pieces

½ cup grated Parmesan cheese

1 tsp. kosher salt

½ tsp. freshly ground black pepper

1. In a pressure cooker over high heat, combine water and salt. Cook, uncovered, for 3 or 4 minutes or until mixture comes to a boil. Reduce heat to medium. Stir in cornmeal and 2 tablespoons unsalted butter, and cook, stirring constantly with a wooden spoon, for 2 or 3 minutes or until mixture begins to bubble.

2. Lock the lid in place. Bring to high pressure, reduce heat to medium, and maintain pressure for 10 minutes. Remove from heat, and reduce pressure using the cold water release method.

3. Stir in ½ cup unsalted butter and Parmesan cheese. Add kosher salt and pepper. Let cool to room temperature.

4. Preheat the oven to 400°F. Coat a 9×13-inch baking dish with nonstick cooking spray.

5. Pour *polenta* into the baking dish, and bake, uncovered, for 25 minutes or until golden brown. Remove from the oven, and transfer to a cooling rack. Let polenta cool for 10 minutes. Cut into 16 squares and serve immediately.

STEAM SPEAK

A staple of Northern Italy, **polenta** is a mush made from cornmeal that can be eaten hot with butter, cooked until firm and cut into squares, or mixed with cheese and served as a hearty dish for breakfast or brunch.

Mini Cabbage Rolls

These aromatic cabbage rolls combine the savory flavors of cabbage and beef in a zesty tomato sauce with hints of garlic and onion.

Yield:	Prep time:	Cook time:	Serving size:
24 rolls	15 minutes	12 minutes	2 rolls

1 large (about 2-lb.) head green or napa cabbage	1 large white or yellow onion, diced small
4 cups water	1 TB. minced garlic
1 lb. lean ground beef or ground turkey	1 TB. kosher salt
	1 tsp. freshly ground black pepper
1 cup white rice	1 cup tomato juice

1. Soak cabbage in a bowl of warm water to soften leaves. Remove leaves when soft.

2. In a pressure cooker over low heat, add cabbage leaves and 3 cups water, ensuring cabbage leaves are completely covered.

3. Lock the lid in place. Bring to low pressure, and maintain for 1 minute. Remove from heat, and release pressure using the quick release method.

4. Using tongs, remove cabbage leaves from the pressure cooker and transfer to a colander. Rinse under cold water for 2 minutes and drain thoroughly, shaking leaves to remove any remaining water. Remove stem from each cabbage leaf, and cut each leaf in half.

5. In a large mixing bowl, combine ground beef, white rice, onion, garlic, kosher salt, and pepper. Place a small ball of meat in the middle of each cabbage leaf, fold sides of leaf together, and roll leaf over until it's closed like a small package. Secure each roll with a wooden toothpick.

6. Transfer stuffed cabbage leaves to the pressure cooker. Add remaining 1 cup water and tomato juice, ensuring cabbage leaves are covered in liquid.

7. Lock the lid in place, and set over high heat. Bring to high pressure, and maintain for 12 minutes. Remove from heat, and reduce pressure using the natural release method.

8. Using a large slotted spoon, transfer cabbage rolls from the pressure cooker to a heat-safe serving platter or tray. Ladle sauce over top of cabbage rolls, and serve immediately.

PRESSURE POINTER

For cabbage rolls that look as good as they taste, choose a compact head of cabbage with fresh, crisp-looking leaves that are firmly packed. When you pick it up, the cabbage should be heavy rather than light for its size.

Artichokes with Lemon Dipping Sauce

A zesty sauce of lemon, mayonnaise, and hot sauce fire up these tender steamed artichokes.

Yield:	Prep time:	Cook time:	Serving size:
4 artichokes	10 minutes	10 minutes	1 artichoke

4 large artichokes	1 tsp. salt
1½ cups water	1 TB. freshly grated lemon zest
¼ cup freshly squeezed lemon juice	1 cup mayonnaise
	½ tsp. hot sauce

1. Wash and trim artichokes, removing stems, tough outside leaves, and the top ½ inch of each.

2. In a pressure cooker over high heat, combine artichokes, water, ½ of lemon juice, and salt.

3. Lock the lid in place. Bring to high pressure, and maintain for 10 minutes. Remove from heat, and reduce pressure using the natural release method.

4. Using tongs, remove artichokes from the pressure cooker and let cool.

5. In a small bowl, whisk together remaining lemon juice, lemon zest, mayonnaise, and hot sauce.

6. Place artichokes on chilled plates, and serve with dipping sauce.

FOODIE FACT

The flower bud of an edible thistle, Romans considered the artichoke a food of the nobles. Today, more than 50 varieties of artichokes are grown around the world. In the United States, most artichokes are grown along the central coast of California.

BBQ Baby Back Ribs

The sweetness of molasses and brown sugar contrasts with the spiciness of mustard, Worcestershire sauce, and apple cider vinegar in these mouth-watering ribs.

Yield:	Prep time:	Cook time:	Serving size:
1 rack of ribs	10 minutes	15 minutes	¼ rack of ribs

1 TB. extra-virgin olive oil	1 tsp. dry mustard
1 small white onion, diced small	2 tsp. Worcestershire sauce
1 clove garlic, finely chopped	1 TB. chili powder
1 cup ketchup	2 cups water
¼ cup apple cider vinegar	¼ tsp. kosher salt
¼ cup molasses	¾ tsp. freshly ground black pepper
2 TB. dark brown sugar, firmly packed	1 cup apple cider
	2 lb. baby back ribs

1. In a pressure cooker over high heat, heat extra-virgin olive oil until hot. Add onion and garlic, and cook, uncovered and stirring constantly, for 3 minutes. Stir in ketchup, apple cider vinegar, molasses, dark brown sugar, dry mustard, Worcestershire sauce, chili powder, 1 cup water, kosher salt, and pepper.

2. Lock the lid in place. Bring to high pressure, and maintain for 7 minutes. Remove from heat, and reduce pressure using the natural release method.

3. Transfer barbecue sauce to a small heat-proof bowl. Set aside.

4. Hand-wash the pressure cooker in hot, soapy water, and dry thoroughly. Insert a rack in the pressure cooker. Add remaining 1 cup water and apple cider. Cut ribs apart in sections and place on rack.

5. Lock the lid in place. Bring to high pressure, and maintain for 20 minutes. Remove from heat, and reduce pressure using the natural release method.

6. Using tongs, remove ribs from the pressure cooker and place on a platter. Brush both sides with barbecue sauce, and transfer to a barbecue grill or broiler. Grill or broil ribs at 450°F for about 8 to 10 minutes on each side. Serve immediately.

FOODIE FACT

Baby back ribs are called "baby" because the cuts are taken from market-weight hogs rather than sows. Because baby back ribs have meat between and on top of the bones, they're often meatier than spare ribs.

Sweet-and-Sour Meatballs

These tangy meatballs are flavored with a feisty sauce that combines the heat of chili sauce and garlic with the sweetness of grape jelly.

Yield:	Prep time:	Cook time:	Serving size:
24 meatballs	15 minutes	10 minutes	4 meatballs

1 lb. lean ground beef	1 tsp. kosher salt
1 large egg, lightly beaten	½ tsp. freshly ground black pepper
½ cup unseasoned breadcrumbs	1 (12-oz.) jar chili sauce
2 tsp. dried parsley flakes	1 cup grape jelly
2 cloves garlic, minced	

1. In a large mixing bowl, combine ground beef, egg, breadcrumbs, parsley flakes, garlic, kosher salt, and pepper. Form mixture into 24 small, 2-inch meatballs. Place meatballs in the pressure cooker, and set over high heat.

2. Lock the lid in place. Bring to high pressure, and maintain for 10 minutes. Remove from heat, and reduce pressure using the quick release method.

3. Remove meatballs from the pressure cooker and drain on paper towels.

4. In the pressure cooker over low heat, combine chili sauce and grape jelly. Cook, uncovered and stirring constantly, for 2 minutes or until mixture is melted and combined. Return meatballs to the pressure cooker, and stir gently until meatballs are coated in sauce.

5. Transfer meatballs and sauce to a fondue pot or chafing dish to keep warm, and serve immediately.

FOODIE FACT

Meatballs aren't originally an Italian food; they're claimed by many cultures. Although no one is sure where the meatball originated, early meatballs were made from leftovers and pounded or minced into balls with primitive tools. Because meat was rare and expensive, meatballs were an economical way to stretch and utilize cuts of meat that would otherwise have been thrown away.

Porcupine Meatballs

These tomato-flavored meatballs are a childhood favorite, combining the richness of lean beef with the crunch of firm rice.

Yield:	Prep time:	Cook time:	Serving size:
24 meatballs	15 minutes	10 minutes	4 meatballs

1 lb. extra-lean ground beef

1 cup cooked white rice

1 tsp. kosher salt

¼ tsp. freshly ground black pepper

2 TB. white or yellow onion, minced

1 large egg

1 (15-oz.) can diced tomatoes, with juice

1½ cups water

1. In a large mixing bowl, combine beef, white rice, kosher salt, pepper, onion, and egg. Shape into 24 large meatballs.

2. In a pressure cooker over high heat, combine tomatoes with juice, water, and meatballs.

3. Lock the lid in place. Bring to high pressure, and maintain for 10 minutes. Remove from heat, and reduce pressure using the quick release method.

4. Transfer meatballs to a serving platter or large bowl. Spear meatballs on cocktail toothpicks, and serve immediately.

FOODIE FACT

Porcupine meatballs are usually made with ground beef, rice, onion, tomato soup, and seasonings, although they can also be made with sour cream or mushroom gravy.

Hot-and-Spicy Chicken Wings

You'll never want another buffalo wing after tasting these Asian-style chicken wings with the rich flavor of brown sugar, chili powder, soy sauce, garlic, and onion.

Yield:	Prep time:	Cook time:	Serving size:
24 wings	20 minutes	15 minutes	6 wings

2 TB. canola oil or vegetable oil

24 chicken wings or mini-drums

½ small red onion, diced small

1 tsp. garlic powder

1 tsp. onion powder

1 cup low-sodium soy sauce

½ cup dark brown sugar, firmly packed

1 cup chili sauce

1 TB. hot sauce

1 tsp. kosher salt

1 tsp. freshly ground black pepper

1. In a pressure cooker over medium heat, heat canola oil until hot. Add chicken wings, and cook, uncovered, for 5 or 6 minutes or until browned on all sides. Remove wings from the pressure cooker, and drain on paper towels.

2. In a small mixing bowl, combine red onion, garlic powder, onion powder, soy sauce, dark brown sugar, chili sauce, hot sauce, kosher salt, and pepper.

3. Return chicken wings to the pressure cooker, and return to medium heat. Add sauce, stirring gently to coat each wing with sauce.

4. Lock the lid in place. Bring to high pressure, reduce heat to low, and maintain for 5 minutes. Remove from heat, and reduce pressure using the quick release method.

5. Using tongs, remove wings from the pressure cooker and transfer to a serving platter. Serve immediately.

PRESSURE POINTER

Although this recipe calls for chicken wings, you can substitute other chicken parts and turn this appetizer into a main dish. Be sure to increase the cooking time based on the size of the parts.

Teriyaki Chicken Strips

This spicy *teriyaki* combines the traditional Japanese flavors of soy sauce and ginger-root with a hint of sherry.

Yield:	Prep time:	Cook time:	Serving size:
24 strips	15 minutes plus 24 hours marinating	5 minutes	6 strips

1 cup low-sodium soy sauce	¼ cup mirin or cooking sherry
2 tsp. freshly grated gingerroot	1 tsp. freshly ground black pepper
½ cup dark brown sugar, firmly packed	4 (4- or 5-oz.) boneless, skinless chicken breasts
1 TB. minced garlic	
2 green onions, white and green parts, sliced into thin rounds	

1. In a small bowl, combine soy sauce, gingerroot, dark brown sugar, garlic, green onions, mirin, and pepper.

2. Place chicken breasts in a large glass bowl. Add marinade, and marinate for at least 15 minutes or up to 24 hours.

3. In a pressure cooker over high heat, add chicken breasts and marinade.

4. Lock the lid in place. Bring to high pressure, and maintain for 5 minutes. Remove from heat, and reduce pressure using the natural release method.

5. Using tongs, transfer chicken breasts from the pressure cooker to a cutting board. Let cool for at least 5 minutes.

6. When cool, cut each chicken breast into 6 strips. Transfer to a serving platter, and serve immediately.

STEAM SPEAK

Teriyaki refers to a Japanese dish in which beef or chicken is marinated in a sauce made of soy sauce, sake or sherry, sugar, ginger, and seasonings and then fried, grilled, or broiled. The sugar in the marinade gives the food a slight glaze.

Stellar Salads

In This Chapter

- Salads around the globe
- Bowled over by nutrients
- Grain, bean, and veggie salads
- Meat and seafood salads

Many people don't realize that pressure cookers can create stellar salads. Whether you're starting with a bed of fresh, leafy greens, or using a mound of grains and beans as the base for your salad, your pressure cooker can provide everything else you need to build a nutritious and delicious bowl—from crunchy roasted veggies, fluffy rice, and hearty grains, to flavorful beans and fork-tender meat, poultry, and seafood.

Whether served as a side dish or as a main meal, the hefty salads in this chapter are more than just big bowls of lettuce. They're loaded with disease-fighting antioxidants and fiber from leafy greens and veggies; packed with protein from beans, meat, poultry, and seafood; and naturally low in calories, fat, and cholesterol. As an extra bonus, these salads are also free of preservatives.

Your pressure cooker can also create scrumptious salad dressings that have a fresh, clean taste and which cost a fraction of what you'd spend on commercial dressings.

Lobster Salad

Celery and lemon enhance the rich, buttery flavor of lobster in this simple yet elegant salad with a touch of tarragon.

Yield:	Prep time:	Cook time:	Serving size:
2 cups	1 hour, 5 minutes	8 minutes	½ cup

4 large lobster tails (at least 6 oz. each)

2 cups water

3 ribs celery, diced fine

1½ cups mayonnaise

1 TB. freshly squeezed lemon juice (or bottled)

1 tsp. dried tarragon

1 tsp. kosher salt

½ tsp. freshly ground black pepper

4 romaine lettuce leaves

4 lemon wedges

1. Rinse lobster tails in cold water. Pour water into the pressure cooker, and insert a rack in the pressure cooker. Place lobster tails on the rack, and set over high heat.

2. Lock the lid in place. Bring to high pressure, and maintain for 8 minutes. Remove from heat, and reduce pressure using the cold water release method. Remove lobster and let cool.

3. Remove shell from lobster, and dice meat into small cubes. Transfer to a mixing bowl. Add celery, mayonnaise, lemon juice, and tarragon. Refrigerate for 1 hour to let flavors mingle.

4. Remove lobster from refrigerator, and add kosher salt and pepper.

5. Serve lobster salad on cold plates, each garnished with 1 lettuce leaf and 1 lemon wedge.

FOODIE FACT

Until the end of the nineteenth century, lobster was so plentiful and cheap that fishermen used it as bait. Today, the rising demand for lobster has driven up both its demand and price. The most popular lobster in the United States is the Maine lobster, which has large, heavy claws chock-full of meat.

Roasted Beet Salad

The sweetness of roasted beets, brown sugar, and orange juice contrasts with the sharpness of the feta cheese and wine vinegar, resulting in an elegant salad with lots of complex flavors and textures.

Yield:	Prep time:	Cook time:	Serving size:
4 cups	10 minutes	20 minutes	1 cup

1½ cups water	¼ tsp. freshly ground black pepper
4 or 5 red and golden beets (1 lb.), skin on, scrubbed, and trimmed	1 TB. dark brown sugar, firmly packed
1 TB. freshly grated orange zest	2 TB. extra-virgin olive oil
2 TB. freshly squeezed orange juice	3 cups mixed salad greens or baby arugula
1 TB. white wine vinegar	
¼ tsp. sea salt	¼ cup crumbled feta cheese

1. Insert a rack in the pressure cooker. Add water, place beets on the rack, and set over high heat.

2. Lock the lid in place. Bring to high pressure, and maintain for 20 minutes. Remove from heat, and reduce pressure using the natural release method.

3. In a small bowl, combine orange zest, orange juice, white wine vinegar, sea salt, pepper, and dark brown sugar. Slowly whisk in extra-virgin olive oil until mixture becomes thick.

4. Cut beets into wedges, and place in a medium bowl. Add 1 tablespoon dressing, and combine gently.

5. Add remaining dressing to salad greens, and toss until combined.

6. Serve salad on cold salad plates. Place beets on top of salad, and sprinkle with feta cheese.

PRESSURE POINTER

Choose small, firm beets that have a smooth skin. Remove the greens as soon as you get home to prevent them from leaching moisture from the beets, and leave about 1 inch of stem on the beets to prevent the nutrients and color from leaching out during cooking.

Chinese Chicken Salad

A rich sesame orange dressing gives this scrumptious salad its Asian flair, while chestnuts and snow peas lend a crunchy bite.

Yield:	Prep time:	Cook time:	Serving size:
6 cups	2 hours, 10 minutes	10 minutes	1 cup

1 (3-lb.) whole chicken

3 cups water

1 rib celery, cut in $\frac{1}{2}$

1 large carrot, peeled and cut in $\frac{1}{2}$ lengthwise

1 large white onion, cut into quarters

8 whole peppercorns

1 tsp. fresh gingerroot, peeled and minced

2 TB. freshly squeezed orange juice

1 TB. freshly grated orange zest

2 TB. low-sodium soy sauce

1 TB. freshly squeezed lemon juice (or bottled lemon juice)

1 tsp. *Chinese five-spice powder*

1 TB. sweet chili paste with garlic

2 tsp. sesame oil

1 tsp. kosher salt

$\frac{1}{2}$ tsp. freshly ground black pepper

$\frac{1}{4}$ cup dark brown sugar, firmly packed

2 cups snow peas, trimmed and strings removed

1 cup fresh or canned water chestnuts, sliced thin

1 cup fresh bean sprouts

1. In a pressure cooker over high heat, place chicken, and cover with 3 cups water or enough to completely cover chicken. Add celery, carrot, onion, and peppercorns.

2. Lock the lid in place. Bring to high pressure, and maintain for 10 minutes. Remove from heat, and reduce pressure using the natural release method.

3. Using tongs, remove chicken from the pressure cooker and place on a cutting board. Discard celery, carrot, onion, and peppercorns. Let chicken cool for 10 minutes, remove skin and bones, and shred or cut chicken into bite-size pieces. Chill chicken for at least 2 hours or until cold.

4. In a small bowl, combine gingerroot, orange juice, orange zest, soy sauce, lemon juice, Chinese five-spice powder, sweet chili paste with garlic, sesame oil, kosher salt, pepper, and dark brown sugar. Whisk slowly until mixture becomes thick.

5. Add dressing to chicken mixture, and toss until combined. Add snow peas and water chestnuts. Refrigerate salad for 1 hour.

6. Serve salad on chilled plates garnished with bean sprouts.

STEAM SPEAK

Chinese five-spice powder is a pungent mixture of equal parts cinnamon, cloves, fennel seed, anise, and Szechuan peppercorns. You can find it in most supermarkets and Asian grocery stores.

Greek Orzo Salad

Mini pasta combined with a savory olive oil dressing, crunchy cucumbers, sweet tomatoes, fruity *kalamata olives*, and zesty feta cheese bring the flavors of the Mediterranean to your salad bowl.

Yield:	Prep time:	Cook time:	Serving size:
4 cups	3 hours, 10 minutes	4 minutes	1 cup

2 cups dried orzo	¾ tsp. freshly ground black pepper
2 cups chicken stock or vegetable broth	1 large cucumber, peeled, seeded, and diced
1 TB. plus ½ cup extra-virgin olive oil	1 cup cherry or grape tomatoes, washed and cut in ½
¼ cup red wine vinegar	¼ cup kalamata olives, pitted and cut in ½
1 tsp. Dijon mustard	½ cup crumbled feta cheese
1 tsp. dried oregano	1 TB. fresh minced Italian parsley (or regular parsley)
1 tsp. dried basil	
½ tsp. kosher salt	

1. In a pressure cooker over high heat, combine orzo, chicken stock, and 1 tablespoon extra-virgin olive oil.

2. Lock the lid in place. Bring to high pressure, reduce heat to low, and maintain for 4 minutes. Remove from heat, and release pressure using the natural release method.

3. In a small bowl, combine red wine vinegar, Dijon mustard, oregano, and basil. Slowly whisk in remaining ½ cup extra-virgin olive oil. Add kosher salt and pepper.

4. Transfer orzo to a large serving bowl. Add cucumber, tomatoes, olives, feta cheese, and dressing, and mix well to distribute dressing.

5. Refrigerate salad for at least 3 hours before serving. Serve on chilled salad plates, and sprinkle each serving with Italian parsley.

STEAM SPEAK

Kalamata olives are large, almond-shape Greek olives that have a rich, fruity flavor and a dark, eggplant color. For the most flavorful olives, purchase kalamata olives that have been pitted and slit.

Cranberry Nut Rice Salad

Brown rice and walnuts give this earthy salad its crunchy texture and nutty flavor, while dried sweetened cranberries add a touch of sour-sweet tartness.

Yield:	Prep time:	Cook time:	Serving size:
3½ cups	15 minutes	12 minutes	1 cup

2 TB. unsalted butter or margarine	½ cup dried sweetened cranberries
1 cup brown rice	2 TB. extra-virgin olive oil
3¼ cups chicken stock	1 tsp. kosher salt
1 TB. fresh minced Italian parsley (or regular parsley)	½ tsp. freshly ground black pepper
½ cup toasted walnuts or almonds, chopped fine	

1. In a pressure cooker over medium heat, melt unsalted butter. Add brown rice, and stir to coat with butter. Add chicken stock.

2. Lock the lid in place. Bring to high pressure, and maintain for 12 minutes. Remove from heat, and reduce pressure using the natural release method. Wait 10 minutes and release any remaining pressure using the quick release method.

3. Transfer rice mixture to a serving bowl and let cool. Stir in Italian parsley, walnuts, cranberries, extra-virgin olive oil, kosher salt, and pepper.

4. Refrigerate until ready to serve.

FOODIE FACT

Cranberries are grown in huge, sandy bogs on low, trailing vines and add a puckery sweetness to dishes.

Tabbouleh Salad

This Middle Eastern dish combines the nutty crunch of *bulgur* wheat with the tartness of lemon juice and the fresh, sweet flavor of tomatoes, onion, celery, and cucumber. Serve it icy cold with crisp bread for a great meal on a hot summer night.

Yield:	Prep time:	Cook time:	Serving size:
4 cups	8 hours, 15 minutes	8 minutes	1 cup

2 TB. plus ¼ cup extra-virgin olive oil	1 large cucumber, peeled, seeded, and diced small
1 cup dried bulgur wheat	1 large tomato, seeded and diced small
1 medium sweet onion, diced small	
3 cups vegetable stock or broth	2 TB. freshly squeezed lemon juice (or bottled)
2 ribs celery, diced small	1 TB. freshly grated lemon zest
4 green onions, white and green parts, sliced thin	¼ cup fresh minced parsley
	¾ tsp. kosher salt
1 large carrot, peeled and diced small	½ tsp. freshly ground black pepper

1. In a pressure cooker over medium heat, heat 2 tablespoons extra-virgin olive oil until hot. Add bulgur wheat and onion, and cook for about 2 minutes or until bulgur is well coated with onion. Add vegetable stock.

2. Lock the lid in place. Bring to high pressure, reduce heat to medium, and maintain pressure for 8 minutes. Remove from heat, and reduce pressure using the quick release method.

3. Transfer mixture to a serving bowl, and let cool for 10 minutes. Stir in celery, green onions, carrot, cucumber, and tomato. Mix in remaining ¼ cup extra-virgin olive oil, lemon juice, lemon zest, parsley, kosher salt, and pepper.

4. Refrigerate salad overnight to let flavors mingle. Salad will keep for up to 2 days in the refrigerator.

STEAM SPEAK

Bulgur is made up of wheat kernels that have been steamed, dried, and crushed. A staple in Middle Eastern cuisine, bulgur is high in protein and has a tender, chewy texture. It's sold in coarse, medium, and fine grinds.

Niçoise Salad

This classic French salad melds the flavors of tuna, eggs, green beans, and potatoes in a zesty dressing with hints of sherry and mustard.

Yield:	Prep time:	Cook time:	Serving size:
6 cups	10 minutes	7 minutes	1½ cups

3 cups water

4 large eggs

8 small red potatoes, scrubbed and unpeeled

¼ cup cider vinegar

¼ cup sherry vinegar or red wine vinegar

1 TB. honey Dijon mustard

1 large head romaine lettuce, rinsed, dried, and cut into bite-size pieces

1 (14-oz.) can white albacore tuna packed in water, drained, and squeezed dry

1 cup fresh, cooked French green beans, cut into 1-in. pieces

1 English cucumber, peeled and cut into thin slices

2 large tomatoes, cut into quarters

1 small red onion, peeled and sliced into thin slices

1 tsp. kosher salt

½ tsp. freshly ground black pepper

½ cup kalamata olives, pitted

1. Insert a steaming basket in the pressure cooker. Add water to the pressure cooker. Place eggs and potatoes in the steaming basket.

2. Lock the lid in place. Bring to high pressure, and maintain for 7 minutes. Remove from heat, and reduce pressure using the cold water release method.

3. Remove eggs and potatoes from the steamer basket, and transfer to a colander. Rinse with cold water to prevent them from overcooking. When eggs are cool, peel and cut into thin slices. Cut potatoes into quarters. Set aside.

4. In a small bowl, whisk together cider vinegar, sherry vinegar, and honey Dijon mustard until thickened.

5. Arrange romaine lettuce on 4 chilled salad plates. Top with eggs, potatoes, tuna, green beans, cucumber, tomatoes, and onion. Add kosher salt and pepper. Drizzle salad dressing over each salad, garnish with kalamata olives, and serve immediately.

FOODIE FACT

Niçoise refers to a garnish that hails from Nice, France, and includes garlic, tomatoes, anchovies, black olives, capers, and lemon juice.

Italian White Bean Salad

This heart-healthy salad combines the mild flavor of *cannelloni beans* with the sweetness of tomatoes, onions, and bell peppers in a light vinaigrette with a hint of white
wine and garlic.

Yield:	Prep time:	Cook time:	Serving size:
5 cups	15 minutes	20 minutes	1 cup

2 cups dried cannelloni beans

6 cups water

2 medium green onions, sliced into
    thin rounds

2 cloves garlic, minced

1 medium red bell pepper, ribs and
    seeds removed, and cut into
    thin strips

1 cup grape tomatoes

¼ cup white wine or champagne
    vinegar

1 tsp. dried Italian seasoning

1 TB. sugar

½ cup extra-virgin olive oil

1 tsp. kosher salt

½ tsp. freshly ground black pepper

1. In a pressure cooker over high heat, combine cannelloni beans and 3 cups water.

2. Lock the lid in place. Bring to high pressure, and maintain for 2 minutes.
   Remove from heat, and reduce the steam using the quick release method. Drain
   and rinse beans under cold water.

3. In the pressure cooker, combine beans and remaining 3 cups water.

4. Lock the lid in place. Bring to high pressure, and maintain for 20 minutes.
   Remove from heat, and release pressure using the quick release method.

5. Let beans cool, and transfer to a large serving bowl. Add green onions, garlic,
   red bell pepper, and grape tomatoes.

6. In a small bowl, combine white wine vinegar, Italian seasoning, and sugar.
   Slowly whisk in extra-virgin olive oil, kosher salt, and pepper.

7. Pour vinaigrette mixture over salad, and toss gently. Serve on chilled plates.

STEAM SPEAK

Cannelloni beans are white kidney beans with a smooth texture and a taste
similar to navy or Great Northern beans. You can buy them dried or canned in
most supermarkets.

Egg-Based Dishes

In This Chapter

- The egg-ceptional egg
- Scrumptious soufflés and scrambles
- No-pressure pancakes
- Delicious brunch custards

Studies have shown that people who skip breakfast are more likely to miss out on important vitamins and minerals. What's more, skipping breakfast to lose weight often backfires by causing you to overeat the rest of the day. Start your day right! Even if you currently don't make time for breakfast at home, this chapter could revolutionize your mornings. With a pressure cooker, you can have a real breakfast on the table in less time than you'd spend waiting in line for your daily latte.

This chapter also provides all the elements you need to create a scrumptious brunch—from sensational soufflés to creamy custards—in less than 20 minutes.

The Incredibly Healthy Egg

Many of the recipes in this chapter revolve around eggs, which may leave you wondering about cholesterol. According to the Mayo Clinic, although eggs are high in cholesterol, and a diet high in cholesterol can contribute to high blood cholesterol levels, how much the cholesterol in your diet can increase your blood cholesterol varies from one person to another.

Dijon Deviled Eggs

Dijon mustard, Worcestershire sauce, hot sauce, and paprika give these deviled eggs a spicy-hot flavor.

Yield:	Prep time:	Cook time:	Serving size:
24 eggs	15 minutes	30 minutes	2 eggs

2 cups water

12 large eggs

¼ cup Dijon mustard

½ cup mayonnaise

1 tsp. Worcestershire sauce

½ tsp. hot sauce

½ tsp. kosher salt

1 tsp. freshly ground black pepper

⅛ tsp. ground paprika

1 TB. minced fresh Italian parsley (or regular parsley)

1. Add water to the pressure cooker. Insert a steamer basket in the pressure cooker, place eggs in the basket, and set over high heat.

2. Lock the lid in place. Bring to high pressure, and maintain for 8 minutes. Remove from heat, and release pressure using the cold water release method.

3. Remove eggs from the pressure cooker and rinse under cold water until cool enough to touch. Place eggs in ice bath, and peel immediately. Rinse eggs thoroughly to remove any traces of shell. Cut eggs in half lengthwise, and using a small spoon, carefully scoop yolks from eggs.

4. In a food processor fitted with a metal blade or a blender, combine egg yolks, Dijon mustard, mayonnaise, Worcestershire sauce, hot sauce, kosher salt, and pepper. Purée for 1 or 2 minutes or until smooth.

5. Spoon mixture into hollowed-out egg halves. Garnish with paprika and Italian parsley, and serve immediately. Or refrigerate, covered, for up to 2 days.

PRESSURE POINTER

Eggs can sometimes be very difficult to peel, especially if they're young eggs. In general, the older the egg, the easier it is to peel. But eggs hard-boiled in the pressure cooker are easy to peel, regardless of their age.

Baked Lemon Eggs

These mini egg casseroles with hints of lemon and parsley are an ideal meal for breakfast, brunch, or whenever you're looking for a light, nutritious dish.

Yield:	Prep time:	Cook time:	Serving size:
4 cups	15 minutes	5 minutes	1 cup

½ cup grated Gouda cheese

2 TB. freshly grated lemon zest

4 large eggs

8 TB. half-and-half or heavy whipping cream

1 tsp. kosher salt

1 tsp. freshly ground black pepper

1½ cups water

2 TB. minced fresh parsley

1. Coat 4 small (4-ounce) ramekins with nonstick cooking spray.

2. Divide Gouda cheese and lemon zest evenly among ramekins. Break 1 egg into each ramekin, and top each with 2 tablespoons half-and-half. Sprinkle each ramekin with kosher salt and pepper. Cover each ramekin tightly with a double layer of aluminum foil.

3. Place a rack in the pressure cooker, and add water. Place ramekins on the rack, and set over high heat.

4. Lock the lid in place. Bring to high pressure, reduce heat to low, and maintain for 4 minutes. Remove from heat, and reduce pressure using the cold water release method.

5. Using tongs or a heat-safe glove, remove the ramekins from the pressure cooker. Remove the aluminum foil. Garnish each ramekin with parsley, and serve immediately.

FOODIE FACT

Depending on the age, the flavor of Gouda ranges from mild and delicate for young cheeses, to fruity, nutty, and rich for aged cheeses. Younger Goudas have a smooth and supple texture, while aged Goudas are hard, flaky, and crunchy.

Swiss Eggs

Heavy cream and cheeses give this scrumptious egg casserole with hints of lemon and parsley a rich, satisfying flavor.

Yield:	Prep time:	Cook time:	Serving size:
4 cups	5 minutes	6 minutes	1 cup

½ cup grated Swiss cheese

¼ cup grated extra-sharp cheddar cheese

4 large eggs

8 TB. half-and-half

2 TB. freshly grated lemon *zest*

½ tsp. kosher salt

1 tsp. freshly ground black pepper

1½ cups water

2 TB. minced fresh parsley

1. Spray 4 small ramekins with nonstick cooking spray. Divide Swiss cheese and extra-sharp cheddar cheese among ramekins. Break 1 egg into each ramekin, and top each with 2 tablespoons half-and-half and lemon zest. Sprinkle each ramekin with kosher salt and pepper, and cover tightly with aluminum foil.

2. Place a rack in the pressure cooker. Add water. Place the ramekins on the rack, and set over high heat.

3. Lock the lid in place. Bring to high pressure, reduce heat to low, and maintain for 6 minutes. Remove from heat, and reduce the pressure using the cold water release method.

4. Using tongs or a heat-safe glove, remove ramekins from the pressure cooker. Allow ramekins to rest for 1 minute. Remove the foil from the ramekins, garnish with parsley, and serve immediately.

STEAM SPEAK

Zest refers to the outer skin of citrus fruit. To remove it, use a vegetable zester or a Microplane. Be careful not to remove the white pith underneath the skin; it's very bitter.

Ham and Cheese Mini Soufflés

Heavy cream makes this ham and cheese soufflé extra rich and creamy.

Yield:	Prep time:	Cook time:	Serving size:
8 cups	15 minutes	6 minutes	1 cup

½ cup grated Gruyère or Swiss cheese	8 TB. half-and-half or heavy cream
½ cup baked ham, diced small	½ tsp. kosher salt
4 large eggs	½ tsp. freshly ground black pepper
	1½ cups water

1. Spray 4 small *ramekins* with nonstick cooking spray. Divide Gruyère cheese and ham among ramekins. Break 1 egg into each ramekin, and top each with 2 tablespoons half-and-half. Sprinkle each ramekin with kosher salt and pepper. Cover each ramekin tightly with a double layer of aluminum foil.

2. Place a rack in the pressure cooker. Add water. Place ramekins on the rack, and set over high heat.

3. Lock the lid in place. Bring to high pressure, reduce heat to low, and maintain for 6 minutes. Remove from heat, and reduce pressure using the cold water release method.

4. Using tongs or a heat-safe glove, remove ramekins from the pressure cooker. Allow ramekins to rest for 1 minute. Remove the foil from each ramekin, and serve immediately.

STEAM SPEAK

A **ramekin** is an individual baking dish 3 or 4 inches in diameter that resembles a small soufflé dish. You can use ramekins to create individual servings of anything, from casseroles to puddings.

Southern-Style Scramble

Spicy sausage, bell peppers, and onions give the eggs, hash browns, and potatoes in this hearty dish extra zest and bite.

Yield:	Prep time:	Cook time:	Serving size:
4 cups	15 minutes	4 minutes	1 cup

2 TB. canola oil or vegetable oil

1 (8-oz.) pkg. spicy breakfast sausage

1 cup water

4 large eggs, slightly beaten

1 (16-oz.) pkg. frozen hash brown potatoes with bell peppers and onion, defrosted

½ tsp. kosher salt

1 tsp. freshly ground black pepper

1 cup grated sharp or medium cheddar cheese

1. In a pressure cooker over high heat, heat canola oil. Break sausage into small pieces and add to the pressure cooker. Cook for 5 to 7 minutes or until brown, and drain in a colander.

2. Using a paper towel, wipe excess fat from the pressure cooker. Pour water into the pressure cooker, and set over medium-low heat. Stir in sausage, and add eggs and hash browns with bell peppers and onions, kosher salt, and pepper.

3. Lock the lid in place. Bring to high pressure, reduce heat to low, and maintain for 4 minutes. Remove from heat, and reduce pressure using the cold water release method.

4. Sprinkle cheese over top of egg mixture. Replace the lid on the pressure cooker, and let sit for 3 minutes to allow cheese to melt. Ladle scramble onto plates, and serve immediately.

UNDER PRESSURE

Don't hesitate to use frozen veggies when pressure cooking. If they've been flash-frozen, they contain the same nutrients and fiber as fresh veggies.

Wild Rice Pancakes

These pancakes combine the chewiness of wild rice with the sweetness of cinnamon, the tartness of lemon, and the richness of real whipped cream.

Yield:	Prep time:	Cook time:	Serving size:
16 pancakes	15 minutes	22 minutes	2 pancakes

1 cup wild rice

4 cups water

1 tsp. kosher salt

2 large egg whites

1 cup baking mix (like Bisquick)

2 tsp. ground ginger

1 tsp. ground cinnamon

1 tsp. ground allspice

1 cup buttermilk

1 TB. freshly grated lemon zest

¼ cup freshly squeezed lemon juice

2 cups heavy whipping cream, whipped

1. In a pressure cooker over medium heat, combine wild rice, water, and kosher salt.

2. Lock the lid in place. Bring to high pressure, and maintain for 22 minutes. Remove from heat, and reduce pressure using the natural release method.

3. Transfer rice to a large bowl and let cool.

4. In a large bowl, and using an electric mixer on medium speed, beat egg whites for 3 or 4 minutes or until soft peaks form. Set aside.

5. In a small bowl, combine baking mix, ginger, cinnamon, and allspice. Stir in buttermilk, lemon zest, and lemon juice, and mix until thoroughly combined. Add to rice, and gently fold egg whites into rice mixture.

6. Preheat a griddle to 350°F.

7. Drop ¼ cup batter 2 inches apart on griddle. Cook for 2 minutes or until bubbles appear. Flip over pancake, and brown on the other side. Serve immediately with fresh whipped cream.

FOODIE FACT

Wild rice isn't rice at all, but a long-grain marsh grass that grows in the northern Great Lakes area, California, and several Midwestern states. Unlike white rice, wild rice has a nutty taste and a chewy texture.

Breakfast Cinnamon Custard

This French toast custard combines the richness of eggs, butter, and heavy cream with the aromatic flavor of cinnamon.

Yield:	Prep time:	Cook time:	Serving size:
4 pieces	10 minutes	10 minutes	1 piece

1 (1-lb.) loaf cinnamon swirl or cinnamon-raisin bread, cut into 1-in. cubes

½ stick unsalted butter or margarine, melted

4 large eggs

½ cup sugar

1 tsp. pure vanilla extract

1 tsp. pure butter extract

½ cup heavy cream or half-and-half

1½ cups water

1. Spray a round or square 1- or 2-quart baking dish or soufflé dish with nonstick cooking spray. Layer bread in the dish.

2. In a mixing bowl, combine unsalted butter, eggs, sugar, vanilla extract, butter extract, and half-and-half, and mix well. Pour over bread. Cover dish tightly with aluminum foil.

3. Place rack in pressure cooker and add water to the pressure cooker. Place dish on rack. Lock pressure cooker lid into place. Bring to high pressure, and maintain for 10 minutes. Remove from heat, and release pressure using the quick release method.

4. Using heat-safe gloves, remove dish from the pressure cooker and place on a cooling rack. Let cool for 5 to 10 minutes. Sprinkle with powdered sugar, cut into 4 slices, and serve immediately with pure maple syrup.

FOODIE FACT

Extracts are concentrated flavorings derived from foods or plants through evaporation or distillation. They give foods a powerful flavor without adding excess volume or changing the texture.

Tequila Flan Custard

This soft, silky custard has the rich flavor of caramel and just enough tequila to give it a little punch.

Yield:	Prep time:	Cook time:	Serving size:
6 cups	15 minutes	10 minutes	½ cup

3 large eggs, beaten

1 (14-oz.) can unsweetened condensed milk

¼ cup tequila

¾ cup whole milk

1 tsp. pure vanilla extract

6 TB. sugar

3 cups water

1. In a large bowl, combine eggs, condensed milk, tequila, whole milk, and vanilla extract. Whisk for about 2 minutes, and set aside.

2. In an aluminum flan mold or a 3-quart baking dish, pour sugar. Place mold or baking dish on a medium-high stove burner, and heat, stirring constantly, for 2 or 3 minutes or until sugar melts down into a caramel-colored liquid. Be careful not to let sugar become too dark or burn.

3. When sugar is fully melted, spread it around so it coats the bottom and sides of the flan mold or baking dish. Use 2 hand towels to hold the flan mold or baking dish so you don't burn your hands. Let sugar rest for 2 minutes or until it sets.

4. Using a mesh strainer, pour egg/custard mixture on top of sugar. Cover the flan mold or baking dish with aluminum foil.

5. Fill a pressure cooker with water. Insert a rack in the pressure cooker, and place flan mold or baking dish in the center of the rack. Set over high heat.

6. Lock the lid into place. Bring to high pressure, and maintain for 10 minutes. Remove from heat, and release pressure using the natural release method.

7. Using heat-safe gloves, remove the flan mold or baking dish from the pressure cooker and place on a cooling rack. Let flan cool to room temperature and then refrigerate overnight.

8. To remove flan from the flan mold or baking dish, use a butter knife to loosen sides of flan all the way around the flan mold or baking dish. Place a large plate upside down on top of the flan mold or baking dish, and carefully invert flan onto the plate. Cut flan into slices, and serve immediately.

FOODIE FACT

Tequila is colorless or pale liquor made from the sweet sap of the blue agave plant, which grows in and around the small border town of Tequila, Mexico, located just south of San Diego.

Soup's On!

"Soup does its loyal best, no matter what undignified conditions are imposed upon it. You don't catch steak hanging around when you're poor and sick, do you?" said Judith Martin, a.k.a. Miss Manners. "I live on good soup, not fine words," wrote playwright Moliere. "A first-rate soup is more creative than a second-rate painting," said renowned psychologist Abraham Maslow. James Duke, a famous cancer and drug expert with the U.S. Department of Agriculture, believed "an old-fashioned vegetable soup, without any enhancement, is a more powerful anti-carcinogen than any known medicine."

Soup warms you in the winter and cools you in the summer, stretches your resources, and transforms humble ingredients into an elegant dish. In Part 3, you find a wide range of recipes for scrumptious soups that satisfy body and soul while providing a host of essential nutrients. James Duke would love the chapter on vegetable soups, which range from light and lively soups to rich and creamy creations. We also give you a chapter on rich and hearty soups that revolve around meat, another on poultry soups that bring out the best in chicken and turkey, and a chapter on savory seafood soups and chowders that showcase the tastes of the sea.

As you'll soon see, your pressure cooker makes savory soups, allowing flavors to mingle to perfection while preserving the colors, flavors, textures, and nutrients of foods that often are destroyed by conventional cooking methods.

Incredible Vegetable Soups

In This Chapter

- Pure, fresh soups
- Nutrient-packed soups
- Bountiful bowls of beans
- Super stock

When you make vegetable soup in the pressure cooker, you'll find proof that less is more. Toss a handful of vegetables and herbs into a pot of water, turn on the pressure cooker, and in less than 20 minutes, you've got soup! Ludwig van Beethoven once said, "Only the pure of heart can make a good soup." To that, we'd add pure, fresh ingredients, including organic vegetables and herbs you've grown in your backyard garden or purchased at a farmers' market. Only the best and freshest vegetables become the finest of soups.

Pressure cookers preserve more nutrients and flavors than other cooking methods, so you get vegetable soup that's naturally more wholesome and tasty. Making homemade vegetable soups is also an easy way to sneak in several extra servings of produce daily, including some veggies you thought your kids would never eat. You don't have to tell them there's a turnip in their soup!

Now You Know Beans

Some of the recipes in this chapter call for canned or dried beans. Either way, beans are packed with protein, fiber, iron, and calcium, and give soups extra thickness, richness, texture, and flavor.

In recipes calling for dried beans, use fresh, well-shaped "young" beans. These beans should have a bright, shiny color, and they shouldn't be shriveled or cracked. Young beans absorb water more quickly than old beans, and they're more tender. To ensure your beans are fresh, buy them in bulk at whole food grocery stores with a high product turnover rate, and avoid buying packaged beans that don't list an expiration date.

PRESSURE POINTER

If a recipe calls for 2 cups or less dried beans, save time by using the quick soak method. Combine 3 cups water for every 1 cup beans in the pressure cooker and set over high heat. Lock the lid in place. Bring to high pressure, and maintain for 2 minutes. Remove from heat, and reduce pressure using the quick release method. Drain and rinse beans, and they're ready to be cooked. Never quick soak more than 2 cups dried beans at a time.

Stock Up on Stock

Homemade vegetable stock dramatically enriches the flavor of homemade soups, stews, and curries. And it's so easy to make, you'll never go back to bouillon cubes or canned stock! Store any leftovers in freezer containers or ice cube trays, and use them for up to 6 months in recipes calling for homemade stock.

Homemade Vegetable Stock

This tasty homemade vegetable stock is flavored with a hint of onion and carrot.

Yield:	Prep time:	Cook time:	Serving size:
1½ quarts	15 minutes	10 minutes	1 cup

2 large white onions, peeled and sliced in ½

4 large carrots, peeled and cross-cut in ½

8 medium tomatoes, quartered

3 ribs celery, chopped in large pieces

1 bunch fresh parsley, cut in ½

1 bay leaf

10 whole black peppercorns

6 cups water

1. In a pressure cooker over high heat, combine onions, carrots, tomatoes, celery, parsley, bay leaf, black peppercorns, and water. Add more water if needed to cover vegetables.

2. Lock the lid in place. Bring to high pressure, and maintain for 10 minutes. Remove from heat, and reduce pressure using the cold water release method.

3. Cool stock and strain. Add to soups, chowders, stews, curries, or any recipe calling for stock. Freeze leftovers for up to 6 months.

UNDER PRESSURE

Never add salt to homemade stock. Stocks are typically added to soups, stews, and other dishes that may already contain a lot of salt. Go easy on the salt shaker until you taste the finished product.

Potato and Leek Soup

The hearty flavors of onion, garlic, and potato dominate this rich soup, while the milk adds a silky creaminess and the vegetables add texture and thickness.

Yield:	Prep time:	Cook time:	Serving size:
5 cups	15 minutes	20 minutes	1 cup

¼ cup extra-virgin olive oil

1 medium white onion, diced small

4 large leeks, both green and white parts, thinly sliced

1 clove garlic, minced

1 tsp. dried thyme

2 TB. dried *Italian parsley* (or regular parsley)

4 large white potatoes, peeled and diced small

4 cups Homemade Vegetable Stock (recipe earlier in this chapter)

1 cup low-fat milk

2 tsp. kosher salt

½ tsp. freshly ground black pepper

1. In a pressure cooker over medium heat, heat extra-virgin olive oil. Add onion and leeks, and cook, stirring frequently, for 2 minutes or until soft. Add garlic, and cook for 30 seconds or until soft. Do not brown.

2. Add thyme, Italian parsley, white potatoes, and Homemade Vegetable Stock.

3. Lock the lid in place. Bring to high pressure, and maintain pressure for 10 minutes. Remove from heat, and reduce pressure using the quick release method.

4. Add low-fat milk, and reheat soup over low heat until warm.

5. Transfer soup to a blender or food processor fitted with a metal blade, and purée until smooth. Be careful not to splatter hot soup on you. Depending on the size of your blender or food processor, you may have to purée in batches.

6. Add kosher salt and pepper, ladle soup into bowls, and serve immediately. This soup is also delicious served chilled on a hot summer's night.

STEAM SPEAK

Italian parsley is the flat-leafed cousin to curled-leafed parsley and is sweeter and more flavorful. Available in most supermarkets, it keeps in the fridge for about 4 days. To keep it fresh, chop off the bottom of the stems, wrap in wet paper towels, and store in a sealed plastic bag.

Minestrone Soup

This hearty soup, with beans and orzo for extra texture and nutrition, has all the sunny flavors of Italy, including a hint of Parmesan cheese, green pepper, tomatoes, and basil.

Yield:	Prep time:	Cook time:	Serving size:
8 cups	15 minutes	25 minutes	1 cup

2 TB. extra-virgin olive oil

1 large leek, white part only, chopped fine

1 medium carrot, peeled and diced

1 medium green bell pepper, ribs and seeds removed, and diced

2 cups Homemade Vegetable Stock (recipe earlier in this chapter)

1 tsp. dried basil

1 tsp. dried thyme

1 cup fresh green beans, trimmed and cut into 1-in. pieces

1 cup dried orzo

1 (15-oz.) can white beans, drained and rinsed

1 medium zucchini, cut into 1-in. chunks

1 (14.5-oz.) can diced tomatoes, with juice

1 tsp. kosher salt

$\frac{1}{2}$ tsp. freshly ground black pepper

$\frac{1}{2}$ cup grated Parmesan cheese

1. In a pressure cooker over medium heat, heat extra-virgin olive oil. Add leek, carrot, and green bell pepper, and cook, stirring frequently, for 5 minutes or until vegetables are soft. Add Homemade Vegetable Stock, basil, and thyme.

2. Lock the lid in place. Bring to high pressure, and maintain for 15 minutes. Remove from heat, and reduce pressure using the quick release method.

3. Stir in green beans, orzo, white beans, and zucchini, and set over low heat.

4. Lock the lid in place. Bring to low pressure, and maintain for 2 minutes. Remove from heat, and reduce pressure using the quick release method.

5. Add diced tomatoes with juice, and cook for 2 minutes.

6. Remove from heat, and add kosher salt and pepper. Ladle soup into bowls, sprinkle with Parmesan cheese, and serve immediately.

Lentil Soup

The rich, complex flavors of this savory soup become full and round as the garlic, basil, and thyme slowly simmer with the lentils. The bay leaf adds a fresh, light touch.

Yield:	Prep time:	Cook time:	Serving size:
7 cups	20 minutes	15 minutes	1 cup

¼ cup extra-virgin olive oil

1 medium white onion, diced

2 large carrots, peeled and diced

2 ribs celery, diced

2 cloves garlic, peeled and minced

1 bay leaf

1 TB. dried basil

1 TB. dried thyme

5 cups Homemade Vegetable Stock (recipe earlier in this chapter)

1 cup water

2 cups dried lentils, sorted and rinsed

1 (14.5-oz.) can diced tomatoes, with juice

1 tsp. kosher salt

½ tsp. freshly ground black pepper

1. In a pressure cooker over medium heat, heat extra-virgin olive oil. Add onion, carrots, and celery, and cook, stirring frequently, for 5 minutes or until soft.

2. Add garlic, and cook, stirring frequently, for 30 seconds or until soft. Do not brown. Add bay leaf, basil, thyme, Homemade Vegetable Stock, water, and lentils.

3. Lock the lid in place. Bring to high pressure, and maintain for 10 minutes. Remove from heat, and reduce pressure using the natural release method.

4. Reduce heat to low, add tomatoes with juice, and cook, stirring frequently, for 2 minutes.

5. Remove from heat, and add kosher salt and pepper. Ladle soup into bowls, and serve immediately.

PRESSURE POINTER

When chopping, slicing, or dicing vegetables for the pressure cooker, try to make the pieces about the same size to ensure the vegetables cook at the same rate.

French Onion Soup

This classic soup has a lively blend of flavors. The sweetness of the caramelized onions contrasts with the sharpness of the Gruyère cheese, while the homemade vegetable broth adds a rich, robust undertone.

Yield:	Prep time:	Cook time:	Serving size:
6 cups	10 minutes	20 minutes	1 cup

½ cup unsalted butter or margarine

6 large white onions, thinly sliced

2 TB. Dijon mustard

6 cups Homemade Vegetable Stock (recipe earlier in this chapter)

1 bay leaf

¼ cup cognac

6 slices toasted French bread, cut into ¼-in.-thick slices

6 slices Gruyère or Swiss cheese

1 tsp. kosher salt

½ tsp. freshly ground black pepper

1. In a pressure cooker over medium heat, heat unsalted butter. Add onions, and cook, stirring frequently, for 15 minutes or until golden brown. Stir in Dijon mustard, and add Homemade Vegetable Stock and bay leaf.

2. Lock the lid in place. Bring to high pressure, and maintain for 10 minutes. Remove from heat, and reduce pressure using the cold release method.

3. Add cognac, and stir until blended. Remove bay leaf.

4. Preheat the broiler to high.

5. Ladle soup into oven-proof bowls. Top each with 1 slice French bread and 1 slice Gruyère cheese. Place the bowls in the oven, and broil for 1 or 2 minutes or until cheese melts.

6. Add kosher salt and pepper, and serve immediately.

PRESSURE POINTER

Contrary to popular belief, alcohol doesn't completely evaporate during pressure cooking. If you're cooking for children or for adults who avoid alcohol, omit the cognac in this recipe. Although it adds richness, leaving it out won't negatively alter the flavor.

Corn Chowder

Pieces of fresh corn, potato, and onion give this chowder a thick, chunky texture. The cream gives the soup a rich, smooth flavor, and the bacon adds a hint of smokiness.

Yield:	Prep time:	Cook time:	Serving size:
6 cups	15 minutes	20 minutes	1 cup

2 slices bacon, uncooked	2 cups fresh white corn, cooked and shucked (2 to 4 ears)
1 TB. unsalted butter or margarine	
1 medium yellow onion, diced small	1 TB. dried chives
1 large white, red, or yellow potato, peeled and diced small	1 TB. minced fresh parsley
	2 cups Homemade Vegetable Stock (recipe earlier in this chapter)
1 bay leaf	
½ tsp. dried sage leaves or sage powder	1 cup heavy cream
	1 tsp. kosher salt
1 tsp. dried cumin	½ tsp. freshly ground black pepper

1. In a pressure cooker over medium heat, fry bacon for about 2 minutes or until crisp. Drain on paper towels, and cut into bite-size pieces. Do not drain bacon fat from the pressure cooker.

2. Add unsalted butter to bacon fat, and stir until melted. Add onion and cook, stirring frequently, for 2 minutes or until golden brown.

3. Add potato, bay leaf, sage leaves, cumin, white corn, chives, parsley, and Homemade Vegetable Stock to the pressure cooker.

4. Lock the lid in place. Bring to high pressure, and maintain for 8 minutes. Remove from heat, and reduce pressure using the quick release method.

5. Reduce heat to low, stir in heavy cream, and reheat soup until warm.

6. Remove from heat, and add kosher salt and pepper. Remove bay leaf, ladle soup into bowls, and serve immediately.

UNDER PRESSURE

Substitute salted butter in recipes calling for unsalted butter, and you may wind up with a dish that tastes too salty! You can use salted butter in a pinch, but it contains anywhere from ¾ to 1 teaspoon salt per stick, or per ½ cup, so be sure to adjust the recipe accordingly.

Pumpkin Pear Soup

Fall flavors abound in this creamy pumpkin soup thickened with potatoes and sweetened with a hint of pear and apple.

Yield:	Prep time:	Cook time:	Serving size:
6 cups	15 minutes	10 minutes	1 cup

¼ cup unsalted butter or margarine	3 cups Homemade Vegetable Stock (recipe earlier in this chapter)
2 large white onions, diced small	1 tsp. freshly ground black pepper
2 large russet potatoes, peeled and diced small	2 bay leaves
3 large Bartlett pears, peeled, cored, and diced small	2 cups heavy cream or half-and-half
1 large red gala apple, peeled, cored, and diced small	1 tsp. kosher salt
2 medium pumpkins, peeled and cut into large cubes	

1. In a pressure cooker over low heat, melt unsalted butter. Add onions, potatoes, pears, apple, and pumpkins, and cook, stirring frequently, for 2 minutes or until vegetables are thoroughly coated in butter.

2. Remove from heat, and add Homemade Vegetable Stock, ½ teaspoon pepper, and bay leaves.

3. Lock the lid in place. Bring to high pressure, and maintain for 5 minutes. Remove from heat, and reduce pressure using the cold release method.

4. Remove bay leaves. Using an immersion blender, purée soup until smooth.

5. Reduce heat to low, add heavy cream, and reheat soup until warm. Add kosher salt and remaining ½ teaspoon pepper. Ladle soup into bowls, and serve immediately.

PRESSURE POINTER

For a festive touch for Halloween or Thanksgiving, serve this soup in a hollowed-out pumpkin and wow your kids with a soup they can't resist slurping.

Zucchini Squash Soup

Creamy and rich with sweet and tart undertones, this soup combines a rich, home-made vegetable stock with a trio of squash, tomato paste, and corn. Onions, leeks, and fennel add some tang.

Yield:	Prep time:	Cook time:	Serving size:
8 cups	15 minutes	20 minutes	2 cups

3 TB. extra-virgin olive oil

2 large yellow squash, diced small (skin on)

2 large zucchini, diced small (skin on)

1 medium butternut squash, seeded, peeled, and cut into 2-in. pieces

2 large leeks, white and light green parts, cut into 2-in. pieces

1 fennel bulb, white part only, diced small

2 TB. minced fresh garlic

6 cups Homemade Vegetable Stock (recipe earlier in this chapter)

1 (6-oz.) can tomato paste

1 cup corn kernels, frozen

1 tsp. kosher salt

½ tsp. freshly ground black pepper

2 medium green onions, white and green parts, sliced thin

1. In a pressure cooker over high heat, heat extra-virgin olive oil until hot. Add yellow squash, zucchini, butternut squash, leeks, and fennel, and cook, stirring frequently, for 2 or 3 minutes or until vegetables are soft. Add garlic, and cook, stirring frequently, for 30 seconds. Do not brown.

2. Lock the lid in place. Bring to high pressure, and maintain for 4 minutes. Reduce pressure using the quick release method.

3. Add Homemade Vegetable Stock.

4. Lock the lid in place. Bring back to high pressure, and maintain for 10 minutes. Remove from heat, and reduce pressure using the quick release method.

5. Add tomato paste and corn, reduce heat to low, and cook, uncovered, for 5 minutes.

6. Remove from heat, and add kosher salt and pepper. Ladle soup into bowls, garnish with green onions, and serve immediately.

FOODIE FACT

We have Christopher Columbus to thank for zucchini. The explorer brought seeds to the Mediterranean from Africa, and the rest is culinary history!

Asparagus Soup

This rich and creamy soup blends the delicate flavors of asparagus and celery with an undertone of garlic, shallots, and thyme.

Yield:	Prep time:	Cook time:	Serving size:
6 cups	15 minutes	20 minutes	1 cup

2 TB. *extra-virgin olive oil*

2 lb. asparagus, woody ends removed, cut into 1-in. pieces

2 large shallots, diced small

2 ribs celery, chopped small

1 clove garlic, minced

4 cups Homemade Vegetable Stock (recipe earlier in this chapter)

1 tsp. dried thyme

1 cup half-and-half or whole milk

1 tsp. kosher salt

½ tsp. freshly ground black pepper

1. In a pressure cooker over medium heat, heat extra-virgin olive oil. Add asparagus, shallots, celery, and garlic, and cook, stirring frequently, for 3 minutes. Add Homemade Vegetable Stock and thyme.

2. Lock the lid in place. Bring to high pressure, and maintain for 10 minutes. Remove from heat, and reduce pressure using the cold release method.

3. Using an immersion blender, purée soup until smooth.

4. Reduce heat to low, stir in half-and-half, and reheat soup until warm. Add kosher salt and pepper, ladle soup into bowls, and serve immediately.

STEAM SPEAK

Extra-virgin olive oil is from the first pressing and is the only type of olive oil extracted without heat and chemical processing. It tastes fresher than regular olive oil and contains more disease-fighting nutrients and antioxidants.

Split Pea Soup

This creamy, full-bodied soup is rich with the flavors of ham, celery, onion, and just a hint of parsley. The croutons add crunch and texture.

Yield:	Prep time:	Cook time:	Serving size:
5 cups	15 minutes	20 minutes	1 cup

1 large ham hock bone, rinsed in cold water

3 qt. water

1 lb. dried split peas, washed and sorted

1 rib celery, diced small

1 tsp. dried parsley or 2 TB. minced fresh parsley

1 medium white or yellow onion, diced small

1 cup whole milk

2 TB. all-purpose flour

2 TB. butter or margarine

2 tsp. kosher salt

½ tsp. freshly ground black pepper

½ cup unseasoned croutons

1. In a pressure cooker over medium heat, add ham hock bone, water, split peas, celery, parsley, and onion. Be sure ham hock bone is covered with water.

2. Lock the lid in place. Bring to high pressure, and maintain for 10 minutes. Remove from heat, and release pressure using the cold water release method.

3. Reduce heat to low, stir in whole milk, and reheat soup for 1 minute.

4. In a small bowl, combine all-purpose flour and butter and roll into small balls, or raw *roux* balls.

5. Set the pressure cooker over medium heat, and add roux balls in small batches. Cook, stirring frequently, for about 1 minute per batch or until soup is thickened.

6. Remove the pressure cooker from heat, and ladle soup into bowls. Add kosher salt and pepper, and garnish with croutons before serving.

STEAM SPEAK

Roux (pronounced *roo*) is a thickening agent for sauces that dates back more than 300 years in French cuisine. Roux thickens soup, gives it a silky-smooth consistency, and imparts a nutty flavor.

Mushroom Cream Soup

This creamy soup has a hint of onion, the soft flavor of mushrooms, and the tang of sour cream and sherry.

Yield:	Prep time:	Cook time:	Serving size:
6 cups	15 minutes	20 minutes	1 cup

4 TB. butter, margarine, or canola oil

½ lb. white button mushrooms, finely chopped

½ lb. brown button mushrooms, finely chopped

½ medium brown onion, diced small

2 cloves garlic, minced

1 TB. minced fresh parsley

½ tsp. ground nutmeg

4 cups Homemade Vegetable Stock (recipe earlier in this chapter)

2½ tsp. freshly ground black pepper

2 cups sour cream

2 TB. all-purpose flour

2 TB. butter or margarine

¼ cup dry sherry or dry white wine

1 tsp. kosher salt

1. In a pressure cooker over medium heat, heat butter. Add white button mushrooms, brown button mushrooms, onion, garlic, parsley, nutmeg, Homemade Vegetable Stock, and pepper.

2. Lock the lid in place. Bring to high pressure, and maintain for 15 minutes. Remove from heat, and reduce pressure using the cold water release method.

3. Reduce heat to low, add sour cream, and reheat soup until warm.

4. In a small bowl, combine all-purpose flour and butter, and roll into small balls, or raw roux balls.

5. Set the pressure cooker over medium heat, and add roux balls in small batches. Cook, stirring frequently, for about 1 minute per batch or until soup is thickened.

6. Reduce heat to low, and stir in sherry. Add kosher salt, ladle soup into bowls, and serve immediately.

PRESSURE POINTER

When selecting button mushrooms for pressure cooking, choose mushrooms that still have tightly closed veils covering the gills. Opt for firm, dry mushrooms that don't have a slimy texture or cracks. Store them in a paper bag in a cool part of the fridge, and use within 1 week.

Black Bean Soup

This chunky vegetarian soup is loaded with garlic, which enhances the flavor of the *black beans*.

Yield:	Prep time:	Cook time:	Serving size:
8 cups	15 minutes	30 minutes	1 cup

1 TB. canola or vegetable oil	2 cups dried black beans, rinsed
1 large white onion, diced small	5 cloves garlic, whole, peeled
2 ribs celery, diced small	1 bay leaf
1 green bell pepper, ribs and seeds removed, and diced small	1 tsp. dried thyme
2 carrots, peeled and diced small	1 tsp. kosher salt
1 tsp. dried cumin	½ tsp. freshly ground black pepper
8 cups water	8 tsp. low-fat sour cream

1. In a pressure cooker over medium heat, heat canola oil. Add onion, celery, green bell pepper, and carrots, and cook, stirring frequently, for 4 minutes or until soft. Add cumin, water, black beans, garlic, bay leaf, and thyme.

2. Lock the lid in place. Bring to high pressure, and maintain for 30 minutes. Reduce pressure using the natural release method.

3. Remove the pressure cooker from heat. Remove bay leaf, and add kosher salt and pepper. Ladle soup into bowls, dollop 1 teaspoon sour cream in the center of each bowl, and serve immediately.

STEAM SPEAK

Packed with protein, fiber, and antioxidants, **black beans** keep you feeling full longer, help reduce bad cholesterol and heart disease, and help fight cancer and slow the aging process. All this for just pennies a serving!

Cream of Tomato Soup

This sophisticated soup is reminiscent of your favorite childhood wintertime soup, but it's richer and creamier. The shallots, garlic, and pepper lend zest to the fresh tomatoes.

Yield:	Prep time:	Cook time:	Serving size:
6 cups	20 minutes	45 minutes	1 cup

1 TB. extra-virgin olive oil

1 TB. unsalted butter or margarine

1 large white or yellow sweet onion, finely chopped

2 large shallots, diced fine

2 cloves garlic, minced

4 lb. medium Roma tomatoes, chopped and diced

1 tsp. dried Italian seasoning

5 cups vegetable broth

1 cup heavy cream or half-and-half

1 tsp. kosher salt

½ tsp. freshly ground black pepper

1. In a pressure cooker over medium heat, heat extra-virgin olive oil and unsalted butter until melted. Add onion and shallots, and cook, stirring frequently, until onion turns translucent.

2. Stir in garlic, and cook for 30 seconds. Do not brown. Add tomatoes, Italian seasoning, and vegetable broth, and set over high heat.

3. Lock the lid in place. Bring to high pressure, and maintain for 10 minutes. Reduce heat to medium, and cook for another 10 minutes. Remove from heat, and reduce pressure using the natural release method.

4. Using an immersion blender, purée soup until smooth, being careful not to spatter yourself with hot soup.

5. Reduce heat to low, stir in heavy cream, and reheat soup until warm. Add kosher salt and pepper, ladle soup into bowls, and serve immediately.

UNDER PRESSURE

Don't substitute high-moisture tomatoes for Roma tomatoes when making this soup or your end product may be thin and runny. Roma tomatoes have a dense, meaty flesh, low moisture content, and very few seeds, which makes them ideal for pressure cooking soups.

Meaty Soups from Around the World

In This Chapter

- Meaty matters
- Beefing up your stock
- Hearty beef soups
- Rich and filling pork soups

Whether you're in the middle of a February deep-freeze or weathering a cold snap in the middle of May, the nourishing meaty soups in this chapter will warm you from the inside out and stick to your ribs.

The soups in this chapter originate from around the world, from a meatball soup that takes its cue from Mexican tortilla soup, to a robust goulash inspired by Hungarian soups, to a sweet-and-sour pork soup that borrows elements from Asian cuisine. By making your own ethnic soups, you can take your taste buds on a trip around the world—and never have to worry about losing your passport!

Making the Cut

At more than $3 a can for some brands, a humble can of soup is no longer the cheap food it used to be! By using your pressure cooker to make soup at home, you not only get delicious results, but you also save a bundle of money.

Just throw an inexpensive cut of meat into the pot—remember, your pressure cooker can transform the toughest cuts of meat into tender morsels—along with a handful of vegetables, grains, and pasta, and you've got soup for just pennies a serving. Beef chuck, bottom round, brisket, shanks, and short ribs; lamb shanks and shoulder, veal shoulder, ribs, and osso bucco; and pork shoulder and ribs are all perfect pressure cooker meats.

If you prefer to make soup using leaner cuts of meat, reduce the cooking time to avoid overcooking or drying out the meat.

Stock Options

The best-tasting meaty soups are made with homemade beef stock, and the recipes in this chapter make a large-enough quantity that you'll have more than enough to go around, plus leftovers. Here are a few tips to follow for savory stock in minutes:

Use roasted bones to make stock that has an intense, rich flavor. To roast the bones, coat them with a thin layer of vegetable oil, place them in a greased roasting pan on top of a layer of chopped onions and carrots, and roast them at 400°F for 40 minutes.

To remove fat from your stock, refrigerate it overnight. The cold will solidify the fat so it rises to the surface, so it's easy to scrape it off with a large spoon. (It's okay to use homemade stock immediately, although it contains more fat than if you refrigerate it overnight.)

To freeze stock for later use, refrigerate and remove the fat from the surface, and pour it into quart-size freezer containers. Or freeze the stock in ice cube trays, and pack the cubes in freezer bags or containers. The stock will keep in the freezer for 6 months.

PRESSURE POINTER

Stock is made from bones and is used as an ingredient in a recipe. Canned *broth* is made from meat, bones, and seasonings and can be enjoyed on its own. The two are interchangeable, but the recipes in this chapter call for homemade stock. Don't substitute canned beef broth or bouillon cubes for homemade beef broth, or your soup will come out thinner and saltier.

Homemade Beef Stock

Made with Madeira wine, this stock has a rich, zesty flavor that's incomparable to canned stock.

Yield:	Prep time:	Cook time:	Serving size:
6 cups	15 minutes	60 minutes	1 cup

2 lb. beef marrow soup bones	1 bay leaf
8 cups hot water	4 whole peppercorns
2 medium white or yellow onions, peeled and sliced	2 sprigs fresh thyme
	4 stems fresh parsley
2 large carrots, peeled and cut into 2-in. chunks	1 cup Madeira wine
4 ribs celery, trimmed and cut into 2-in. chunks	

1. Wash soup bones thoroughly in cold water to remove blood.

2. Insert a trivet in the pressure cooker. Place bones on the trivet. Add hot water, onions, carrots, celery, bay leaf, peppercorns, thyme, and parsley.

3. Lock the lid in place. Bring to high pressure, and maintain for 1 hour. Remove from heat, and reduce pressure using the cold water release method.

4. Strain stock, let cool, and refrigerate overnight.

5. Using a large spoon, skim fat from surface of stock. Stir in Madeira wine. Pour into 1-pint or 1-quart freezer containers, and freeze for up to 6 months.

PRESSURE POINTER

When buying bones for stock, use shanks, marrow bones, oxtails, calves feet, or knuckle bones, and ask the butcher to cut or split them into small pieces.

Oxtail Soup

Similar to beef stew but with a softer flavor, this soup combines the flavors of oxtail, tomatoes, and sherry.

Yield:	Prep time:	Cook time:	Serving size:
6 cups	15 minutes	20 minutes	1 cup

½ cup unsalted butter or margarine

1 medium yellow or white onion, diced small

1 large carrot, peeled and diced small

2 ribs celery, diced small

1 small white turnip, peeled and diced small

2 large leeks, white part only, thinly sliced

2 lb. oxtail bones, rinsed in cold water

2 qt. Homemade Beef Stock (recipe earlier in this chapter)

2 bay leaves

3 black peppercorns

4 large Roma tomatoes, diced small

1 tsp. kosher salt

2 tsp. freshly ground black pepper

¼ cup dry sherry

1. In a pressure cooker over medium heat, heat unsalted butter. Add onion, carrot, celery, turnip, and leeks, and sauté for 1 minute. Add oxtail bones, Homemade Beef Stock, bay leaves, and black peppercorns.

2. Lock the lid in place. Bring to high pressure, and maintain for 30 minutes. Remove from heat, and release pressure using the cold water release method.

3. Using tongs, remove meat from broth and place on a cutting board. When cool, dice meat into bite-size pieces.

4. Strain broth.

5. Return broth and meat to the pressure cooker, and set over low heat. Add Roma tomatoes, and simmer for 5 minutes. Add kosher salt and pepper, and stir in sherry. Cook for 1 minute. Ladle soup into warmed soup bowls, and serve immediately.

 PRESSURE POINTER

Oxtail was once part of an ox, but today the term refers to beef or veal tail. Oxtail is very bony and flavorful, but it's also very tough, which makes it a natural choice for the pressure cooker.

Hearty Beef Soup

This thick, rich soup combines a rich beef broth with the flavors of tomato, onion, and garlic.

Yield:	Prep time:	Cook time:	Serving size:
6 cups	15 minutes	15 minutes	1 cup

1½ lb. chuck or soup bone with meat

6 ribs celery, cut into 2-in. pieces

1 medium brown or white onion, diced small

2 large carrots, peeled and cut into 1-in. rounds

2 cloves garlic, minced

1 tsp. kosher salt

6 whole *peppercorns*

½ cup canned diced tomatoes, with juice

1 small white or red potato, skin on and diced medium

¼ cup dry lima beans

1 tsp. freshly ground black pepper

½ cup water

1. Wash meat and bones thoroughly in cold water to remove blood. Place in the pressure cooker, pour enough water into the cooker to cover the bones by 1 inch, and set over high heat.

2. Lock the lid in place. Bring to high pressure, and maintain for 15 minutes. Remove from heat, and release pressure using the cold water release method.

3. Using a large spoon, carefully skim foam from top of broth. Add celery, onion, carrots, garlic, kosher salt, peppercorns, tomatoes with juice, potato, lima beans, pepper, and water. Set the pressure cooker over high heat.

4. Lock the lid in place. Bring to high pressure, and maintain for 10 minutes. Remove from heat, and release pressure using the natural release method.

5. Ladle soup into bowls, and serve immediately.

STEAM SPEAK

Peppercorns were once so valuable they were used as currency, and many European fleets sailed the seas in pursuit of the rare spice. Today, you can find peppercorns in any grocery store. They give foods a strong, fresh, peppery flavor you can't get from a typical pepper shaker.

Traditional Goulash

This thick, rich stew combines the sunny flavors of the Mediterranean—including paprika, tomato, onion, and bay leaves—in a hearty *goulash*.

Yield:	Prep time:	Cook time:	Serving size:
4 to 6 cups	15 minutes	27 minutes	1 cup

4 TB. unsalted butter, margarine, or canola oil	1 cup water
2 lb. beef chuck or beef round steak, cut into 1-in. pieces	4 medium white or brown onions, thinly sliced
2 TB. paprika	1 clove garlic, minced
2 bay leaves	1 large green bell pepper, ribs and seeds removed, and thinly diced
1 (6-oz.) can tomato paste	$\frac{1}{8}$ tsp. allspice
2 tsp. kosher salt	

1. In a pressure cooker over medium heat, heat unsalted butter until hot. Add beef chuck, and brown on both sides. Add paprika, bay leaves, and tomato paste, and stir until paprika is well blended into butter mixture. Add kosher salt and water.

2. Lock the lid in place. Bring to high pressure, and maintain for 20 minutes. Remove from heat, and release pressure using the cold water release method.

3. Set the pressure cooker over high heat, and add onions, garlic, green bell pepper, and allspice.

4. Lock the lid in place. Bring to high pressure, and maintain for 7 minutes. Remove from heat, and release pressure using the cold water release method.

5. Remove bay leaves. Using a large serving spoon, ladle goulash onto dinner plates and serve immediately.

STEAM SPEAK

Goulash, which originated in Hungary, refers to a stew made with beef and vegetables and flavored with paprika, a spice that also hails from Hungary.

Beef Borscht

With chunks of beef and vegetables, this *borscht* is so thick and chunky you might want to eat it with a fork. Beets, tomatoes, and garlic lend a savory flavor, and sour cream adds richness and bite.

Yield:	Prep time:	Cook time:	Serving size:
6 cups	10 minutes	20 minutes	1 cup

4 TB. unsalted butter, margarine, or canola oil

1 medium white or yellow onion, diced small

1 TB. garlic, minced

4 or 5 medium beets (1 lb.), washed and diced

2 bay leaves

2 cups Homemade Beef Stock (recipe earlier in this chapter)

1 lb. beef chuck, cut into bite-size cubes

1 large carrot, peeled and sliced into 1-in. rounds

1 medium parsnip or medium turnip, peeled and cubed

2 large russet potatoes, peeled and cubed

4 medium Roma tomatoes, cubed

1 cup sour cream

1 tsp. kosher salt

½ tsp. freshly ground black pepper

1. In a pressure cooker over medium heat, heat unsalted butter for about 30 seconds or until fragrant. Do not brown. Add onion, garlic, beets, bay leaves, Homemade Beef Stock, and beef chuck.

2. Lock the lid in place. Bring to high pressure, and maintain for 20 minutes. Remove from heat, and release pressure using the cold water release method.

3. Set the pressure cooker over high heat. Add carrot, parsnip, and potatoes.

4. Lock the lid in place. Bring to high pressure, and maintain for 8 minutes. Remove from heat, and release pressure using the cold water release method.

5. Set the pressure cooker over low heat. Add Roma tomatoes, and cook for 5 minutes. Add sour cream, and heat, stirring, for 1 or 2 minutes or until soup is warm. Add kosher salt and pepper. Remove bay leaves. Ladle soup into soup bowls, and serve immediately.

STEAM SPEAK

Originating in Russia and Poland, **borscht** is a rich soup made with beets and sour cream, although it may also include vegetables. Borscht can be served piping hot or icy cold as gazpacho.

Hamburger Soup

Almost like spaghetti and meatballs in a bowl, this soup is loaded with beef and *orzo* and combines the zesty flavors of onions, peppers, tomatoes, and a variety of hot spices.

Yield:	Prep time:	Cook time:	Serving size:
8 cups	15 minutes	20 minutes	1 cup

1 lb. lean ground beef

1 small yellow or white onion, diced

1 large green bell pepper, ribs and seeds removed, and thinly sliced

2 large ribs celery, finely diced

2 large carrots, peeled and finely diced

2 large russet potatoes, skin on and diced

½ small head green cabbage, shredded

3 cups hot water

2 cups Homemade Beef Stock (recipe earlier in this chapter)

3 cups tomato juice

¼ tsp. ground black pepper

1 TB. kosher salt

1 bay leaf

¼ tsp. cayenne

1 TB. paprika

½ tsp. dried basil

¾ cup dried orzo

8 TB. sour cream

1. In a pressure cooker over medium heat, add ground beef, onion, green bell pepper, celery, carrots, potatoes, and cabbage, and cook for 5 to 10 minutes or until beef is browned. Add hot water, Homemade Beef Stock, tomato juice, pepper, kosher salt, bay leaf, cayenne, paprika, and basil.

2. Lock the lid in place. Bring to high pressure, and maintain for 15 minutes. Remove from heat, and release pressure using the quick release method.

3. Set the pressure cooker over medium heat, and stir in orzo. Bring heat to high until mixture begins to boil, reduce heat to low, and cook orzo for 5 minutes or until soft.

4. Ladle soup into bowls, garnish each with 1 tablespoon sour cream, and serve immediately.

STEAM SPEAK

Orzo is a tiny, rice-shape pasta made from semolina wheat. A close cousin to couscous, orzo can be substituted for couscous, rice, barley, and many other grains.

Beef Stroganoff Soup

Dry sherry, sour cream, and butter combine with beef to give this classic comfort food a distinctively rich taste and aroma.

Yield:	Prep time:	Cook time:	Serving size:
6 cups	15 minutes	15 minutes	1 cup

4 TB. butter, margarine, or canola oil

2 lb. top round steak, cut into strips

1 lb. white button mushrooms, brushed free of dirt and sliced thin

½ medium white or yellow onion, diced small

2 ribs celery, diced

2 cloves garlic, minced

1 TB. fresh minced parsley

1 tsp. ground nutmeg

1 large green bell pepper, ribs and seeds removed, and thinly sliced

4 cups Homemade Beef Stock (recipe earlier in this chapter)

2½ tsp. freshly ground black pepper

1 cup sour cream

2 TB. all-purpose flour

2 TB. butter or margarine

¼ cup dry sherry or dry white wine

1 tsp. kosher salt

1. In a pressure cooker over medium heat, heat 4 tablespoons butter. When hot, add top round steak, and brown on both sides. Add mushrooms, onion, celery, garlic, parsley, nutmeg, green bell pepper, Homemade Beef Stock, and pepper.

2. Lock the lid in place. Bring to high pressure, and maintain for 15 minutes. Remove from heat, and release pressure using the cold water release method.

3. Add sour cream, and reheat soup over low heat until warm.

4. In a small bowl, combine all-purpose flour and 2 tablespoons butter, and roll into small balls, or roux.

5. Increase heat to medium, and add roux to the pressure cooker in small batches. Cook, stirring frequently, for about 1 minute per batch or until soup is thickened.

6. Reduce heat to low, and stir in sherry and kosher salt. Ladle soup into bowls, and serve immediately.

UNDER PRESSURE

If a recipe calls for wine or liquor, never use cooking wines or inexpensive liquor, which could ruin the taste of the dish. Instead, use a high-quality wine or liquor you'd enjoy drinking.

Meatball Soup

Carrots and peas flavor this rich meatball soup in a beefy stock with hints of Worcestershire sauce, garlic, and nutmeg.

Yield:	Prep time:	Cook time:	Serving size:
6 cups	15 minutes	5 minutes	1 cup

1½ lb. lean ground beef

1 large egg, lightly beaten

2 slices white bread, crusts removed, soaked in 1 cup skim milk, and squeezed dry

2 TB. fresh Italian parsley, minced

½ tsp. ground nutmeg

1 TB. Worcestershire sauce

2 cloves garlic, minced

2 TB. extra-virgin olive oil

¾ cup frozen peas

2 large carrots, peeled and diced small

2 medium white potatoes, peeled and cut into 1-in. cubes

1 TB. Homemade Beef Stock (recipe earlier in this chapter)

¼ cup dry red wine

1 bay leaf

1 tsp. kosher salt

½ tsp. freshly ground black pepper

1. In a large bowl, combine ground beef, egg, bread, Italian parsley, nutmeg, Worcestershire sauce, and garlic. Form mixture into about 25 (2-inch) meatballs.

2. In a pressure cooker over medium heat, heat extra-virgin olive oil. When hot, add meatballs and brown on all sides. Add peas, carrots, potatoes, Homemade Beef Stock, red wine, and bay leaf.

3. Lock the lid in place. Bring to high pressure, and maintain for 5 minutes. Remove from heat, and release pressure using the quick release method. Using tongs, remove and discard bay leaf.

4. Set the pressure cooker over low heat, and reheat soup for 2 minutes. Add kosher salt and pepper, ladle soup into bowls, and serve immediately.

PRESSURE POINTER

To save time, you can prepare the meatballs a day in advance and refrigerate them. Don't brown them until you're ready to cook them in the pressure cooker because dangerous bacteria can develop in partially cooked meats.

Sausage with Black-Eyed Peas

This Southern classic combines the rich flavors of sausage and black-eyed peas with a hot tomato sauce spiced with garlic, chili powder, and cumin.

Yield:	Prep time:	Cook time:	Serving size:
5 cups	15 minutes	25 minutes	1 cup

2 cups dried black-eyed peas

3 cups water

2 TB. vegetable oil or olive oil

1 medium white or yellow onion, diced small

1 (16-oz.) pkg. kielbasa or other sausage, cut into 1-in. cubes

1 bay leaf

1 TB. chili powder

1 tsp. ground cumin

3 cloves garlic, minced

3 cups Homemade Beef Stock (recipe earlier in this chapter)

1 (32-oz.) can diced tomatoes, with juice

¼ cup dark brown sugar, firmly packed

1 tsp. kosher salt

½ tsp. freshly ground black pepper

1. In a pressure cooker over high heat, combine black-eyed peas, water, and vegetable oil, ensuring peas are completely covered with water.

2. Lock the lid in place. Bring to high pressure, and maintain for 10 minutes. Remove from heat, and release pressure using the natural release method.

3. Drain peas in a colander, and set aside in a bowl.

4. In the pressure cooker over low heat, combine onion, kielbasa, bay leaf, chili powder, cumin, and garlic.

5. Lock the lid in place. Bring to low pressure, and maintain for 3 minutes. Remove from heat, and release pressure using the quick release method.

6. Set the pressure cooker over high heat, and add Homemade Beef Stock, tomatoes with juice, dark brown sugar, and peas.

7. Lock the lid in place. Bring to high pressure, and maintain for 15 minutes. Remove from heat, and release pressure using the natural release method.

8. Add kosher salt and pepper, ladle soup into large soup bowls, and serve immediately.

PRESSURE POINTER

If your supermarket doesn't sell sausage in bulk, you can use sausage links. Just remove the casings and push out the sausage before using because the casings have the texture and flavor of wet rubber bands.

Sweet-and-Sour Soup with Pork

The sweet-and-sour sauce, soy sauce, and garlic in this scrumptious dish infuse the pork and vegetables with spicy Asian flavors.

Yield:	Prep time:	Cook time:	Serving size:
6 cups	15 minutes	20 minutes	1 cup

4 TB. butter, margarine, or vegetable oil

1 medium white or yellow onion, diced small

1 large red bell pepper, ribs and seeds removed, and thinly sliced

1 large yellow bell pepper, ribs and seeds removed, and thinly sliced

1 lb. pork tenderloin, trimmed of fat and cut into 2-in. cubes

2 cloves garlic, minced

⅓ cup low-sodium soy sauce

1 cup sweet-and-sour sauce

1 TB. white vinegar

¼ cup water

2 green onions, white part only, thinly sliced

¼ cup sherry or mirin

½ tsp. kosher salt

½ tsp. freshly ground black pepper

1. In a pressure cooker over high heat, heat butter. When hot, add onion, red bell pepper, and yellow bell pepper, and cook for 5 minutes or until soft.

2. Add pork, garlic, and soy sauce, and cook for 2 minutes. Stir in sweet-and-sour sauce, white vinegar, water, and green onions.

3. Lock the lid in place. Bring to high pressure, and maintain for 10 minutes. Remove from heat, and release pressure using the quick release method.

4. Set the pressure cooker over low heat, and stir in sherry. Cook for 30 seconds. Add kosher salt and pepper, ladle soup into bowls, and serve immediately.

PRESSURE POINTER

To reduce the alcohol content of a dish calling for wine, substitute mirin, a low-alcohol, sweet golden wine made from glutinous rice. You can find it in the gourmet section of many supermarkets, and in Asian markets.

Perfect Poultry Soups

Chapter 9

In This Chapter

- Perfect poultry for your pressure cooker
- Making savory chicken stock
- Old-fashioned chicken soups
- Hearty poultry gumbos

France's King Henry IV knew what he was talking about when he stated in his coronation speech that he hoped every peasant would have "a chicken in his pot every Sunday," a phrase later paraphrased by President Herbert Hoover. Unfortunately, until after World War II, only the wealthy could afford the proverbial chicken in every pot. Today, modern production methods have turned chicken (and eggs) into some of the most affordable and accessible meats and sources of protein.

Chicken has such a mild, delicate flavor it can serve as a blank culinary slate for a world's worth of flavors. That may explain why nearly every region on Earth has its own chicken specialties, from Italy's chicken cacciatore and India's tandoori chicken, to China's sweet-and-sour chicken and the Lone Star state's fiery Tex-Mex grilled chicken. With a pressure cooker, you can duplicate ethnic chicken recipes in no time flat, and take your family and friends on a culinary taste tour around the globe.

A Cut Above

Fortunately, you won't have to worry about buying low-quality chicken or turkey because the U.S. Department of Agriculture grades poultry. Only the highest-quality poultry, or grade A, is sold in supermarkets and grocery stores. Whether you're making stock, soup, chowders, or gumbos, poultry is virtually foolproof to prepare in the pressure cooker. It comes out tender, moist, and flavorful.

Chicken backs, which have a lot of bones and skin, make the tastiest stock. If you don't have chicken backs, you can substitute chicken bones. To remove excess fat, chill the stock so the fat rises to the top and then skim it off using a large spoon.

For extra-rich and savory stock, start with a chicken or turkey carcass you've been storing in the freezer. If you're buying bones to make stock, purchase the cheapest, boniest parts of a chicken, including the back, neck, and wings. Remember, it's the bones, not the meat, that makes the best stock.

FOODIE FACT

The ultimate comfort food, poultry soup is warming, easy to digest, and the perfect thing to sip when you're under the weather. And it's not just folklore; many studies have, in fact, shown that sipping hot chicken soup helps relieve the symptoms of colds and the flu.

Homemade Chicken Stock

This all-purpose chicken stock adds intense flavor and richness to any soup, stew, curry, or main dish it's added to. You'll never use bouillon cubes again!

Yield:	Prep time:	Cook time:	Serving size:
6 cups	15 minutes	20 minutes	1 cup

2 lb. chicken bones	6 large ribs celery, sliced into 2-in. chunks
8 cups water	1 bay leaf
2 medium white or yellow onions, sliced	4 whole peppercorns
2 large carrots, peeled and cut into 2-in. chunks	2 sprigs fresh thyme
	4 stems fresh parsley

1. Wash bones well in cold water to remove all traces of blood.

2. Insert a rack in the pressure cooker. Place bones on the rack.

3. Set the pressure cooker over high heat, and add water, onions, carrots, celery, bay leaf, peppercorns, thyme, and parsley.

4. Lock the lid in place. Bring to high pressure, and maintain for 20 minutes. Remove from heat, and reduce pressure using the cold water release method.

5. Strain stock, transfer to a bowl, and refrigerate overnight. Using a large spoon, skim fat from surface of stock.

6. Use stock immediately in recipes, or freeze in 1-pint or 1-quart containers for up to 6 months.

FOODIE FACT

When making poultry soups, it's okay to use frozen instead of fresh chicken and turkey. Just remember that larger cuts of frozen meat, such as a whole chicken, require up to a third more cooking time. For the best results, use small, individual cuts of frozen meat no thicker than 1 inch (patties, chops, thin cuts) and thaw partially before cooking.

Grandma's Chicken Noodle Soup

This old-fashioned chicken soup is packed with onions, carrots, and celery for a sweet, mellow flavor and lots of chicken and noodles for a chunky, stewlike consistency.

Yield:	Prep time:	Cook time:	Serving size:
5 cups	15 minutes	20 minutes	2 cups

1 TB. extra-virgin olive oil or canola oil	1 tsp. kosher salt
1 TB. unsalted butter or margarine	1 tsp. dried parsley
4 medium carrots, peeled and sliced into ½-in. rounds	1 tsp. dried thyme
3 ribs celery, cut into ½-in. slices	2 cups Homemade Chicken Stock (recipe earlier in this chapter)
1 large sweet onion, diced fine	1 (8-oz.) pkg. spaghetti noodles, cooked
4 lb. boneless, skinless chicken breasts	½ tsp. freshly ground black pepper

1. In a pressure cooker over medium heat, heat extra-virgin olive oil and unsalted butter. When hot, add carrots and celery, and cook for 3 minutes. Add onion, and cook for 5 minutes or until very soft. Add chicken, kosher salt, parsley, thyme, and Homemade Chicken Stock.

2. Lock the lid in place. Bring to low pressure, and maintain for 20 minutes. Remove from heat, and reduce pressure using the quick release method.

3. Transfer chicken to a cutting board, and let cool for 10 minutes. Cut into bite-size pieces.

4. Return chicken to the pressure cooker.

5. Lock the lid in place. Bring to a boil over high heat. Remove from heat, and reduce pressure using the quick release method.

6. Increase heat to high. Add spaghetti noodles and cook, covered, for about 10 minutes or until soft. Add pepper, ladle soup into bowls, and serve immediately.

FOODIE FACT

There are more than 30 varieties of parsley, the most common being curly leaf parsley and the stronger-flavored Italian or flat-leaf parsley. Parsley is widely available in supermarkets, sold in bunches. Choose bunches with bright-green leaves and no sign of wilting.

Spicy Chicken Dumpling Soup

Cayenne, garlic, cumin, and onion kick up the flavor of this fun-to-eat chicken soup with homemade *dumplings*.

Yield:	Prep time:	Cook time:	Serving size:
5 cups	15 minutes	8 minutes	1 cup

2 cups all-purpose flour

1 TB. baking powder

1 tsp. salt

5 TB. unsalted butter

¾ cup buttermilk

2 TB. canola oil or vegetable oil

1 large white or yellow onion, diced small

4 cloves garlic, minced

2 lb. boneless, skinless chicken breasts

2 tsp. ground cumin

1 tsp. dried Italian seasoning

4 cups Homemade Chicken Stock (recipe earlier in this chapter)

1 tsp. cayenne

1 tsp. kosher salt

½ tsp. freshly ground black pepper

1. In a large bowl, combine all-purpose flour, baking powder, and salt. Using a pastry blender, 2 knives, or a fork, cut unsalted butter into flour mixture. Stir in buttermilk, and mix until combined. Form into small dumpling balls using an ice-cream scoop, and set aside.

2. In a pressure cooker over high heat, heat canola oil for about 2 minutes or until hot. Add onion, and cook for 2 or 3 minutes or until soft. Add garlic, and cook for 30 seconds. Do not brown.

3. Add chicken, cumin, and Italian seasoning, and cook, stirring frequently, for 1 or 2 minutes or until chicken is lightly browned. Stir in 2 cups Homemade Chicken Stock.

4. Lock the lid in place. Bring to high pressure, and maintain for 8 minutes. Remove from heat, and reduce pressure using the quick release method.

5. Reduce heat to medium, stir in remaining 2 cups Homemade Chicken Stock, and bring to a low simmer. Stir in cayenne.

6. Drop dumpling balls into soup in small batches.

7. Lock the lid in place. Cook for 10 minutes on medium heat. Remove from heat, and reduce pressure using the quick release method. Dumplings are done if a toothpick inserted in the center comes out clean.

8. Add kosher salt and pepper, ladle soup into large bowls, and serve immediately.

STEAM SPEAK

Dumplings are an ancient food found in many cuisines around the world. They range from Czech *knedliky* and Hungarian *tesztak* to Jewish *matzo balls,* Chinese *wontons,* Italian *ravioli* and *gnocchi,* and Southern *slicks.*

Chicken and Rice Soup

The bay leaf, peppercorns, and parsley lend this old-fashioned classic extra zest, depth, and flavor.

Yield:	Prep time:	Cook time:	Serving size:
6 cups	10 minutes	10 minutes	1 cup

2 TB. extra-virgin olive oil

1 medium white or yellow onion, diced small

1 large carrot, peeled and cut into 1-in. rounds

3 ribs celery, cut in ½

½ cup uncooked white rice

4 (5-oz.) bone-in chicken breasts

6 cups water

3 whole peppercorns

1 bay leaf

¼ cup fresh parsley leaves, minced

1 tsp. kosher salt

½ tsp. freshly ground black pepper

2 sprigs parsley

1. In a pressure cooker over medium heat, combine extra-virgin olive oil, onion, carrot, celery, and white rice. Cook uncovered for 1 minute. Add chicken, water, peppercorns, bay leaf, and parsley leaves.

2. Lock the lid in place. Bring to high pressure, and maintain for 20 minutes. Remove from heat, and reduce pressure using the quick release method.

3. Transfer chicken to a cutting board, and let cool for 10 minutes. Remove chicken from bones and return chicken to the pressure cooker. Using tongs, remove and discard bay leaf.

4. Reduce heat to low, and reheat soup for 10 minutes. Add kosher salt and pepper, ladle soup into bowls, garnish each serving with parsley sprigs, and serve immediately.

UNDER PRESSURE

Salmonella bacteria are present on most poultry. After cutting or handling raw chicken, wash utensils, cutting boards, and your hands with an antibacterial soap to kill germs and avoid contamination. Don't let any raw juices come into contact with cooked chicken, which should have an internal temperature of 165°F.

Summer Vegetables with Chicken Soup

This light and flavorful soup combines the fresh and lively flavors of squash, zucchini, and corn.

Yield:	Prep time:	Cook time:	Serving size:
8 cups	15 minutes	14 minutes	2 cups

3 TB. canola oil or vegetable oil

2 large yellow squash, skin on and diced small

2 large zucchini, skin on and diced small

2 large leeks, white and green parts, cut into 2-in. pieces

1 large red bell pepper, ribs and seeds removed, and diced small

2 TB. freshly minced garlic

6 cups Homemade Chicken Stock (recipe earlier in this chapter)

2 (4-oz.) boneless, skinless chicken breasts, diced small

2 cups corn kernels, fresh or frozen

1 tsp. kosher salt

1 tsp. freshly ground black pepper

2 large green onions, sliced into small rounds

1. In a pressure cooker over medium heat, heat canola oil for about 2 minutes or until very hot. Add yellow squash, zucchini, leeks, and red bell pepper, and cook for 2 or 3 minutes or until vegetables are soft. Add garlic, and cook for about 30 seconds or until aromatic. Do not brown.

2. Lock the lid in place. Bring to high pressure, and maintain for 4 minutes. Remove from heat, and reduce pressure using the quick release method.

3. Add Homemade Chicken Stock and chicken.

4. Lock the lid in place. Bring to high pressure, and maintain for 10 minutes. Remove from heat, and reduce pressure using the quick release method.

5. Reduce heat to low, and stir in corn. Cook, uncovered, for 5 minutes. Add kosher salt and pepper, ladle soup into bowls, garnish with sliced green onions, and serve immediately.

PRESSURE POINTER

Technically, zucchini is a summer squash, but you can find it year-round in most supermarkets. For the best flavor, buy small, young zucchini. The skin should be a bright, vibrant green and free of dings and blemishes.

White Bean and Chicken Soup

Italian seasoning, garlic, onions, and *white beans* bring the flavors of Italy right to your soup bowl.

Yield:	Prep time:	Cook time:	Serving size:
6 cups	15 minutes	13 minutes	2 cups

2 TB. extra-virgin olive oil

1 large white or yellow onion, diced small

4 cloves garlic, minced

2 lb. boneless, skinless chicken breasts, diced small

1 tsp. kosher salt

1 tsp. freshly ground black pepper

2 tsp. ground cumin

2 tsp. dried Italian seasoning

4 cups Homemade Chicken Stock (recipe earlier in this chapter)

2 (16-oz.) cans white beans, rinsed and drained

1 TB. hot sauce

1. In a pressure cooker over medium heat, heat extra-virgin olive oil for about 2 minutes or until very hot. Add onion, and cook for 2 or 3 minutes or until soft. Add garlic, and cook for about 30 seconds or until aromatic. Do not brown.

2. Sprinkle chicken pieces with kosher salt, pepper, cumin, and Italian seasoning, and add chicken to the pressure cooker. Add 2 cups Homemade Chicken Stock.

3. Lock the lid in place. Bring to high pressure, and maintain for 8 minutes. Remove from heat, and reduce pressure using the quick release method.

4. Add remaining 2 cups Homemade Chicken Stock and white beans.

5. Lock the lid in place. Bring to low pressure, and maintain for 5 minutes. Remove from heat, and reduce pressure using the quick release method.

6. Taste and season with any additional kosher salt and pepper if needed. Add hot sauce. Ladle soup into bowls, and serve immediately.

STEAM SPEAK

The term **white bean** is actually a generic name for beans that fall into one of four categories: Great Northern beans, navy beans, pea beans, and marrow beans. Unless a recipe specifies type of white bean, you can use any type you choose.

Cream of Chicken Soup

Whole milk and cheddar cheese make this soup extra rich and creamy, while parsley and thyme add just a hint of flavor.

Yield:	Prep time:	Cook time:	Serving size:
5 cups	15 minutes	10 minutes	1 cup

4 TB. unsalted butter or margarine	1 tsp. kosher salt
1 TB. extra-virgin olive oil or canola oil	1 tsp. dried parsley
	1 tsp. dried thyme
2 medium carrots, peeled and sliced into ½-in. rounds	2 cups Homemade Chicken Stock (recipe earlier in this chapter)
3 ribs celery, cut into ½-in. slices	⅓ cup all-purpose flour
1 large yellow or white onion, diced fine	2 cups whole milk
	2 cups shredded cheddar cheese
2 lb. boneless, skinless chicken breasts	½ tsp. freshly ground black pepper

1. In a pressure cooker over medium heat, heat 1 tablespoon unsalted butter and extra-virgin olive oil until hot. Add carrots and celery, and cook for 3 minutes. Add onion, and cook for 3 minutes or until soft. Add chicken, kosher salt, parsley, thyme, and Homemade Chicken Stock.

2. Lock the lid in place. Bring to high pressure, and maintain for 10 minutes. Remove from heat, and reduce pressure using the quick release method.

3. Using tongs, transfer chicken to a cutting board, and let cool for 10 minutes. Cut chicken into bite-size pieces, and return it to the pressure cooker.

4. In a medium saucepan over medium-low heat, melt remaining 3 tablespoons unsalted butter. Add all-purpose flour, and mix well. Reduce heat to low, and gradually whisk in whole milk until creamy. Stir mixture into the pressure cooker, and cook over low heat for 5 minutes or until mixture becomes slightly thickened. Add cheddar cheese and pepper, and stir over low heat until melted.

5. Ladle soup into shallow soup bowls, and serve immediately.

PRESSURE POINTER

To avoid lumps when making creamy soups in your pressure cooker, combine the butter, flour, and milk in a saucepan before adding to the pressure cooker. Add to the pressure cooker in small batches, stirring constantly, until the flour is blended thoroughly.

Thai Chicken Noodle Soup

This spicy soup is a unique mix of flavors, with the sweetness of the carrots and onion contrasting with the tartness of the jalapeño peppers. The *cilantro* and herbs add zest and spice.

Yield:	Prep time:	Cook time:	Serving size:
5 cups	15 minutes	10 minutes	1 cup

1 TB. extra-virgin olive oil or canola oil

1 TB. unsalted butter or margarine

3 medium carrots, peeled and sliced into ½-in. rounds

3 ribs celery, cut into ½-in. slices

1 large sweet onion, diced fine

1 (8-oz.) pkg. spaghetti noodles

3 (5-oz.) boneless, skinless chicken breasts

1 tsp. kosher salt

1 tsp. dried parsley

1 tsp. dried thyme

4 cups Homemade Chicken Stock (recipe earlier in this chapter)

2 medium jalapeño peppers, seeded and diced fine

½ tsp. freshly ground black pepper

2 large green onions, sliced into thin rounds

¼ cup fresh cilantro, minced

1. In a pressure cooker over medium heat, heat extra-virgin olive oil and unsalted butter until hot. Add carrots and celery, and cook for about 3 minutes or until soft. Add sweet onion, and cook for about 2 minutes or until very soft.

2. Add noodles, and stir to coat with oil and butter mixture. Add chicken, kosher salt, parsley, thyme, Homemade Chicken Stock, and jalapeño peppers.

3. Lock the lid in place. Bring to low pressure, and maintain for 10 minutes. Remove from heat, and reduce pressure using the quick release method.

4. Using tongs, transfer chicken to a cutting board, and let cool. Remove skin and cut meat into bite-size pieces. Return chicken to the pressure cooker.

5. Add pepper, ladle soup into bowls, and garnish with sliced green onions and cilantro.

STEAM SPEAK

Cilantro is actually the bright green leaves of the coriander plant. It has a pungent and lively flavor that adds kick and fire.

Turkey Gumbo

Traditional gumbo flavors of okra, turkey, and *filé powder* combine with hints of cayenne and red pepper in this spicy gumbo.

Yield:	Prep time:	Cook time:	Serving size:
3 cups	15 minutes	20 minutes	2 cups

2 TB. extra-virgin olive oil

2 lb. turkey breast, skin and bones removed

2 large white or yellow onions, sliced thin

2 large cloves garlic, minced

¼ tsp. dried red pepper flakes

1¾ tsp. freshly ground black pepper

½ tsp. cayenne

¾ cup dry white wine

2 ribs celery, cut into ½-in. slices

1 large green bell pepper, ribs and seeds removed, and diced fine

1 lb. fresh okra, trimmed and sliced, or 1 (12-oz.) pkg. frozen okra

1 (28-oz.) can diced tomatoes, with juice

2 cups Homemade Chicken Stock (recipe earlier in this chapter)

2 bay leaves

1 tsp. kosher salt

1 tsp. filé powder

1. In a pressure cooker over medium heat, heat extra-virgin olive oil for about 2 minutes or until very hot. Add turkey, and brown on all sides.

2. Using tongs, transfer turkey to a cutting board. Let cool for 2 minutes, and cut into bite-size pieces. Return turkey to the pressure cooker.

3. Reduce heat to medium-low. Add onions, and cook, stirring constantly, for about 5 minutes or until soft. Add garlic, and cook for 30 seconds or until fragrant.

4. Drain fat from the pressure cooker, reserving 2 teaspoons. Add fat, red pepper flakes, ¾ teaspoon pepper, and cayenne to the pressure cooker. Increase heat to medium, and cook, uncovered, for about 20 seconds.

5. Add white wine, and deglaze by using a heat-safe spatula or wooden spoon to scrape up brown bits from the bottom of the pressure cooker.

6. Add celery, green bell pepper, okra, tomatoes with juice, Homemade Chicken Stock, and bay leaves. Stir until blended well.

7. Lock the lid in place. Bring to high pressure, and maintain for 15 minutes. Remove from heat, and reduce pressure using the natural release method.

8. Remove and discard bay leaves. Add kosher salt and remaining 1 teaspoon pepper. Stir in filé powder, and cook for 1 or 2 more minutes or until gumbo is thickened. Ladle gumbo into large soup bowls, and serve immediately.

STEAM SPEAK

A popular ingredient in Creole cooking, **filé powder** comes from the dried leaves of the sassafras tree and has a woodsy taste similar to root beer. Too much heat can make filé tough and stringy, so add it at the last minute or after the dish has been removed from the heat.

Seaside Soups and Chowders

In This Chapter

- Delicious DIY fish stock
- Great soups from crustaceans and fin
- Nutritious and delicious chowders

Fish brings a delicate, rich flavor to stock, soups, chowders, and bisques. And talk about variety! Wherever there's water, there's some sort of seafood-based soup. With so many different varieties—from New England clam chowder to Alaskan salmon chowder—you'd have to eat fish soup every day for nearly 5 months to repeat the same fish twice.

When it comes to fish, three basic types are used in cooking: crustaceans, mollusks, and finfish. Crustaceans have 10 legs, antennae, and a hard exoskeleton, and are absolutely delicious. Some of the most popular for making soups include shrimp, crab, lobster, and crayfish. Mollusks are soft-bodied invertebrates and may or may not have shells. Just a few you're likely to find in fish soup include oysters, clams, and mussels.

If it's not a crustacean or a mollusk, it's a finfish, or a true fish with fins. Many kinds of finfish offer meat in a variety of colors, textures, and tastes. Here are a few of the more popular fish:

- Cod, yellowtail snapper, and haddock are white-meat finfish and have a delicate, light flavor and flaky, tender texture.

- Catfish, sea trout, and whiting are finfish with white meat and a strong taste.

- Sea bass, mahi mahi, rainbow trout, walleye, and red snapper are finfish with light meat, a moderately firm texture, and a strong taste.

- Pink or silver salmon, freshwater perch, striped bass, tuna, and swordfish are finfish with dark meat, a moderately firm texture, and a moderate flavor.

Easy Fish Stock

Fish stock is one of the fastest stocks to make because fish bones are thinner than the bones found in meat and poultry. The pressure cooker extracts the flavor from the bones and turns it into scrumptious stock in no time.

Fish stock has an extremely delicate flavor and tastes best when used immediately. You can freeze leftover fish stock for up to 2 months, compared to 6 months for stocks made from meat, poultry, and vegetables.

Seafood bones tend to foam during cooking, so be sure to skim off any foam that forms as the stock comes to a boil. To reduce foaming, drizzle a small amount of oil on top of the stock before closing the lid.

Homemade Fish Stock

This delicate stock is made from haddock or cod bones and pieces, and gives any soup or stews a fresh, delicate flavor.

Yield:	Prep time:	Cook time:	Serving size:
6 cups	10 minutes	20 minutes	1 cup

2 lb. fish bones and pieces

6 cups cold water

¼ cup freshly squeezed lemon juice

2 large white or yellow onions, quartered

3 large carrots, peeled and quartered

3 ribs celery, sliced into 2-in. chunks

1 bay leaf

10 whole peppercorns

2 sprigs fresh thyme

3 stems fresh parsley

1. In a pressure cooker over high heat, combine fish bones and pieces, cold water, lemon juice, onions, carrots, celery, bay leaf, peppercorns, thyme, and parsley.

2. Lock the lid in place. Bring to high pressure, and maintain for 20 minutes. Remove from heat, and reduce pressure using the cold water release method.

3. Strain fish stock through a large sieve. Discard bones, fish pieces, and vegetables.

4. Use stock immediately, or pour into pint- or quart-size containers, and freeze for up to 2 months.

UNDER PRESSURE

When making fish stock, avoid oily fish such as salmon or herring because they'll give the broth a very strong, fishy flavor. Instead, use mild-flavored whitefish such as cod, snapper, or whiting.

Seafood Soup Cioppino-Style

This classic seafood *cioppino* in a rich broth flavored with tomato, fish, and clams is made with a variety of seafood—including shrimp, scallops, and whitefish—and has undertones of oregano, thyme, bay leaf, and basil.

Yield:	Prep time:	Cook time:	Serving size:
6 cups	15 minutes	5 minutes	1 cup

½ cup extra-virgin olive oil

½ cup unsalted butter or margarine

1 medium yellow or white onion, diced small

1 large leek, white part only, diced fine

2 cloves garlic, minced

2 medium carrots, peeled and diced small

1 rib celery, diced small

1 green bell pepper, ribs and seeds removed, and diced small

1 (28-oz.) can crushed Italian-style tomatoes, with juice

1 (6-oz.) can tomato paste

3 cups Homemade Fish Stock (recipe earlier in this chapter) or clam juice

1 cup water

1 cup dry red wine

2 bay leaves

1 tsp. dried oregano

1 tsp. dried thyme

1 tsp. dried basil

1 tsp. kosher salt

1 tsp. freshly ground black pepper

20 large shrimp, peeled, deveined, and rinsed well

1 lb. whitefish

20 large sea scallops, rinsed

¼ cup fresh minced Italian parsley (or regular parsley)

1. In a pressure cooker over medium heat, heat extra-virgin olive oil and unsalted butter until hot. Add onion, leek, and garlic, and cook for 2 or 3 minutes or until soft. Add carrots, celery, and green bell pepper, and cook for 5 minutes.

2. Add crushed tomatoes with juice, tomato paste, Homemade Fish Stock, water, red wine, bay leaves, oregano, thyme, basil, kosher salt, and pepper.

3. Lock the lid in place. Bring to high pressure, and maintain for 15 minutes. Remove from heat, and reduce pressure using the quick release method.

4. Return the pressure cooker to medium heat, and bring liquid to a low simmer. Add shrimp, whitefish, and scallops, and cook for 2 minutes or until fish is cooked.

5. Using tongs, remove and discard bay leaves. Ladle soup into bowls, garnish with Italian parsley, and serve immediately.

STEAM SPEAK

San Francisco's Italian immigrants created **cioppino,** a savory fish stew made with tomatoes and a variety of fish, inspired by the various regional fish soups and stews of Italian cuisine.

New Orleans-Style Shrimp Gumbo

This classic shrimp gumbo gets its zesty taste from bell peppers and okra and its rich tomato flavor from diced tomatoes and tomato juice.

Yield:	Prep time:	Cook time:	Serving size:
6 cups	15 minutes	10 minutes	1 cup

½ cup unsalted butter or margarine

4 ribs celery, finely diced

2 medium yellow or white onions, finely diced

2 green bell peppers, ribs and seeds removed, and diced fine

2 red bell peppers, ribs and seeds removed, and chopped fine

1 lb. fresh okra, trimmed and sliced

4 cups Homemade Chicken Stock (recipe in Chapter 9)

1 (32-oz.) can diced tomatoes, with juice

2 cups tomato or spicy vegetable juice

2 bay leaves

2 tsp. garlic salt

1 tsp. freshly ground black pepper

2 lb. large shrimp (24 to 30), peeled and deveined

6 cups steamed rice

1. In a pressure cooker over medium heat, melt unsalted butter. Add celery, onions, green bell peppers, and red bell peppers, and cook, stirring, for 5 minutes or until soft. Add okra, and stir for 5 minutes.

2. Add Homemade Chicken Stock, tomatoes with juice, tomato juice, bay leaves, garlic salt, and pepper.

3. Lock the lid in place. Bring to high pressure, and maintain for 10 minutes. Remove from heat, and reduce pressure using the natural release method.

4. Add shrimp, and simmer over low heat for about 3 or 4 minutes or until seafood is cooked. Using tongs, remove and discard bay leaves.

5. Ladle gumbo over plates of steamed rice, and serve immediately.

FOODIE FACT

Shrimp should always be deveined because the intestinal vein contains grit.

Lobster Gazpacho

This fresh, zesty *gazpacho* is accented with huge chunks of lobster, cucumber, and bell peppers and has a zesty tomato flavor.

Yield:	Prep time:	Cook time:	Serving size:
4 cups	15 minutes	5 minutes	1 cup

2 cups water

2 fresh (8-oz.) lobster tails, rinsed in cold water

2 lb. Roma tomatoes, seeded and diced small

1 large sweet onion, diced small

½ green bell pepper, ribs and seeds removed, and diced small

½ red bell pepper, ribs and seeds removed, and diced small

1 small cucumber, peeled, seeded, and diced small

1 (15-oz.) can corn, drained and rinsed

1 jalapeño, ribs and seeds removed, and diced fine

2 cloves garlic, minced

¼ cup freshly squeezed lime juice

1 TB. freshly grated lime zest

½ tsp. kosher salt

¾ tsp. freshly ground black pepper

4 tsp. sour cream

1 large avocado, peeled and sliced into strips

1. Place a rack in the bottom of a pressure cooker. Add water. Place lobster tails on the rack, and set over high heat.

2. Lock the lid in place. Bring to high pressure, reduce heat to reach low pressure, and maintain for 5 minutes. Remove from heat, and reduce pressure using the cold water release method.

3. Using tongs, transfer lobster tails to a cutting board, and let cool for 10 minutes. Remove lobster from shell, and dice into small pieces. Set aside.

4. In a blender or food processor fitted with a metal blade, purée Roma tomatoes, onion, green bell pepper, red bell pepper, cucumber, corn, jalapeño, and garlic. Stir in lime juice, lime zest, kosher salt, and pepper.

5. Transfer purée to a large bowl, and stir in lobster. Cover the bowl tightly with aluminum foil, and refrigerate for 6 to 24 hours.

6. Ladle gazpacho into chilled bowls. Garnish the center of each bowl with 1 teaspoon sour cream and 1 slice avocado, and serve immediately.

STEAM SPEAK

Gazpacho, a cold, uncooked soup that hails from southern Spain, is made from a puréed mixture of fresh tomatoes, sweet bell peppers, onions, celery, and cucumber.

Steamed Lobster Soup

This lively lobster soup in a light, fresh tomato broth with undertones of garlic and onion gets an extra kick from *brandy* and white wine.

Yield:	Prep time:	Cook time:	Serving size:
3 cups	15 minutes	30 minutes	½ cup

2 cups water

4 (6- to 8-oz.) fresh lobster tails, rinsed in cold water

2 TB. extra-virgin olive oil

½ cup minced onion

4 cloves garlic, minced

2 TB. brandy

2 large tomatoes, seeded and chopped small

2 TB. all-purpose flour

2 ribs celery, diced small

1 cup tomato sauce

1 cup dry white wine

1 cup Homemade Fish Stock (recipe earlier in this chapter) or clam juice

½ tsp. kosher salt

½ tsp. freshly ground black pepper

1 TB. fresh minced parsley

1. Place a rack in the bottom of a pressure cooker. Add water. Place lobster tails on the rack, and set over high heat.

2. Lock the lid in place. Bring to high pressure, reduce heat to low, and maintain low pressure for 5 minutes. Remove from heat, and reduce pressure using the cold water release method.

3. Using tongs, transfer lobster tails to a cutting board, and let cool for 10 minutes. Remove lobster from shell, and dice into small pieces. Set aside.

4. In a pressure cooker over medium heat, heat extra-virgin olive oil. When hot, add onion and garlic, and cook for 2 or 3 minutes or until onion is soft. Add brandy, and cook for 1 minute. Add tomatoes, and cook for 1 more minute.

5. Stir in all-purpose flour. Add celery, tomato sauce, white wine, and Homemade Fish Stock, and stir until thickened.

6. Lock the lid in place. Bring to high pressure, and maintain for 10 minutes. Remove from heat, and reduce pressure using the quick release method.

7. Reduce heat to low, add lobster, and simmer for about 2 or 3 minutes or until lobster is heated through.

8. Add kosher salt and pepper. Ladle soup into bowls, garnish with minced parsley, and serve immediately.

STEAM SPEAK

Made from apples and grapes, and usually aged in wood, **brandy** gives soups and stews extra depth and sweet, spicy undertones.

New England–Style Clam Chowder

This creamy, hearty soup is chock-full of clams and combines the flavors of clam, onion, and potato in a thick and hearty chowder.

Yield:	Prep time:	Cook time:	Serving size:
6 cups	15 minutes	20 minutes	1 cup

¼ cup *salt pork* or bacon, diced

2 TB. extra-virgin olive oil

2 ribs celery, diced fine

1 medium yellow onion, diced small

3 cups canned clams, with liquid

1 clove garlic, minced

2 cups Homemade Chicken Stock (recipe in Chapter 9)

1 tsp. dried thyme

2 lb. small white potatoes, peeled and diced small

½ cup unsalted butter

½ cup all-purpose flour

1 cup half-and-half

1 cup heavy cream

½ tsp. kosher salt

½ tsp. freshly ground black pepper

1. In a pressure cooker over medium heat, combine salt pork, extra-virgin olive oil, celery, and onion, and fry until pork is crisp.

2. Add clams with liquid, garlic, Homemade Chicken Stock, and thyme. Add potatoes, and stir until well coated with fat.

3. Lock the lid in place. Bring to high pressure, and maintain for 15 minutes. Remove from heat, and reduce pressure using the quick release method.

4. In a large bowl, make roux by combining unsalted butter and all-purpose flour with your hands. Form mixture into small balls of dough, and add roux balls to the pressure cooker, set over medium heat, and stir constantly until chowder thickens.

5. Add half-and-half and heavy cream, and stir until well blended. Add kosher salt and pepper.

6. Ladle chowder into soup bowls, and serve immediately.

STEAM SPEAK

Salt pork is cured with salt and is leaner than bacon. If you can't find salt pork, substitute lean bacon.

Shrimp Creole Chowder

Cayenne, paprika, and garlic fire up the taste of the shrimp and veggies in this classic Cajun chowder.

Yield:	Prep time:	Cook time:	Serving size:
8 cups	15 minutes	10 minutes	1 cup

1 TB. canola oil or vegetable oil	1 large white or russet potato, peeled and diced small
1 large white onion, diced small	1/2 tsp. kosher salt
2 ribs celery, diced small	4 cups Homemade Chicken Stock (recipe in Chapter 9)
1 medium green or red bell pepper, ribs and seeds removed, and finely diced	1 (14.5-oz.) can diced tomatoes, with juice
2 cloves garlic, minced	1/4 cup all-purpose flour
2 TB. paprika	2 cups fresh okra, trimmed and sliced into rounds
1 TB. dried basil	1 lb. large shrimp (16 to 20), peeled and deveined
1 TB. dried thyme	1 tsp. freshly ground black pepper
1 tsp. garlic powder	
1/4 tsp. cayenne	
1 bay leaf	

1. In a pressure cooker over medium heat, heat canola oil. When hot, add onion, celery, bell pepper, and garlic, and cook for about 3 minutes or until soft.

2. Add paprika, basil, thyme, garlic powder, and cayenne, and mix well to coat vegetables. Add bay leaf, potato, kosher salt, Homemade Chicken Stock, and tomatoes with juice.

3. Lock the lid in place. Bring to high pressure, and maintain for 10 minutes. Remove from heat, and reduce pressure using the quick release method.

4. Using tongs, remove and discard bay leaf.

5. To make roux, place all-purpose flour in a small skillet over medium heat and cook, stirring constantly with a wooden spoon, for about 5 minutes or until flour becomes toasted and turns light brown. Ladle 1/2 cup cooking liquid from the pressure cooker, and whisk it into flour until it forms a smooth paste, or roux. Stir into the pressure cooker.

6. Add okra and shrimp, and cook, uncovered, for about 5 minutes or until okra is soft and chowder has thickened. Add pepper.

7. Ladle chowder into bowls, and serve immediately.

FOODIE FACT

Okra thickens any liquid to which it's added, making it a popular ingredient in thick and hearty Cajun soups, chowders, gumbos, and stews.

Salmon Chowder

This creamy chowder blends the simple flavors of salmon, *leek*, sweet fennel, and potato.

Yield:	Prep time:	Cook time:	Serving size:
5 cups	10 minutes	7 minutes	1 cup

20 oz. salmon fillets, skinless	4 cups water
1 TB. extra-virgin olive oil or canola oil	1 bay leaf
1 large leek, white part only, sliced thin	1½ tsp. kosher salt
1 large fennel bulb, cut into thin slices	½ tsp. freshly ground black pepper
4 medium red or white potatoes, peeled and diced	5 tsp. sour cream

1. Rinse salmon fillets under cold water. Gently pat dry.

2. In a pressure cooker over medium heat, heat extra-virgin olive oil. When hot, add leek and fennel, and cook for about 2 minutes or until soft.

3. Add potatoes, water, bay leaf, and ½ teaspoon kosher salt.

4. Lock the lid in place. Bring to high pressure, and maintain for 5 minutes. Remove from heat, and reduce pressure using the quick release method.

5. Insert a rack in the pressure cooker. Place salmon fillets on the rack.

6. Lock the lid in place. Bring to high pressure, and maintain for 1 minute. Remove from heat, and reduce pressure using the natural release method.

7. Using tongs, remove and discard bay leaf. Using a spatula, gently transfer salmon to a cutting board, and let cool for 10 minutes. Cut into large chunks.

8. Remove the rack from the pressure cooker, and return salmon to pressure cooker. Stir chowder over low heat for 2 minutes or until warm.

9. Add remaining 1 teaspoon kosher salt and pepper. Ladle chowder into warmed soup bowls, garnish the center of each bowl with 1 teaspoon sour cream, and serve immediately.

STEAM SPEAK

Although a relative of garlic and onions, **leeks** have a milder flavor and fragrance than its cousins. Leeks resemble giant scallions and have been prized by gourmands for thousands of years.

Tomato Crab Bisque

In this classic Maryland soup, the crab absorbs the flavors of tomato, butter, milk, onion, and bell pepper, resulting in a rich, thick soup with complex flavors.

Yield:	Prep time:	Cook time:	Serving size:
5 cups	10 minutes	5 minutes	1 cup

½ cup unsalted butter or margarine

2 shallots, peeled and minced

¼ cup red bell pepper, diced fine

¼ cup all-purpose flour

1 (6-oz.) can tomato paste

4 cups Homemade Chicken Stock (recipe in Chapter 9) or Homemade Vegetable Stock (recipe in Chapter 7)

1 (18-oz.) can blue crabmeat, drained and squeezed dry

6 Roma tomatoes, washed and diced small

1 cup half-and-half

½ tsp. kosher salt

½ tsp. freshly ground black pepper

1. In a pressure cooker over medium heat, melt unsalted butter. Add shallots and red bell pepper, and cook for about 3 minutes or until soft.

2. Stir in all-purpose flour and tomato paste. Using a wire whisk, stir in Homemade Chicken Stock.

3. Lock the lid in place. Bring to high pressure, and maintain for 5 minutes. Remove from heat, and reduce pressure using the quick release method.

4. Stir in blue crabmeat, Roma tomatoes, and half-and-half. Cook for 3 to 5 minutes. Add kosher salt and pepper.

5. Ladle bisque into soup bowls, and serve immediately.

PRESSURE POINTER

If you prefer a rich, creamy chowder—calories be damned!—go ahead and use the half-and-half or heavy cream. For chowder that's lighter, thinner, and has fewer calories and fat, substitute whole milk or low-fat milk.

Sultry Stews and Curries

The ultimate convenience meal, stews combine any combination of meat, poultry, fish, vegetables, grains, pasta, sauces, and gravies into a mouth-watering and nourishing one-pot meal that makes getting dinner on the table fast, easy, and affordable. Stews are also extremely versatile. Depending on the herbs and spices you use, you can create anything from a soothing, children-pleasing stew to a four-alarm curry that sets your guests' taste buds on fire.

In Part 4, we give you recipes for vegetarian, meat, poultry, and seafood stews and curries that showcase a world of flavor, from Indian-Style Chickpea Curry and German Knockwurst, to Pork Alsace and Russian Fish Stew.

If you're new to pressure cooking or just getting back to it after a long hiatus, you'll be happy to hear that stews are a great place to start, requiring little or no pressure cooking expertise. Just toss everything into the pot, and your pressure cooker does the rest, turning tough cuts of meat into tender morsels, and mingling myriad flavors into a savory stew that's ready in minutes.

Vegetarian Stews, Chilies, and Curries

In This Chapter

- The secret to perfect stews
- Stews from around the globe
- Stick-to-your-ribs chilies
- Flavorful curries

Stews have been around for at least 8,000 years, when Amazonian tribes used the turtle shells as a pot to boil the entrails of the turtle with nuts, seeds, and roots. Other early cultures used large clam shells as their cooking pot.

In those days, making stew was an all-day affair, slowly cooking the dish over the campfire so the different flavors would mingle. Today, you can make vegetarian stew in just minutes in your pressure cooker and enjoy nature's bounty in a flavorful dish that offers a variety of flavors, textures, colors, and nutrients in every bite.

In this chapter, you'll find recipes for stews that go by many names, such as curries, tagines, ragouts, and ratatouilles. Basically, they are all stews, or dishes made with a variety of ingredients that are boiled or simmered to mingle the flavors of the various ingredients. But they have subtle differences that make all the difference when it comes to taste.

No-Stress Stew

The most important thing to remember when making vegetable stew in your pressure cooker is that vegetables don't all cook at the same rate. Harder vegetables, such as green beans, potatoes, turnips, and onions, take 10 minutes or less to cook, while softer vegetables, such as mushrooms, tomatoes, and squash, cook in 60 seconds or less.

There are two ways to ensure all the vegetables in your stew cook to perfection. You can use the interrupted cooking method (see Chapter 2) and cook the vegetables in two or more stages, putting the hardest veggies in the pot first and the softest vegetables in the pot last. When using this method, cut the vegetables in pieces that are roughly the same size to ensure uniform cooking.

If you don't want to use the interrupted cooking method but instead cook all the vegetables together for the same length of time, you can cheat by cutting the hard vegetables into small pieces so they cook faster and cutting the softer vegetables into large pieces so they cook more slowly.

Spicy Vegetable Stew

This four-alarm stew gets its fire from coriander, cumin, cayenne, and jalapeño. The coconut milk adds rich, mellow undertones and cools the heat, while the golden raisins add a sweet surprise.

Yield:	Prep time:	Cook time:	Serving size:
6 cups	15 minutes	15 minutes	1 cup

2 TB. extra-virgin olive oil

1 tsp. ground coriander

1 tsp. ground cumin

1 tsp. cayenne

½ tsp. ground cinnamon

4 cloves garlic, minced

3 cups Homemade Vegetable Stock (recipe in Chapter 7)

1 (15-oz.) can unsweetened coconut milk

4 large carrots, peeled and cut into 1-in. rounds

1 large eggplant, peeled and diced small

2 large zucchini, diced small

1 large white or yellow onion, diced small

1 (28-oz.) can diced tomatoes, with juice

1 (15-oz.) can chickpeas, drained and rinsed

¾ cup golden raisins

1 tsp. kosher salt

1 tsp. freshly ground black pepper

2 large jalapeños, ribs and seeds removed, and diced fine

1. In a pressure cooker over medium heat, heat extra-virgin olive oil. When hot, stir in coriander, cumin, cayenne, cinnamon, and garlic, and cook, stirring, for about 2 minutes or until fragrant.

2. Add Homemade Vegetable Stock, coconut milk, carrots, eggplant, zucchini, onion, tomatoes with juice, chickpeas, raisins, and kosher salt.

3. Lock the lid in place. Bring to high pressure, and maintain for 15 minutes. Remove from heat, and reduce pressure using the quick release method.

4. Add pepper. Ladle stew into bowls, garnish with jalapeños, and serve immediately.

PRESSURE POINTER

You can find canned coconut milk in the supermarket or in Asian grocery stores. Or make your own by combining equal parts water with shredded fresh coconut and simmering in a saucepan over low heat until foamy.

Eggplant Ratatouille Stew

This hearty and flavorful stew blends the mellow flavors of eggplant, zucchini, and bell pepper with hints of garlic and parsley.

Yield:	Prep time:	Cook time:	Serving size:
4 cups	15 minutes	3 minutes	1 cup

4 TB. extra-virgin olive oil

1 small eggplant, peeled and cut into 1-in. cubes

1 large zucchini, skin on and sliced into ½-in. slices

1 large green bell pepper, ribs and seeds removed, and cut into strips

1 medium white or russet potato, peeled and diced small

1 large white or yellow onion, diced small

2 cloves garlic, minced

2 medium tomatoes, seeds removed and diced small

2 TB. minced fresh parsley

3 cups Homemade Vegetable Stock (recipe in Chapter 7) or canned broth

1 tsp. kosher salt

1 tsp. freshly ground black pepper

1. In a pressure cooker over medium heat, heat 2 tablespoons extra-virgin olive oil. When hot, add eggplant, zucchini, green bell pepper, and potato in small batches, and cook for 1 minute. Transfer to a bowl, and set aside.

2. Add remaining 2 tablespoons extra-virgin olive oil to the pressure cooker. When hot, add onion and garlic, and cook for 2 minutes or until onion is soft. Do not brown.

3. Return cooked eggplant-zucchini mixture to the pressure cooker. Add tomatoes, parsley, and Homemade Vegetable Stock.

4. Lock the lid in place. Bring to high pressure, and maintain for 3 minutes. Remove from heat, and reduce pressure using the quick release method.

5. Add kosher salt and pepper, ladle stew into soup bowls, and serve immediately.

STEAM SPEAK

Ratatouille refers to a popular stew that hails from the French region of Provence. A combination of eggplant, tomatoes, onions, bell peppers, zucchini, garlic, and herbs simmered together in olive oil, the dish can be served as a hot or cold entrée or at room temperature with baguettes as an appetizer.

Vegetable Stew with Pineapple Chutney

Pineapple *chutney* brings out the sweet flavors of yam, zucchini, and bell peppers in this rich and spicy stew, while cumin, curry, and turmeric add feisty undertones.

Yield:	Prep time:	Cook time:	Serving size:
4 cups	15 minutes	5 minutes	1 cup

2 TB. extra-virgin olive oil or vegetable oil

1 large yam, peeled and cut into ½-in. cubes

1 medium yellow or white onion, diced small

1 large zucchini, peeled, and diced small

1 large green bell pepper, ribs and seeds removed, and diced small

1 large red bell pepper, ribs and seeds removed, and diced small

2 tsp. ground curry

1 tsp. ground turmeric

1 tsp. ground cumin

2 cups Homemade Vegetable Stock (recipe in Chapter 7)

1 (14-oz.) can stewed tomatoes, with juice

1 tsp. kosher salt

½ tsp. freshly ground black pepper

1 (15-oz.) can chickpeas, drained and rinsed

2 cups steamed jasmine rice

4 TB. pineapple chutney

1. In a pressure cooker over medium heat, heat extra-virgin olive oil. When hot, add yam, onion, zucchini, green bell pepper, and red bell pepper, and cook for 5 minutes or until vegetables turn golden brown.

2. Add curry, turmeric, and cumin, and stir well so all vegetables are coated in oil and spices. Add Homemade Vegetable Stock and stewed tomatoes with juice.

3. Lock the lid in place. Bring to high pressure, and maintain for 5 minutes. Remove from heat, and reduce pressure using the cold water method.

4. Add kosher salt, pepper, and chickpeas, and heat over low heat for 2 or 3 minutes.

5. Ladle stew into soup bowls over a mound of steamed jasmine rice, garnish each serving with 1 tablespoon pineapple chutney, and serve.

STEAM SPEAK

Chutney is an East Indian condiment made from fruit, vinegar, sugar, and spices. It can range from smooth to chunky, and from mild to four-alarm. You can find chutney in most supermarkets. For a wider variety, look for it in Indian grocery stores.

Spicy Cauliflower, Potato, and Carrot Stew

The cauliflower, carrots, and potatoes soak up the flavors of ginger, green chile, garlic, and numerous spices in this hearty and belly-warming vegetarian curry.

Yield:	Prep time:	Cook time:	Serving size:
4 cups	15 minutes	5 minutes	1 cup

4 TB. extra-virgin olive oil or vegetable oil

1 medium yellow or white onion, diced small

2 cloves garlic, minced

2 large white potatoes, peeled and diced small

1 medium head cauliflower, broken into florets

2 large carrots, peeled and sliced into 1-in. rounds

1 (1-in.) piece fresh gingerroot, peeled and minced

1 tsp. ground *coriander*

1 tsp. ground cumin

1 tsp. ground turmeric

2 cups Homemade Vegetable Stock (recipe in Chapter 7)

1 cup tomato or vegetable juice

1 (8-oz.) can mild green chiles, drained and diced

1 tsp. kosher salt

1 tsp. freshly ground black pepper

1. In a pressure cooker over medium heat, heat extra-virgin olive oil. When hot, add onion, garlic, potatoes, cauliflower, and carrots, and cook for about 5 minutes or until well coated with oil and slightly browned.

2. Stir in gingerroot, coriander, cumin, turmeric, Homemade Vegetable Stock, tomato juice, and green chiles.

3. Lock the lid in place. Bring to high pressure, and maintain for 5 minutes. Remove from heat, and reduce pressure using the cold water release method.

4. Add kosher salt and pepper, ladle stew into soup bowls, and serve immediately.

STEAM SPEAK

Coriander is a cousin of parsley and originated in the Orient and Mediterranean. Coriander is popular for its aromatic seeds as well as for its dark, lacy leaves, called cilantro. The seeds have a distinctive flavor that combines undertones of lemon, sage, and caraway.

Black Bean and Lentil Chili

Spiced with chile pepper, jalapeño, and chili powder, this four-alarm chili turns black beans and lentils into a feisty bite.

Yield:	Prep time:	Cook time:	Serving size:
6 cups	15 minutes	22 minutes plus overnight soaking	1 cup

1 cup dried black beans

8 cups water

3 TB. extra-virgin olive oil or vegetable oil

1 medium yellow or white onion, diced small

1 Serrano chile pepper, seeded and minced

1 jalapeño, seeded and minced

2 tsp. garlic, minced

1 cup dried brown lentils

3 TB. chili powder

1 tsp. dried oregano

1 tsp. ground cumin

½ tsp. ground turmeric

1 (32-oz.) can diced tomatoes, with juice

4 cups Homemade Vegetable Stock (recipe in Chapter 7)

1 tsp. kosher salt

1 tsp. freshly ground black pepper

6 TB. low-fat sour cream

1. In a large bowl, soak black beans in 3 cups water, or enough to cover beans, overnight. Drain beans, and discard soaking water.

2. Place soaked beans in the pressure cooker with 3 cups water and 1 tablespoon extra-virgin olive oil, and set over high heat.

3. Lock the lid in place. Bring to high pressure, and maintain for 12 minutes. Remove from heat, and reduce pressure using the quick release method.

4. Drain black beans in a colander, and set aside.

5. In the pressure cooker over medium heat, heat remaining 2 tablespoons extra-virgin olive oil. When hot, add onion, Serrano chile pepper, and jalapeño, and cook for 1 or 2 minutes or until soft.

6. Stir in garlic, and cook for 30 seconds, or until fragrant. Do not brown. Add lentils, chili powder, oregano, cumin, turmeric, tomatoes with juice, Homemade Vegetable Stock, and remaining 2 cups water.

7. Lock the lid in place. Bring to high pressure, and maintain for 10 minutes. Remove from heat, and reduce pressure using the natural release method.

8. Return the pressure cooker to low heat. Stir in black beans, and cook for 5 to 10 minutes or until warm. Add kosher salt and pepper, ladle stew into soup bowls, garnish each with 1 tablespoon sour cream, and serve immediately.

STEAM SPEAK

Serrano chile peppers are small, super-hot peppers grown in Spain that add extra fire and spice to any dish. You can find them in most large supermarkets and in Hispanic grocery stores.

Three-Bean Vegetarian Chili

Flavors of beans and onion dominate this spicy vegetarian chili that's thick with chunks of zucchini, squash, tomatoes, and corn.

Yield:	Prep time:	Cook time:	Serving size:
8 cups	15 minutes	12 minutes	1 cup

1 cup dried pinto beans

1 cup dried white beans

1 cup dried red beans

6 cups water

3 TB. extra-virgin olive oil or vegetable oil

2 medium yellow or white onions, diced small

4 cloves garlic, minced

2 large yellow squash, skin on and diced small

1 large zucchini, skin on and diced small

6 large Roma tomatoes, seeded and diced small

1 cup frozen corn, defrosted

2 cups Homemade Vegetable Stock (recipe in Chapter 7)

1 TB. Italian seasoning

1 tsp. kosher salt

1 tsp. freshly ground black pepper

1. In a large bowl, soak pinto beans, white beans, and red beans in 3 cups water, or enough water to cover beans, overnight. Drain beans, and discard soaking water.

2. Place soaked beans in the pressure cooker with remaining 3 cups water. Add 1 tablespoon extra-virgin olive oil.

3. Lock the lid in place. Bring to high pressure, and maintain for 10 minutes. Remove from heat, and reduce pressure using the quick release method. Drain beans in a colander, and set aside.

4. In the pressure cooker over medium heat, heat remaining 2 tablespoons extra-virgin olive oil. When hot, add onions, and cook for 5 minutes or until soft and slightly browned.

5. Add garlic, yellow squash, zucchini, Roma tomatoes, corn, Homemade Vegetable Stock, Italian seasoning, kosher salt, and pepper. Return beans to the pressure cooker, and stir until combined with vegetables.

6. Lock the lid in place. Bring to high pressure, and maintain for 2 minutes. Remove from heat, and reduce pressure using the natural release method.

7. Ladle chili into soup bowls, and serve immediately.

UNDER PRESSURE

Don't substitute black beans for the red or white beans in this recipe. Although black beans won't significantly change the flavor, they will give the chili a blackish tint.

Mushroom Curry with Vegetables and Rice

This curry fires up the mellow flavors of mushrooms, onions, and zucchini with spicy cumin, chili powder, and turmeric. The *jasmine rice* adds sweet undertones.

Yield:	Prep time:	Cook time:	Serving size:
6 cups	15 minutes	5 minutes	1 cup

3 TB. extra-virgin olive oil

15 brown or white mushrooms, brushed clean and sliced thin

1 large sweet onion, finely chopped

4 cloves garlic, minced

1 tsp. ground cumin

1 tsp. chili powder

1 tsp. ground curry

1 tsp. ground turmeric

1 large zucchini, skin on and diced small

1 large yellow squash, skin on and diced small

1 medium eggplant, peeled and cut into small cubes

1 (14.5-oz.) can diced tomatoes, with juice

1 tsp. kosher salt

1/2 tsp. freshly ground black pepper

2 cups steamed jasmine rice

1. In a pressure cooker over medium heat, heat extra-virgin olive oil. When hot, add mushrooms and onion, and cook for 3 minutes.

2. Add garlic, cumin, chili powder, curry, and turmeric, and stir until vegetables are well coated with oil. Add zucchini, yellow squash, eggplant, and tomatoes with juice.

3. Lock the lid in place. Bring to high pressure, and maintain for 5 minutes. Remove from heat, and reduce pressure using the cold water release method.

4. Add kosher salt and pepper. Place 1/2 cup steamed jasmine rice into each bowl, ladle curry over rice, and serve immediately.

STEAM SPEAK

Jasmine rice is sweet, aromatic rice from Thailand with a flavor and fragrance similar to basmati rice from India. It's okay to substitute basmati rice for jasmine rice.

Indian-Style Chickpea Curry

Turmeric gives this hearty stew its vivid yellow color, while cumin, curry powder, and garlic fire up the meaty chickpeas.

Yield:	Prep time:	Cook time:	Serving size:
4 cups	10 minutes	30 minutes	1 cup

2 cups chickpeas

3 cups water

2 TB. extra-virgin olive oil

1 medium yellow or white onion, diced small

1 clove garlic, minced

1 tsp. ground cumin

1/2 tsp. ground turmeric

1/2 tsp. cayenne

2 tsp. ground curry

1 cup Homemade Vegetable Stock (recipe in Chapter 7)

1 (14.5-oz.) can diced tomatoes, with juice

1/4 cup freshly squeezed lemon juice

1 tsp. kosher salt

1 tsp. freshly ground black pepper

1/4 cup fresh cilantro, minced

1. In a large bowl, soak chickpeas in 3 cups water, or enough water to completely cover beans, overnight. Drain water and discard. Set beans aside.

2. In a pressure cooker over medium-high heat, heat extra-virgin olive oil. When hot, add onion and garlic, and cook for 30 seconds or until soft.

3. Add cumin, turmeric, cayenne, and curry, and stir until onion and garlic are coated with oil and spices. Add chickpeas, Homemade Vegetable Stock, and tomatoes with juice.

4. Lock the lid in place. Bring to high pressure, and maintain for 30 minutes. Remove from heat, and reduce pressure using the quick release method.

5. Add lemon juice, kosher salt, and pepper. Ladle stew into soup bowls, garnish with cilantro, and serve immediately.

STEAM SPEAK

Used in cooking since 600 B.C.E., **turmeric** is an ancient spice related to ginger that has a bitter, pungent flavor and an intense yellow-orange color that's used to give mustard its vivid color.

Vegetable Tagine with Couscous

Cinnamon and molasses enhance the sweet flavors of the onion, carrot, and sweet potatoes in this spicy, Moroccan-style chickpea stew.

Yield:	Prep time:	Cook time:	Serving size:
5 cups	15 minutes	3 minutes	1 cup

3 TB. unsalted butter or margarine

2 large sweet potatoes, peeled and diced small

1 large white onion, diced small

1 large carrot, peeled and diced small

4 cloves garlic, minced

1 large eggplant, peeled and diced small

1 small head (about 1 lb.) cauliflower, cut into florets

1 TB. ground cumin

1 tsp. ground cinnamon

2 TB. molasses

3 cups Homemade Vegetable Stock (recipe in Chapter 7)

1 (14-oz.) can chickpeas, drained and rinsed

1 tsp. kosher salt

1 tsp. freshly ground black pepper

3 cups cooked couscous

1. In a pressure cooker over medium heat, melt unsalted butter. Add sweet potatoes, onion, and carrot, and cook for 2 minutes.

2. Add garlic, eggplant, cauliflower, cumin, cinnamon, molasses, and Homemade Vegetable Stock, and stir well.

3. Lock the lid in place. Bring to high pressure, and maintain for 3 minutes. Remove from heat, and reduce pressure using the cold water release method.

4. Return the pressure cooker to low heat. Stir in chickpeas, kosher salt, and pepper.

5. Ladle stew into large soup bowls over a mound of couscous, and serve immediately.

STEAM SPEAK

Tagine is a North African stew that contains meat or poultry gently simmered with vegetables, olives, preserved lemons, garlic, and various spices, including turmeric, cinnamon, cumin, ginger, pepper, and saffron. The stew is named after the heavy clay pot in which the stew is traditionally cooked.

Fork-Tender Meat Stews and Curries

Chapter 12

In This Chapter

- Stewing in stages
- Browning basics
- All-American classic beef stews
- Exotic curries

Stews are an economical way to stretch a pound or two of inexpensive meat. Just add a handful of vegetables, pasta, and spices, and you've got dinner for eight, plus leftovers. Because stews meld flavors, be sure to use vegetables and spices that complement each other and the meat.

Your pressure cooker actually prefers tough, less-expensive cuts of beef over expensive, lean cuts because its super-high temperatures break down tough fibers and turn the meat into tender morsels. Talk about a thrifty appliance!

Building the Perfect Stew

You might think the prepackaged "stew meat" you find in the supermarket is the perfect thing to buy for your stew, but it's actually the *last* thing you should use. Because it's made up of odds and ends, you never know what you're getting. For the tastiest stews, use cuts like steak, shanks, short rib, skirt steak, or flank.

The most flavorful stews begin with browned meat. Browning meat in hot oil seals in the flavors and natural juices and gives the meat's exterior a golden finish. Before browning meat, dry it with paper towels to remove moisture. Brown the meat in very hot oil and in small batches to prevent too much meat from lowering the temperature of the oil. Browning in small batches also prevents the meat from sputtering and releasing its natural juices. To save time, you can brown some of the meat in a skillet and add it to the pressure cooker.

If your stew recipe calls for wine, don't use "cooking wine," which is made from low-quality wines and contains a lot of added salt. Instead, use a high-quality wine you would enjoy drinking. If the wine isn't good enough for your wine glass, it's not good enough for your stew. (If you're making a dish that calls for wine or beer and are planning on serving it to children or adults who don't drink alcohol, you can substitute nonalcoholic options such as nonalcoholic beer, apple juice, or grape juice.)

To rev up the taste of stews, consider using bay leaves, thyme, oregano, sage, or Italian parsley. For feisty spices, try cumin, curry, cayenne, and turmeric for a hint of fire. Milder spices like cinnamon and nutmeg give stews a touch of sweetness.

Mild Beef Curry

Cumin, turmeric, garlic, gingerroot, and *curry* give the beef just a hint of fire in this two-alarm curry. No fire engines required!

Yield:	Prep time:	Cook time:	Serving size:
3 cups	15 minutes	10 minutes	1 cup

2 TB. ground curry

1 tsp. ground cumin

1 tsp. ground turmeric

2 large cloves garlic, minced

2 TB. fresh gingerroot, minced

2 tsp. kosher salt

2 TB. extra-virgin olive oil or vegetable oil

1 large onion, diced

1 (16-oz.) can diced tomatoes, with juice

2 lb. round steak, trimmed of fat and cut into 1-in. cubes

1½ cups water

1 tsp. freshly ground black pepper

1. In a small bowl, combine curry, cumin, and turmeric. Stir in garlic, gingerroot, and 1 teaspoon kosher salt. Set aside.

2. In a pressure cooker over medium heat, heat extra-virgin olive oil. When hot, add onion, and cook, stirring occasionally, for about 15 minutes or until golden brown. Do not burn.

3. Add spice mixture and tomatoes with juice, and cook for 2 minutes. Add round steak and water.

4. Lock the lid in place. Bring to high pressure, and maintain for 10 minutes. Remove from heat, and reduce pressure using the quick release method.

5. Add remaining 1 teaspoon kosher salt and pepper. Ladle curry into large bowls, and serve immediately.

STEAM SPEAK

The word **curry** comes from the Indian word *kari,* which means "sauce." Over time, curry has come to refer to a variety of spicy, hot sauce–based specialties of East Indian origin.

Chili Con Carne

Rich and chunky, the chili powder gives the beef and beans in this old-fashioned beef chili extra fire and zest, while the cheese mellows out the flavors and adds richness and creaminess.

Yield:	Prep time:	Cook time:	Serving size:
6 cups	15 minutes	15 minutes	1 cup

2 lb. lean ground beef

1 tsp. kosher salt

1 tsp. freshly ground black pepper

1 TB. canola oil or vegetable oil

1 medium green bell pepper, ribs and seeds removed, and diced small

2 large white onions, diced

2 (15-oz.) cans dark red kidney beans, drained and rinsed

2 ribs celery, diced small

1 (28-oz.) can diced tomatoes, with juice

2 tsp. chili powder

½ cup shredded medium cheddar cheese

1. In a pressure cooker over medium-high heat, brown ground beef on both sides. Sprinkle with kosher salt and pepper. Remove beef from the pressure cooker, and drain on paper towels.

2. Drain fat from the pressure cooker into a colander. Wipe the inside of the pressure cooker with a paper towel to remove excess fat.

3. Return beef to the pressure cooker, and set over medium heat. Add canola oil. When hot, add green bell pepper and 1 onion, and cook for about 2 minutes or until soft.

4. With a fork or potato masher, mash 1 cup kidney beans, and add to the pressure cooker along with remaining whole beans. Add celery, tomatoes with juice, and chili powder.

5. Lock the lid in place. Bring to high pressure, and maintain for 15 minutes. Remove from heat, and reduce pressure using the cold water release method. Reduce heat to low, and simmer, uncovered, for 10 minutes or until chili thickens slightly.

6. Ladle chili into large bowls, garnish with cheddar cheese and remaining 1 diced onion, and serve immediately.

STEAM SPEAK

Chile con carne is Spanish for "chili with meat." The dish is traditionally made with ground beef, chiles, and chili powder. Beans are sometimes added, but they're not considered to be part of the traditional dish.

German Knockwurst and Sauerkraut

This one-pot dinner straight from Bavaria combines the meaty flavors of *knockwurst*, the tangy taste of sauerkraut and mustard, and the rich finish of dark beer.

Yield:	Prep time:	Cook time:	Serving size:
4 cups	10 minutes	10 minutes	1 cup

6 slices bacon, cut into 2-in. pieces

1 large yellow or white onion, diced small

4 ribs celery, diced small

2 large carrots, peeled and diced small

2 cloves garlic, minced

1 bay leaf

1½ lb. beef knockwurst, cut in ½

1 (16-oz.) can sauerkraut, rinsed, drained, and squeezed dry

1 TB. mustard seed

1 tsp. dried sage

1 tsp. dried thyme

1 tsp. dried rosemary

1 tsp. kosher salt

1 tsp. freshly ground black pepper

1 (16-oz.) bottle or can dark beer

1. In a pressure cooker over medium heat, cook bacon for 3 or 4 minutes or until crisp. Remove bacon from the pressure cooker, and drain on paper towels.

2. Add onion to the pressure cooker, and cook in bacon fat for about 5 minutes or until crisp.

3. Add celery, carrots, garlic, bay leaf, knockwurst, sauerkraut, mustard seed, sage, thyme, rosemary, kosher salt, pepper, and beer.

4. Lock the lid in place. Bring to high pressure, and maintain for 10 minutes. Remove from heat, and reduce pressure using the natural release method.

5. Remove bay leaf. Serve immediately on large dinner plates.

STEAM SPEAK

Knockwurst is a short link of beef or pork sausage flavored with garlic. The name originated from the German words *knack* and *wurst,* which mean "crack" and "sausage," respectively.

Beef Provençal

This flavorful combo of braised beef, onions, garlic, tomatoes, and red wine is seasoned with sunny herbs, which give the dish a distinctively French twist.

Yield:	Prep time:	Cook time:	Serving size:
4 cups	10 minutes	10 minutes	1 cup

2 lb. round steak, trimmed of fat and cut into $\frac{1}{2}$-in. strips

$\frac{1}{2}$ tsp. kosher salt

$\frac{1}{4}$ tsp. freshly ground black pepper

3 TB. extra-virgin olive oil

$\frac{1}{4}$ cup unsalted butter or margarine

2 large white or yellow onions, thinly sliced

4 cloves garlic, peeled and thinly sliced

$1\frac{1}{2}$ cups Homemade Beef Stock (recipe in Chapter 8)

$\frac{1}{2}$ cup dry red wine

2 TB. *herbes de Provence*

1 (14.5-oz.) can diced tomatoes, with juice

6 sprigs Italian parsley, minced (or regular parsley)

1. Sprinkle round steak with kosher salt and pepper.

2. In a pressure cooker over medium heat, heat 1 tablespoon extra-virgin olive oil. When hot, add round steak, and brown on all sides. Remove steak from the pressure cooker, and drain on paper towels.

3. In the pressure cooker over low heat, melt remaining 2 tablespoons extra-virgin olive oil and unsalted butter. Add onions, increase heat to medium, and cook, stirring constantly, for 10 minutes or until onions begin to caramelize and turn golden brown. Do not let onions burn.

4. Add garlic, Homemade Beef Stock, red wine, herbes de Provence, tomatoes with juice, and browned round steak to the pressure cooker.

5. Lock the lid in place. Bring to high pressure, and maintain for 10 minutes. Remove from heat, and reduce pressure using the quick release method.

6. Ladle stew into large soup bowls, garnish with Italian parsley, and serve immediately.

STEAM SPEAK

Herbes de Provence is a combination of dried herbs commonly found in the south of France, including basil, fennel seed, lavender, marjoram, sage, savory, and thyme. You can find it in the spice section of large supermarkets.

Grandma's Beef Stew with Vegetables

This childhood favorite combines the earthy flavors of tomatoes, onion, and celery with just a touch of bay leaf and parsley.

Yield:	Prep time:	Cook time:	Serving size:
4 cups	15 minutes	20 minutes	1 cup

2 lb. chuck roast, cut into 1-in. cubes	6 small white or yellow medium onions, peeled
2 tsp. kosher salt	3 large ribs celery
¼ tsp. freshly ground black pepper	4 medium red potatoes, quartered
2 TB. vegetable oil	4 medium carrots, peeled and sliced
1 bay leaf	
1 TB. ketchup or tomato paste	2 cups canned or fresh tomatoes (with juice, if canned)
1¼ cups water	3 TB. all-purpose flour
1½ cups Homemade Beef Stock (recipe in Chapter 8)	2 TB. freshly minced parsley

1. Sprinkle chuck roast with kosher salt and pepper.

2. In the pressure cooker over medium-high heat, heat vegetable oil. When hot, add chuck roast, and brown on all sides. Add bay leaf, ketchup, 1 cup water, and Homemade Beef Stock.

3. Lock the lid in place. Bring to high pressure, and maintain for 20 minutes. Remove from heat, and reduce pressure using the cold water release method.

4. Add onions, celery, potatoes, carrots, and tomatoes.

5. Lock the lid in place. Bring to high pressure, and maintain for 5 minutes. Remove from heat, and reduce pressure using the cold water release method. Remove bay leaf.

6. In a small bowl, combine all-purpose flour and remaining ¼ cup water. Add to the pressure cooker, reduce heat to medium-high, and cook for 2 minutes or until slightly thickened. Stir in minced parsley.

7. Ladle stew into large soup bowls, and serve immediately.

PRESSURE POINTER

For extra-fresh parsley whenever you need it, wash fresh parsley with cold water, trim off the stems, and wrap it in bundles and freeze. Whenever you need a little, just chop off a little with the blunt end of a sharp knife, and you're cooking.

Spicy Yam and Peanut Beef Stew

This zesty beef stew combines peanut butter, jalapeño, and tomato in a spicy dish packed with the flavors of both America and Asia.

Yield:	Prep time:	Cook time:	Serving size:
4 cups	15 minutes	20 minutes	1 cup

1½ lb. lean chuck boneless beef, cut into 1-in. cubes

1½ tsp. kosher salt

1 tsp. freshly ground black pepper

2 TB. vegetable oil or canola oil

1 medium white or yellow onion, finely diced

2 large yams, peeled and cut into 1-in. cubes

1 bay leaf

½ cup tomato paste

1 cup Homemade Beef Stock (recipe in Chapter 8)

2 cups water

¾ cup smooth peanut butter

½ small jalapeño, seeds removed and diced fine

1. Sprinkle beef with ½ teaspoon kosher salt and ½ teaspoon pepper.

2. In a pressure cooker over medium heat, heat vegetable oil. Add beef, and brown on all sides. Add onion and yams, and stir until vegetables are coated with oil. Add bay leaf, tomato paste, Homemade Beef Stock, and water.

3. Lock the lid in place. Bring to high pressure, and maintain for 20 minutes. Remove from heat, and reduce pressure using the quick release method.

4. Using a whisk, stir peanut butter into the pressure cooker until well blended. Add diced jalapeño, remaining 1 teaspoon kosher salt, and remaining ½ teaspoon pepper.

5. Ladle stew into soup bowls, and serve immediately.

UNDER PRESSURE

Don't substitute sweet potatoes for yams. They may look similar, but yams have more natural sugar and a higher moisture content than sweet potatoes. Sweet potatoes are often mislabeled and sold as yams, so be sure you know what you're buying.

Chinese Pepper Steak

The colorful vegetables remain crisp in this dish flavored with garlic and orange as well as crunchy bean sprouts.

Yield:	Prep time:	Cook time:	Serving size:
6 cups	15 minutes	20 minutes	1 cup

1½ lb. boneless beef round steak

2 cloves garlic, minced

¼ cup low-sodium soy sauce

1 TB. *hoisin sauce*

2 TB. freshly grated orange zest

1 tsp. sugar

½ tsp. kosher salt

½ tsp. freshly ground black pepper

1 large tomato, peeled, seeded, and chopped

2 medium red bell peppers, ribs and seeds removed, and cut into ¼-in. strips

3 TB. cornstarch

3 TB. cold water

1 cup fresh bean sprouts

2 cups cooked white rice

4 large green onions, white and green parts, peeled and finely chopped

1. Trim fat from beef round steak, and slice into thin strips.

2. In a pressure cooker over high heat, combine steak, garlic, soy sauce, hoisin sauce, orange zest, sugar, kosher salt, and pepper.

3. Lock the lid in place. Bring to high pressure, and maintain for 20 minutes. Remove from heat, and reduce pressure using the natural release method.

4. Reduce heat to low. Add tomato and red bell peppers, and simmer, uncovered, for 10 minutes.

5. In a small bowl, combine cornstarch and cold water. Add to the pressure cooker, and stir until stew is thickened. Stir in bean sprouts.

6. Ladle stew over white rice in large bowls, garnish with green onions, and serve immediately.

STEAM SPEAK

Hoisin sauce, also called Peking sauce, is a rich, thick, reddish-brown sweet-and-sour sauce widely used in Asian cooking. It's a combination of soy beans, garlic, chile peppers, and other spices. Look for it in large supermarkets and in Asian groceries.

Drunken Corned Beef in Beer

The carrots and potatoes in this hearty stew absorb the flavors of a tangy broth infused with the flavors of ale, *pickling spices*, mustard, and a hint of tarragon.

Yield:	Prep time:	Cook time:	Serving size:
6 cups	10 minutes	50 minutes	1 cup

3 lb. corned beef brisket, rinsed and patted dry

1 (12-oz.) bottle amber ale

1 tsp. dried pickling spices

1 lb. large carrots, peeled and cut into 2-in. rounds

6 medium red potatoes, washed and cut in ½

2 TB. coarse-grain mustard

¾ cup sour cream

1 TB. chopped fresh tarragon or 1 tsp. dried

½ tsp. kosher salt

½ tsp. freshly ground black pepper

1. In a pressure cooker over high heat, combine corned beef, amber ale, and pickling spices.

2. Lock the lid in place. Bring to high pressure, and maintain for 45 minutes. Remove from heat, and reduce pressure using the quick release method.

3. Transfer corned beef to a cutting board, cover with foil, and set aside.

4. Insert a steamer basket in the pressure cooker. Add carrots and potatoes.

5. Lock the lid in place. Bring to high pressure, and maintain for 5 minutes. Remove from heat, and reduce pressure using the quick release method.

6. In a small bowl, combine coarse-grain mustard, sour cream, tarragon, kosher salt, and pepper.

7. Slice corned beef, and serve on dinner plates with carrots, potatoes, and mustard sauce.

STEAM SPEAK

Pickling spices is a spice blend used to pickle foods and certain dishes. Although blends vary widely, ingredients typically include allspice, bay leaves, cinnamon, cardamom, coriander, cloves, ginger, mustard seeds, and peppercorns.

Chuck Roast Beef Stew

An American classic, this old-fashioned beef stew is made with onions, carrots, and potatoes in a savory beef broth.

Yield:	Prep time:	Cook time:	Serving size:
4 cups	10 minutes	28 minutes	1 cup

3 lb. chuck beef roast

¾ tsp. *kosher salt*

½ tsp. freshly ground black pepper

2 TB. vegetable oil or canola oil

2 medium yellow onions, diced small

2 cups Homemade Beef Stock (recipe in Chapter 8)

4 medium carrots, peeled and cut into 2-in. rounds

4 medium red potatoes, cut in ½

1. Sprinkle chuck roast with kosher salt and pepper.

2. In a pressure cooker over medium heat, heat vegetable oil. When hot, add chuck roast, and brown on all sides. Remove meat and drain on paper towels. Add onions, and cook for about 2 minutes or until soft.

3. Return chuck roast to the pressure cooker, and add Homemade Beef Stock.

4. Lock the lid in place. Bring to high pressure, and maintain for 20 minutes. Remove from heat, and reduce pressure using the quick release method.

5. Add carrots and potatoes to the pressure cooker.

6. Lock the lid in place. Bring to high pressure, and maintain for 8 minutes. Remove from heat, and reduce pressure using the cold water release method.

7. Ladle stew into large soup bowls, and serve immediately.

STEAM SPEAK

Because **kosher salt** has larger crystals than table salt, it dissolves more slowly and draws out more moisture from food, making the food more flavorful. Kosher salt is also free of additives and iodine. *Kosher* means "pure" and refers to how food is stored, prepared, and served to comply with Jewish law described in the Old Testament.

White Meat Stews

In This Chapter

- The best poultry for stews
- Stew-worthy pork
- Safety tips for handling chicken and pork
- A world of white meat stews

White meat stews—those made with poultry or pork—are a light alternative to red meat stews because they contain fewer calories and less saturated fat. And thanks to their mild flavor, white meats can be paired with other meats and fish as well as a wide variety of vegetables, grains, pasta, spices, and herbs. With the addition of just a few seasonings, the ethnic stews in this chapter reflect the cuisines of Italy, France, Russia, Germany, China, and the United States.

Perfect Poultry Stews

For the tastiest chicken stew, use stewing chickens, which are also called hens. Stewing chickens weigh from 3 to 6 pounds and are anywhere from 10 to 18 months old. Because of their age, stewing chickens are tastier but also less tender than young chickens, making them ideal for pressure cooker stews.

Choose chickens with a soft, smooth skin that's cream or yellow in color. Avoid chickens with bruised or torn skin, or those that have a bad odor. Remove the chicken from the cellophane wrapping and rewrap it loosely in waxed paper, removing any giblets from the body cavity and storing those separately. Refrigerate raw chicken in the coldest, lowest part of the refrigerator for up to 2 days, or up to 3 days for cooked chicken.

To avoid the risk of salmonella, never eat or taste raw chicken, and wash utensils, cutting boards, and your hands after handling raw chicken. Always use a bleach/water solution to sanitize your cutting board and other areas that the chicken has touched. (For more information on handling and cooking chicken, see Chapters 9 and 16.)

To make turkey stew, purchase or use leftover thighs and legs with the skin on and the bone in.

The Other White Meat

When it comes to white meat, don't forget about pork! Most pork today is leaner and tenderer with more protein and less fat than the pork of 10 years ago. Thanks to improved feeding methods, trichinosis is extremely rare today.

Choose pork that's pale pink and has a little marbling and white (not yellow) fat. The darker the flesh, the older the animal was when it was slaughtered. If you plan to use pork within 6 hours of purchasing it, you can refrigerate it in its store container. Otherwise, remove the pork from the package, wrap it in waxed paper, and refrigerate it for up to 2 days in the coldest part of the refrigerator. Pork that's wrapped in an airtight package can be frozen for up to 6 months.

To avoid any possible contamination, you should wash your hands as well as knives, cutting boards, and other utensils when handling raw pork, and you should never eat or taste uncooked pork.

Cacciatore-Style Chicken with Mushrooms

This hearty dish combines the flavor of bacon and chicken in an elegant mushroom sauce with a hint of brandy.

Yield:	Prep time:	Cook time:	Serving size:
4 cups	15 minutes	8 minutes	1 cup

4 (5-oz.) boneless chicken breasts, cut into bite-size pieces	12 pearl onions, peeled
1½ tsp. kosher salt	1 tsp. all-purpose flour
2 slices bacon	2 TB. brandy
3 medium white or russet potatoes, peeled and diced small	¼ cup dry white wine
½ cup fresh mushrooms, brushed clean and cut into slices	2 cups Homemade Chicken Stock (recipe in Chapter 9)
	½ tsp. freshly ground black pepper

1. Sprinkle chicken pieces with 1 teaspoon kosher salt. Set aside.

2. In a pressure cooker over medium heat, cook bacon for 3 or 4 minutes or until crisp. Remove bacon from the pressure cooker, and drain on paper towels. Cut into bite-size pieces.

3. Add potatoes to the pressure cooker, and cook in bacon fat for about 6 minutes or until golden brown. Remove from the pressure cooker, and drain on paper towels.

4. Add chicken pieces to the pressure cooker in small batches, and brown well on all sides. Transfer chicken to a cutting board, and let cool.

5. Add mushrooms and onions to the pressure cooker, and cook for 1 minute. Sprinkle with all-purpose flour, and using a wooden spoon, stir in brandy, white wine, and Homemade Chicken Stock. Return chicken, bacon, and potatoes to the pressure cooker.

6. Lock the lid in place. Bring to high pressure, and maintain for 8 minutes. Remove from heat, and release pressure using the quick release method. Add remaining ½ teaspoon kosher salt and pepper.

7. Ladle chicken and stew into large bowls or onto dinner plates, and serve immediately.

FOODIE FACT

Cacciatore is Italian for "hunter," and refers to dishes prepared "hunter style," or with tomatoes, onions, mushrooms, herbs, and wine. The term originated with Italian hunters, who prepared small game hunter style out in the open.

Chicken Stroganoff

The combination of white wine, hickory-flavored barbecue sauce, and Worcestershire sauce gives the vegetables and sauce in this classic comfort food a distinctively zesty flavor and bite.

Yield:	Prep time:	Cook time:	Serving size:
6 cups	15 minutes	10 minutes	1 cup

3 TB. canola oil or vegetable oil

2 medium yellow onions, peeled and sliced into rings

1 large green bell pepper, ribs and seeds removed, and cut into strips

1 cup white mushrooms, brushed clean and sliced thin

4 (4- or 5-oz.) boneless, skinless chicken breasts, cut into 1-in. strips

1 tsp. kosher salt

$\frac{1}{2}$ tsp. freshly ground black pepper

1 cup dry white wine

2 cups Homemade Chicken Stock (recipe in Chapter 9)

1 tsp. Worcestershire sauce

3 TB. hickory-flavored barbecue sauce

1 tsp. hot sauce

1. In a pressure cooker over medium heat, heat 1 tablespoon canola oil. When hot, add onions and green bell pepper, and cook for about 5 minutes or until brown.

2. Add mushrooms, and cook for 2 minutes. Using a slotted spoon, remove vegetables from the pressure cooker, and drain on paper towels.

3. Sprinkle chicken strips with kosher salt and pepper.

4. In the pressure cooker over medium heat, heat remaining 2 tablespoons canola oil. When hot, add chicken and cook for 4 or 5 minutes or until golden brown.

5. Return vegetables to the pressure cooker. Add white wine, Homemade Chicken Stock, Worcestershire sauce, barbecue sauce, and hot sauce.

6. Lock the lid in place. Bring to high pressure, and maintain for 10 minutes. Remove from heat, and reduce pressure using the cold water release method.

7. Return the pressure cooker to low heat, and cook for 5 minutes or until broth thickens slightly.

8. Ladle stroganoff into soup bowls, and serve immediately.

FOODIE FACT

Named after a nineteenth-century Russian diplomat, traditional stroganoff consists of thin slices of tender beef, onions, and mushrooms sautéed in butter and combined with a sour cream sauce and served over rice or pasta.

Brunswick Stew

The tangy sweet-and-sour tomato sauce gives this Southern-style stew its rich, spicy flavor.

Yield:	Prep time:	Cook time:	Serving size:
6 cups	10 minutes	12 minutes	1 cup

2 TB. canola oil or vegetable oil

1 large yellow or white onion, diced small

1 large green bell pepper, ribs and seeds removed, and diced small

2 (4- or 5-oz.) boneless, skinless chicken breasts, diced small

2 tsp. kosher salt

2 tsp. freshly ground black pepper

1 (28-oz.) can diced tomatoes, with juice

1 (8-oz.) can tomato sauce

¼ cup sugar

3 TB. apple cider vinegar

2 TB. Worcestershire sauce

1 lb. small red potatoes, unpeeled and cut into 2-in. cubes

1 (16-oz.) can corn, drained and rinsed

2 TB. all-purpose flour

1 cup cold water

1 (16-oz.) can pork and beans

1. In a pressure cooker over medium-high heat, heat canola oil. When hot, add onion and green bell pepper, and cook for about 5 minutes or until brown.

2. Season chicken with 1 teaspoon kosher salt and 1 teaspoon pepper, and add to the pressure cooker. Cook for 5 to 7 minutes or until chicken is light golden brown.

3. Add tomatoes with juice, tomato sauce, sugar, apple cider vinegar, Worcestershire sauce, and red potatoes.

4. Lock the lid in place. Bring to high pressure, and maintain for 12 minutes. Remove from heat, and reduce pressure using the cold water release method.

5. Set the pressure cooker over medium-low heat, and stir in corn. Cook for 2 or 3 minutes or until mixture is hot throughout.

6. In a small bowl, mix all-purpose flour with cold water to make slurry. Stir slurry into stew, and cook over medium-high heat for about 3 minutes or until thickened.

7. Stir in pork and beans, remaining 1 teaspoon kosher salt, and remaining 1 teaspoon pepper.

8. Ladle stew into warm soup bowls, and serve immediately.

FOODIE FACT

Brunswick County, Virginia, was the 1828 birthplace of Brunswick stew. In the early days, the stew was made with squirrel meat and onions. Today, it's made with chicken or rabbit and a variety of vegetables.

Chicken and Vegetable Stew

This hearty, easy-to-make stew combines the flavors of chicken, onions, bell peppers, tomatoes, squash, and corn in a spicy tomato sauce.

Yield:	Prep time:	Cook time:	Serving size:
8 cups	15 minutes	8 minutes	1 cup

3 TB. canola or vegetable oil

1 large sweet white or yellow onion, diced small

1 large yellow squash, skin on and diced small

1 large zucchini, skin on and diced small

1 green bell pepper, ribs and seeds removed, and finely diced

1 red bell pepper, ribs and seeds removed, and finely diced

1 large carrot, peeled and cut into 1-in. rounds

2 ribs celery, diced small

6 cups Homemade Chicken Stock (recipe in Chapter 9)

2 (4- or 5-oz.) boneless, skinless chicken breasts, cut into 1-in. cubes

2 large tomatoes, seeded and diced

1 cup frozen corn kernels, defrosted

1 tsp. kosher salt

1 tsp. freshly ground black pepper

2 medium green onions, white and green parts, sliced into thin rounds

1. In a pressure cooker over medium-high heat, heat canola oil. When hot, add onion, yellow squash, zucchini, green bell pepper, red bell pepper, carrot, and celery, and cook for 2 or 3 minutes or until vegetables are soft. Add Homemade Chicken Stock and chicken.

2. Lock the lid in place. Bring to high pressure, and maintain for 8 minutes. Remove from heat, and reduce pressure using the quick release method.

3. Add tomatoes and corn, reduce heat to low, and cook, uncovered, for 5 minutes. Add kosher salt and pepper.

4. Ladle stew into warm bowls, and garnish with sliced green onions.

PRESSURE POINTER

How do you get the seeds out of a pepper without ruining it? One way is to slice off the ends of the pepper and then slice it lengthwise. Use a paring knife to scrape out the ribs and seeds.

Turkey Chili

This dish has all the flavors you'd expect from traditional chili but is made with lean turkey instead of beef for a lighter, fresher-tasting chili lower in calories and saturated fat.

Yield:	Prep time:	Cook time:	Serving size:
6 cups	15 minutes	15 minutes	1 cup

1 TB. canola oil or vegetable oil

2 lb. ground turkey

1 medium green bell pepper, ribs and seeds removed, and finely diced

2 large white sweet onions, diced small

1 (15-oz.) can light red kidney beans, drained and rinsed

2 ribs celery, diced

1 (28-oz.) can diced tomatoes, with juice

1 tsp. kosher salt

1½ tsp. freshly ground black pepper

1 TB. sugar

2 tsp. chili powder

1 TB. dried taco seasoning

½ cup shredded medium cheddar cheese

1. In a pressure cooker over medium-high heat, heat canola oil. When hot, add ground turkey, and brown. Add green bell pepper and 1 sweet onion, and cook for about 2 minutes or until soft.

2. Using a fork, mash 1 cup kidney beans and add to the pressure cooker along with remaining whole beans. Add celery, tomatoes with juice, kosher salt, pepper, sugar, chili powder, and taco seasoning.

3. Lock the lid in place. Bring to high pressure, and maintain for 15 minutes. Remove from heat, and reduce pressure using the cold water release method. Return cooker to low heat, and let simmer for 10 minutes or until chili begins to thicken.

4. Ladle chili into large bowls, garnish with cheddar cheese and remaining 1 sweet onion, and serve immediately.

FOODIE FACT

The first chili cook-off was a showdown between two men in the remote city of Terlingua, Mexico. After the Terlingua event, chili fever spread throughout the country and chili societies formed to organize other cook-offs. Today, the tiny town of Terlingua hosts two international chili cook-offs every November.

Pork Chop Suey Stew

In this Asian-inspired stew, bean sprouts join celery, bell peppers, potatoes, and garlic in a savory sauce flavored with soy sauce and sweet molasses.

Yield:	Prep time:	Cook time:	Serving size:
3 cups	15 minutes	11 minutes	1 cup

1 lb. pork tenderloin, or 4 (5-oz.) boneless pork chops

2 tsp. kosher salt

½ tsp. freshly ground black pepper

4 TB. vegetable oil

¼ cup all-purpose flour

2 cups water

2 TB. low-sodium soy sauce

2 TB. molasses

4 ribs celery, finely diced

1 medium green bell pepper, ribs and seeds removed, and finely diced

1 large white or yellow onion, peeled and thinly sliced

1 clove garlic, minced

1 cup white or brown mushrooms, brushed clean and sliced thin

1½ cups bean sprouts

2 cups steamed white rice

1. Cut pork into 1-inch strips, and sprinkle with kosher salt and pepper.

2. In a pressure cooker over medium heat, heat vegetable oil. When hot, add pork. Add all-purpose flour, and stir well. Add water, soy sauce, and molasses.

3. Lock the lid in place. Bring to high pressure, and maintain for 8 minutes. Remove from heat, and reduce pressure using the cold water release method.

4. Add celery, green bell pepper, onion, garlic, mushrooms, and bean sprouts to the pressure cooker.

5. Lock the lid in place. Bring to high pressure, and maintain for 3 minutes. Remove from heat, and reduce pressure using the cold water release method.

6. Ladle stew into large bowls over white rice, and serve immediately.

STEAM SPEAK

Chop suey may sound Chinese, but it actually doesn't exist as a dish in China. Rather, it was invented by Chinese Americans in the nineteenth century. The dish includes small pieces of meat or fish, bean sprouts, onions, and other vegetables cooked together and served over rice.

Pork Chops and Potatoes

This one-pot meal combines the rich flavors of pork, garlic, nutmeg, and white wine for a fast and easy dinner with just one pot to wash afterward.

Yield:	Prep time:	Cook time:	Serving size:
4 pork chops	10 minutes	10 minutes	1 pork chop

4 (5-oz.) boneless pork chops

1 tsp. kosher salt

1 tsp. freshly ground black pepper

2 TB. canola or vegetable oil

2 cups Homemade Chicken Stock (recipe in Chapter 9)

3 cloves garlic, minced

3 medium red or Yukon Gold pota-toes, peeled and thinly sliced

1 large white or yellow onion, thinly sliced

2 bay leaves

¾ tsp. ground nutmeg

¾ tsp. dried sage

¾ cup dry white wine

1. Sprinkle both sides of pork chops with ½ teaspoon kosher salt and ½ teaspoon pepper.

2. In a pressure cooker over medium heat, heat canola oil. When hot, add pork chops, and brown on both sides. Using tongs, transfer chops to a cutting board, and set aside.

3. Stir in Homemade Chicken Stock. Using a heat-safe spatula or a wooden spoon, deglaze the pan by scraping meat particles from the bottom of the pressure cooker. Add garlic, and cook for about 30 seconds or until fragrant.

4. Remove the pressure cooker from heat, and layer the bottom with ½ of potato and onion slices. Top with pork chops and 1 bay leaf. Cover pork chops with a second layer of potato and onion. Sprinkle with remaining ½ teaspoon kosher salt, remaining ½ teaspoon pepper, nutmeg, and sage. Pour white wine over mixture, and add another bay leaf.

5. Lock the lid in place. Bring to high pressure, and maintain for 10 minutes. Remove from heat, and release pressure using the quick release method.

6. Remove bay leaves. Transfer chops and potatoes to warm dinner plates, and serve immediately.

FOODIE FACT

North Americans couldn't enjoy yellow potatoes until 1980, when the Yukon Gold potato was developed in Canada following years of intensive experimenting. The Yukon Gold is a cross-breed between the North American white potato and a wild yellow-fleshed South American potato.

Pork Butt in Beer

Dark beer and *liquid smoke* combine to give the pork and vegetables in this hearty stew a rich, smoky flavor.

Yield:	Prep time:	Cook time:	Serving size:
6 pounds	15 minutes	35 minutes	½ pound

6 lb. pork butt roast

1 TB. sea salt

1 TB. coarse-grain black pepper

3 TB. vegetable or canola oil

2 ribs celery, diced fine

2 large carrots, peeled and cut into 1-in. rounds

2 large white or yellow sweet onions, diced small

4 cloves garlic, minced

2 tsp. liquid smoke

1 (8-oz.) can tomato sauce

4 cups dark beer

1. Rub pork butt with sea salt and pepper.

2. In a pressure cooker over medium-high heat, heat vegetable oil. When hot, add pork roast, and cook for 3 minutes or until brown on all sides.

3. Remove roast from the pressure cooker, and drain on paper towels. Drain fat from the pressure cooker, reserving 2 tablespoons.

4. Add fat, celery, carrots, and onions to the pressure cooker, and cook for about 5 to 7 minutes or until golden brown. Stir in garlic, liquid smoke, tomato sauce, and beer. Return roast to the pressure cooker.

5. Lock the lid in place. Bring to high pressure, and maintain for 35 minutes. Remove from heat, and reduce pressure using the natural release method.

6. Transfer roast to a cutting board, cover loosely with aluminum foil, and let sit for 10 minutes to let juices lock in. Discard vegetables.

7. Slice roast into thick slices, transfer to large dinner plates, and serve immediately.

STEAM SPEAK

Liquid smoke is a brownish-yellow liquid created from the vapors of burning wet wood chips. It adds a smoky flavor to foods so they taste like they were grilled over a wood fire. Liquid smoke is readily available in supermarkets, usually near the barbecue sauces.

Pork Alsace

The fragrant aroma of sauerkraut, bacon, and pork will permeate the entire house when you make this elegant and traditional Old-World dish.

Yield:	Prep time:	Cook time:	Serving size:
2 pounds	15 minutes	28 minutes	½ pound

2 (11-oz.) cans sauerkraut, drained and rinsed

10 small red potatoes, skin on and scrubbed well

2 large carrots, peeled and sliced into 1-in. rounds

2 lb. smoked boneless ham

4 knockwurst, cut in ½ lengthwise

4 bratwurst, cut in ½ lengthwise

½ lb. bacon, cooked medium (not crisp)

3 bay leaves

¼ tsp. whole peppercorns

8 whole *juniper berries*

½ small red onion, minced

2 cups Homemade Beef Stock (recipe in Chapter 8)

1 cup water

1 cup dry white wine

1. In the bottom of a pressure cooker, layer ½ of sauerkraut, potatoes, and carrots. Add ham, knockwurst, and bratwurst, and cover with a second layer of sauerkraut. Top with cooked bacon, bay leaves, peppercorns, juniper berries, and onion. Pour Homemade Beef Stock, water, and white wine over mixture.

2. Lock the lid in place. Bring to high pressure, and maintain for 15 minutes. Remove from heat, and reduce pressure using the cold water release method.

3. Add remaining potatoes and carrots to the pressure cooker.

4. Lock the lid in place. Bring to high pressure, and maintain for 8 minutes. Remove from heat, and reduce pressure using the natural release method.

5. Using a slotted spoon, remove meat, potatoes, and carrots from the pressure cooker, transfer to dinner plates, and serve immediately.

STEAM SPEAK

Best known as the flavoring in gin, **juniper berries** grow on Juniper trees in Europe and America. Although you can find whole juniper berries in supermarkets, the berries are too bitter and astringent to eat raw. They're usually crushed and sold dried to flavor sauces and meats.

Stews from the Sea

In This Chapter

- Nutrition from the sea
- The best catch for your stew
- Great seafood gumbos
- Spicy seafood curries

Fish stews and curries are a seafood-lover's delight. Delicious, nutritious, and versatile, fish takes just a few minutes to cook in the pressure cooker. In fact, it's easier to overcook than undercook seafood, which can make it dry and tough.

Fish is also highly nutritious, packed with protein and B complex vitamins, along with iron, potassium, calcium, and phosphorous. Compared to meat, fish is low in sodium, fat, cholesterol, and calories.

Fatty fish, such as salmon, tuna, herring, and mackerel, are high in omega-3 fatty acids, the primary polyunsaturated fatty acids found in the fat and oils of fish. These fats lower low-density lipoprotein levels (LDL), the "bad" cholesterol that increases your risk of heart disease and stroke, and raise "good" high-density lipoproteins (HDL), which help decrease your risk.

And as you'll see in the recipes in this chapter, one of the best things about stews is that you can combine a wide variety of ingredients into one dish and reap the nutritional benefits of each!

The Complete Idiot's Guide to Seafood

When it comes to making seafood entrées, a bounty of choices are available from oceans, lakes, and streams. From fabulous finfish to savory crustaceans and shellfish, each brings its own distinctive flavors, textures, fragrances, and colors to your meal.

Fabulous Finfish

Finfish are divided into two broad categories: fish with fins, backbones, and gills, and fish and shellfish with shells. In this chapter, we look at fish without shells, which are grouped into two categories: freshwater fish and saltwater fish.

In addition, finfish are grouped into categories based on their shape—flatfish and roundfish—as well as on their fat content.

Lean fish such as halibut, perch, and snapper have mild, light-colored flesh and less than $2\frac{1}{2}$ percent fat. Moderate-fat fish like swordfish, bonita tuna, and whiting have less than 6 percent fat. High-fat fish, including yellowtail, tuna, and salmon, can contain as much as 30 percent fat, which gives their flesh a dark color, firm texture, and distinctive flavor.

Come Out of Your Shell

In addition to finfish, you can make scrumptious entrées with a wide variety of shellfish like mollusks and crustaceans. Mollusks such as clams, oysters, and scallops have soft bodies covered by a shell in one or more pieces. Crab, lobster, shrimp, and other crustaceans have elongated bodies and soft, jointed, crustlike shells.

Crustaceans and mollusks should have a pleasant smell like fresh ocean water, and the shells should be undamaged and closed. (For more information on pressure cooking with seafood, see Chapter 10.)

Seafood Gumbo

This spicy gumbo combines the flavors of oysters, ham, and crab in a zesty tomato sauce.

Yield:	Prep time:	Cook time:	Serving size:
8 cups	15 minutes	15 minutes	1 cup

3 TB. vegetable oil or bacon fat drippings

2½ cups fresh okra, cut into small slices

1 large white or yellow sweet onion, chopped fine

2 cloves garlic, minced

1 medium green bell pepper, ribs and seeds removed, and chopped fine

¼ cup diced ham

1 cup Homemade Fish Stock (recipe in Chapter 10) or clam juice

3½ cups water

1 tsp. dried thyme

2 bay leaves

1 cup blue crabmeat, drained and squeezed dry

1 pt. fresh or frozen oysters, with liquid

1 (8-oz.) can tomato sauce

½ cup all-purpose flour

1 tsp. kosher salt

¼ tsp. freshly ground black pepper

4 cups steamed brown rice

1 tsp. fresh flat-leaf parsley, minced

1. In a pressure cooker over medium heat, heat vegetable oil. When hot, add okra, and cook for about 5 minutes or until browned. Add onion, garlic, green bell pepper, and ham, and cook for 5 minutes or until golden brown. Add Homemade Fish Stock, 3 cups water, thyme, and bay leaves.

2. Lock the lid in place. Bring to high pressure, and maintain for 10 minutes. Remove from heat, and reduce pressure using the cold water release method.

3. Return pressure cooker to medium heat. Add crabmeat, oysters, and tomato sauce.

4. In a small bowl, combine all-purpose flour and remaining ½ cup water, and stir until smooth. Add to pressure cooker, increase heat to high, and cook, stirring frequently, for about 5 minutes.

5. Using tongs, remove bay leaves from the pressure cooker. Add kosher salt and pepper.

6. Ladle gumbo over brown rice in deep bowls, sprinkle with parsley, and serve immediately.

PRESSURE POINTER

When selecting oysters for the pressure cooker, look for fresh, shucked oysters that are plump, uniform in size, fresh smelling, and packaged in clear oyster liquor. You'll find the freshest oysters in fish stores with high turnover. If you can't find fresh oysters, you can substitute frozen oysters canned in their own liquor.

Elegant Sea Scallops

The buttery citrus sauce brings out the delicate, sweet flavors of sea scallops.

Yield:	Prep time:	Cook time:	Serving size:
1 pound	5 minutes	5 minutes	⅓ pound

½ lb. sea scallops, rinsed

½ tsp. kosher salt

¼ tsp. freshly ground black pepper

Zest of 1 large lemon

Zest of 1 large lime

½ cup water

½ cup dry white wine

½ cup Grand Marnier or other orange liqueur, or orange juice

1 TB. cornstarch

Juice of 1 large lemon

Juice of 1 large lime

1 TB. unsalted butter, cold and cut into cubes

1. Pat scallops dry and season with kosher salt, pepper, lemon zest, and lime zest.

2. Spray a rack with nonstick cooking spray, and insert it into a pressure cooker. Place scallops on the rack. Add water and white wine.

3. Lock the lid in place. Bring to high pressure, and maintain for 2 minutes. Remove from heat, and reduce pressure using the cold water release method.

4. Using tongs, remove scallops from the pressure cooker and transfer to a warm platter. Cover with aluminum foil to keep warm. Using a heat-safe glove, remove the rack from the pressure cooker.

5. In a small bowl, combine Grand Marnier with cornstarch until well blended.

6. In the pressure cooker over medium heat, combine orange mixture, lemon juice, and lime juice. Cook, stirring constantly, for 2 or 3 minutes or until sauce boils and thickens.

7. Reduce heat to low. Add unsalted butter, stirring constantly with a wooden spoon until butter is melted.

8. Transfer scallops to warmed dinner plates, top with sauce, and serve immediately.

UNDER PRESSURE

When buying scallops, avoid those that are stark white, which is a telltale sign they've been soaked in water to increase their weight. Instead, look for scallops that are pale beige to creamy pink in color. Fresh scallops should also have a fresh, sweet smell.

Southern-Style Shrimp Stew

Cayenne and garlic lend a pungent flavor to this thick and spicy stew that's chock-full of shrimp, carrots, and onions.

Yield:	Prep time:	Cook time:	Serving size:
4 cups	10 minutes	5 minutes	1 cup

2 TB. extra-virgin olive oil	1½ tsp. freshly ground black pepper
1 lb. medium gold or red potatoes, washed, cut in ½, and cut into 1-in. cubes	2 TB. all-purpose flour
2 large carrots, peeled and sliced into 1-in. rounds	2 cups Homemade Fish Stock (recipe in Chapter 10) or clam juice
2 cloves garlic, minced	½ cup water
2 large sweet onions, cut into quarters	1½ lb. shrimp (24 to 30), rinsed, peeled, and deveined
2 tsp. cayenne	1 bay leaf
1 tsp. dried thyme	½ cup Italian parsley, minced, or 2 tsp. dried
1 tsp. kosher salt	

1. In a pressure cooker over medium heat, heat extra-virgin olive oil. When hot, add potatoes, carrots, garlic, onions, cayenne, thyme, ½ teaspoon kosher salt, and ¾ teaspoon pepper. Cook, stirring occasionally, for about 5 minutes or until potatoes are soft.

2. Add all-purpose flour, and stir with a wooden spoon until blended. Increase heat to high. Add Homemade Fish Stock, water, shrimp, and bay leaf.

3. Lock the lid in place. Bring to high pressure, and maintain for 5 minutes. Remove from heat, and release pressure using the cold water release method.

4. Using tongs, remove bay leaf from the pressure cooker.

5. Stir in Italian parsley, remaining ½ teaspoon kosher salt, and remaining ¾ teaspoon pepper.

6. Ladle stew into warmed bowls, and serve immediately.

FOODIE FACT

Of the hundreds of species of shrimp, most can be categorized as cold-water or warm-water shrimp. Shrimp range in size from colossal (10 or less per pound) to miniature (80 to 100 per pound). In general, the colder the water, the smaller and juicier the shrimp. Most shrimp consumed in the United States come from the Atlantic and Pacific Oceans and the Gulf Coast.

Shrimp à la King

This old-time favorite has a soft, buttery flavor, thanks to the mushroom soup, and a hint of lemon. The peppers, mushrooms, onions, and shrimp give it a thick, chunky texture.

Yield:	Prep time:	Cook time:	Serving size:
4 cups	10 minutes	2 minutes	1 cup

2 TB. unsalted butter

1 medium green bell pepper, ribs and seeds removed, and diced small

1 medium red bell pepper, ribs and seeds removed, and diced small

1 cup white button mushrooms, brushed clean and sliced thin

1 medium sweet onion, diced small

Zest of 1 medium lemon

Juice of 1 medium lemon

1 cup water

2 lb. large shrimp (32 to 40), deveined, and shells and tails removed

1 (14.5-oz.) can cream of mushroom soup

½ tsp. freshly ground black pepper

2 cups steamed white rice

1. In a pressure cooker over medium heat, melt unsalted butter. Add green bell pepper, red bell pepper, mushrooms, and onion, and cook for 3 minutes or until vegetables are soft. Add lemon zest, lemon juice, water, and shrimp.

2. Lock the lid in place. Bring to high pressure, and maintain for 2 minutes. Remove from heat, and reduce pressure using the cold water release method.

3. Return the pressure cooker to low heat. Add cream of mushroom soup and pepper, and cook for 5 minutes.

4. Ladle stew over white rice in large bowls, and serve immediately.

FOODIE FACT

Shrimp à la King was created in the 1880s by the chef at the original Delmonico's Restaurant in lower Manhattan. The dish was made with shrimp cooked briefly with shallots and topped with a sauce made from sautéed red peppers, mushrooms, sherry, and cream.

Russian Fish Stew

This savory stew infuses whitefish with the zesty flavors of bacon and garlic and the sweetness of carrots, onions, and tomatoes.

Yield:	Prep time:	Cook time:	Serving size:
4 cups	15 minutes	5 minutes	1 cup

½ lb. bacon, chopped into 1-in. pieces

1 large sweet onion, diced small

2 TB. unsalted butter

1 large zucchini, skin on and cut into 1-in. cubes

2 large carrots, peeled and cut into ½-in. cubes

2 cups small mushrooms, brushed clean and sliced thin

2 TB. fresh garlic, minced

2 lb. whitefish fillets, rinsed and cut into 2-in. cubes

1 (32-oz.) can peeled tomatoes, with juice

2 tsp. freshly ground black pepper

1 bay leaf

2 cups Homemade Fish Stock (recipe in Chapter 10) or water

1 cup dry white wine

½ tsp. kosher salt

1. In a pressure cooker over medium heat, add bacon, and cook for 3 or 4 minutes or until crisp. Add onion, and cook for 2 minutes or until soft.

2. Add unsalted butter, zucchini, carrots, and mushrooms, and cook for about 2 minutes or until vegetables are browned.

3. Add garlic, and cook, stirring constantly, for 30 seconds. Add whitefish fillets, tomatoes with juice, 1 teaspoon pepper, bay leaf, Homemade Fish Stock, and white wine, and stir well.

4. Lock the lid in place. Bring to high pressure, and maintain for 5 minutes. Remove from heat, and release pressure using the natural release method.

5. Using tongs, remove bay leaf from pressure cooker.

6. Add kosher salt and remaining 1 teaspoon pepper, ladle stew into warmed bowls, and serve immediately.

FOODIE FACT

Russian fish stew, or *Ukha,* is traditionally made by simmering potatoes, onions, and parsley with cubes of whitefish fillets and freshly squeezed lemon juice, although there are hundreds of varieties using different vegetables; wine instead of lemon juice; and pike, perch, cod, or salmon instead of whitefish.

Whitefish in White Wine Sauce

The white wine sauce gives the fish a rich, buttery flavor. For best results, use white, flaky fish such as halibut, cod, or sole.

Yield:	Prep time:	Cook time:	Serving size:
4 fillets	10 minutes	5 minutes	1 fillet

6 oz. halibut, cod, or sole fish fillets

½ tsp. kosher salt

¼ tsp. freshly ground black pepper

2 shallots, minced

4 TB. unsalted butter, cold and cut into small cubes

1 cup Homemade Fish Stock (recipe in Chapter 10) or clam juice

½ cup dry white wine

1 cup dry white wine or sherry

2 cups water

2 TB. fresh parsley, minced

1. Rinse halibut under cold water, and pat dry. Season with kosher salt and pepper, and set aside.

2. In a small frying pan over high heat, cook shallots in 2 tablespoons unsalted butter for 1 or 2 minutes or until golden brown.

3. Add Homemade Fish Stock and ½ cup white wine, and bring to a boil. Reduce heat to medium, and continue cooking for about 5 to 10 minutes or until liquid is reduced by ½.

4. Add remaining 2 tablespoons butter, stirring constantly until mixture thickens.

5. Coat a rack with nonstick cooking spray, and insert it into the pressure cooker. Place fish on the rack. Cover with 1 cup white wine and water.

6. Lock the lid in place. Bring to high pressure, and maintain for 5 minutes. Remove from heat, and reduce pressure using the cold water release method.

7. Using a spatula, transfer fish from the pressure cooker to warmed dinner plates. Ladle wine sauce over fish, sprinkle with parsley, and serve immediately.

FOODIE FACT

Whitefish refers to several species of oceanic deep-water fish with fins, particularly cod, whiting, haddock, hake, and pollock. The term doesn't refer to the color of the fish's flesh.

Halibut with Fennel, Onion, and Tomatoes

Sweet, crunchy fennel, onions, and tomatoes give halibut a sweet kiss, while white wine lends richness and zest.

Yield:	Prep time:	Cook time:	Serving size:
4 fillets	10 minutes	5 minutes	1 fillet

6 oz. halibut fillets

¾ tsp. kosher salt

½ tsp. freshly ground black pepper

½ tsp. dried thyme

1 large fennel bulb, sliced thin

1 large sweet white or yellow onion, sliced

1 cup water

1 cup dry white wine or sherry

2 large Roma tomatoes, diced small and seeds removed

1. Rinse halibut under cold water, and pat dry. Season with ½ teaspoon kosher salt, ¼ teaspoon pepper, and thyme.

2. Place fennel and ½ of onion slices in the bottom of a pressure cooker.

3. Spray a rack with nonstick cooking spray, and insert it into the pressure cooker. Place halibut on the rack, and cover with water and white wine.

4. Lock the lid in place. Bring to high pressure, and maintain for 5 minutes. Remove from heat, and reduce pressure using the cold water release method.

5. Using a spatula, transfer halibut to warmed dinner plates. Top with remaining onion and Roma tomatoes, season with remaining ¼ teaspoon kosher salt and remaining ¼ teaspoon pepper, and serve immediately.

FOODIE FACT

Fennel is often mislabeled as "sweet anise" and shunned by those who dislike licorice. In fact, fennel has a sweeter and more delicate flavor than anise and is hard to detect when cooked.

Sweet-and-Spicy Seafood Curry

Cayenne, curry, and turmeric give this hot-and-spicy Indian-style curry its four-alarm flavor.

Yield:	Prep time:	Cook time:	Serving size:
4 cups	5 minutes	2 minutes	1 cup

2 TB. extra-virgin olive oil

1 large sweet onion, finely chopped

1 medium red bell pepper, ribs and seeds removed, and chopped fine

1 TB. garlic, minced

1 TB. curry powder

1 tsp. ground turmeric

1 tsp. cayenne

2 lb. large fresh shrimp (32 to 40), rinsed and deveined

1½ cups Homemade Fish Stock (recipe in Chapter 10), Homemade Vegetable Stock (recipe in Chapter 7), or canned low-sodium broth

¼ tsp. dried red pepper flakes

½ tsp. kosher salt

1 tsp. freshly ground black pepper

2 cups cooked white rice

1. In a pressure cooker over medium heat, heat extra-virgin olive oil. When hot, add onion and red bell pepper, and cook for 3 minutes.

2. Stir in garlic, curry powder, turmeric, and cayenne, and cook for 20 seconds.

3. Spray a rack with nonstick cooking spray, and insert it into the pressure cooker. Place shrimp on the rack, and cover with Homemade Fish Stock.

4. Lock the lid in place. Bring to high pressure, and maintain for 2 minutes. Remove from heat, and reduce pressure using the cold water release method.

5. Using tongs, remove shrimp from the rack. Drain vegetables in a colander, and discard liquid.

6. In a large bowl, combine vegetables and shrimp. Add red pepper flakes, kosher salt, and pepper.

7. Ladle stew into large bowls over white rice, and serve immediately.

FOODIE FACT

Curry powder, widely used in Indian cooking, is a combination of up to 20 different pulverized herbs, spices, and seeds, including cardamom, chiles, cinnamon, cloves, coriander, cumin, fennel seeds, mace, nutmeg, red and black pepper, poppy seeds, sesame seeds, saffron, tamarind, and turmeric. Curry powder loses its pungency within 2 months, so store it in an airtight container.

Everyday Entrées

If you don't have time on workdays to make and enjoy your favorite entrées, let your pressure cooker come to the rescue! In less time than it would take to order a take-out pizza, you could be serving your family the sort of scrumptious entrées you once reserved for guests. Instead of spending an entire afternoon making a pot roast, you can have dinner on the table in less than an hour using a pressure cooker. In addition to making meals up to 70 percent faster, your pressure cooker takes less electricity, so it helps you save on energy bills.

In Part 5, you'll find a range of recipes for hearty, stick-to-your-ribs entrées that are as delicious as they are nutritious and filling. We give you a chapter on hearty, stick-to-your-ribs beef entrées ranging from pot roast and chili to beef stroganoff, barbecued beef, and brisket. And we provide another chapter on a wide range of poultry pleasers, from barbecued, roasted, and shredded poultry entrées, to elegant recipes that pair poultry with everything from artichokes and garlic to orange sauce and wine. In Chapter 17, you'll find delicious and heart-healthy ways to pig out on pork, ham, and lamb entrées that are high in protein but contain less saturated fats than red meats.

Beefy Entrées

Chapter

15

In This Chapter

- The best cuts of beef
- BBQ without the grill
- Old-fashioned pot roasts, briskets, and stroganoff
- Mouth-watering tacos and beef strips

When you pair beef and your pressure cooker, the possibilities for delicious and tantalizing entrées are nearly endless, as you'll see by the recipes in this chapter. Turn the page to see how easy it is to use your pressure cooker to turn that 3-hour "company" roast into a 50-minute workaday quickie, create zesty tacos, and make finger-licking barbecue beef in half the time and without the smoke or mess.

Getting the Best Cuts

Fortunately for anyone on a budget, the best cuts of beef for pressure cooking—chuck, round, tri-tip, round tip, rump, bottom round, eye round, top sirloin, and chuck eye—are also the least expensive. The pressure cooker's moist heat turns these toughies into tender bites.

Ground beef is another good bet for the pressure cooker and is also extremely versatile and inexpensive. Lean ground beef has 2 percent fat, while regular ground beef has 15 percent fat. If you're trying to cut fat from your diet, use the lean version. If you're trying to save money, buy the higher-fat version.

You can also use choice cuts of beef in the pressure cooker, including T-bone, porterhouse, rib-eye, rib, and tenderloin. But with these cuts, you must lower the heat and reduce the cooking time to prevent the meat from becoming dry and tough.

BBQ Wizardry

If you love barbecue beef but hate the hassle of lighting the grill and heating the coals, your pressure cooker can make mouth-watering barbecue beef in less than 45 minutes—and you won't have to hassle with marinating, either.

Auntie's Pork Roast

This tender pork roast combines the zesty flavors of onion and garlic with the sweet taste of apples, apple cider, and white wine.

Yield:	Prep time:	Cook time:	Serving size:
3½ pounds	15 minutes	41 minutes	¾ pound

3½ lb. boneless pork roast

1 tsp. kosher salt

1 tsp. freshly ground black pepper

2 TB. canola or vegetable oil

1 large white or yellow onion, thinly sliced

3 cloves garlic, minced

1 cup dry white wine

1 cup Homemade Chicken Stock (recipe in Chapter 9)

1 cup apple cider

4 large Granny Smith apples, cores removed, and thinly sliced

1. Season pork roast with kosher salt and pepper.

2. In a pressure cooker over medium heat, heat canola oil. When hot, add pork roast, and brown on all sides. Using tongs, remove pork roast from the pressure cooker and set aside.

3. Add onion and garlic, and cook for about 3 minutes or until onion is soft.

4. Using tongs, return pork roast to the pressure cooker, and place on top of onion mixture. Add white wine, Homemade Chicken Stock, and apple cider.

5. Lock the lid in place. Bring to high pressure, and maintain for 35 minutes. Remove from heat, and reduce pressure using the cold water release method.

6. Using tongs, remove pork roast from the pressure cooker, and place on a cutting board. Cover with aluminum foil to keep warm.

7. Return the pressure cooker to high heat, and add Granny Smith apples.

8. Lock the lid in place. Bring to high pressure, and maintain for 3 minutes. Remove from heat, and reduce pressure using the natural release method.

9. Slice pork roast into thick slices and transfer to warmed dinner plates. Top with apple-onion mixture and juices, and serve immediately.

FOODIE FACT

Canola oil is one of the healthiest oils. At 6 percent, it contains less saturated fat than other oils, compared to 18 percent for peanut oil and a whopping 79 percent for palm seed oil.

Fruity Pot Roast

Allspice, cinnamon, and cloves give this tender beef a sweet flavor, while the onion gives it extra zest.

Yield:	Prep time:	Cook time:	Serving size:
4 cups	10 minutes	28 minutes	1 cup

4 lb. chuck beef roast

¾ tsp. kosher salt

½ tsp. freshly ground black pepper

2 TB. vegetable or canola oil

2 medium yellow or white onions, diced small

2 cups Homemade Beef Stock (recipe in Chapter 8)

2 TB. pickling spices

2 cups mixed dried fruit (plums, apricots, cherries, raisins, etc.)

1. Season chuck roast with kosher salt and pepper, and set aside.

2. In a pressure cooker over medium heat, heat vegetable oil. When hot, add chuck roast to the pressure cooker, and brown on all sides. Using tongs, remove chuck roast from the pressure cooker and set aside. Add onions to the pressure cooker, and cook for about 3 minutes or until soft.

3. Using tongs, return roast to pressure cooker. Add Homemade Beef Stock and pickling spices.

4. Lock the lid in place. Bring to high pressure, and maintain for 20 minutes. Remove from heat, and reduce pressure using the natural release method.

5. Return the pressure cooker to high heat, and add dried fruit.

6. Lock the lid in place. Bring to high pressure, and maintain for 8 minutes. Remove from heat, and reduce pressure using the cold water release method.

7. Ladle pot roast into large, warmed dinner bowls, and serve immediately.

FOODIE FACT

Drying depletes fruit's levels of vitamins A and C, but it has no effect on many other nutrients. Dried fruit contains nearly five times the calories by weight of fresh fruit, so a little goes a long way.

Beef Stroganoff

A rich and creamy gravy infuses the beef with the flavors of mushrooms, sour cream, and sherry.

Yield:	Prep time:	Cook time:	Serving size:
6 cups	15 minutes	15 minutes	1 cup

2 lb. top round steak, cut into strips

1 tsp. kosher salt

4 TB. unsalted butter or margarine, or vegetable oil

1 medium white or yellow onion, diced small

1 lb. brown button mushrooms, brushed clean of dirt and thinly sliced

2 cloves garlic, minced

1 TB. fresh Italian parsley, minced

4 cups Homemade Beef Stock (recipe in Chapter 8)

2 tsp. freshly ground black pepper

1 cup sour cream

¼ cup dry sherry or dry white wine

1. Season steak with kosher salt, and set aside.

2. In a pressure cooker over medium heat, heat unsalted butter. When hot, add beef and brown well on all sides. Using a slotted spoon, remove beef from the pressure cooker, and set aside.

3. In the pressure cooker over medium heat, add onion, mushrooms, garlic, Italian parsley, and Homemade Beef Stock. Cook for about 3 minutes or until onions are soft.

4. Return beef to the pressure cooker.

5. Lock the lid in place. Bring to high pressure, and maintain for 15 minutes. Remove from heat, and reduce pressure using the cold water release method.

6. Return the pressure cooker to low heat. Add pepper and sour cream, and cook for 3 minutes. Stir in sherry, and cook for 30 seconds.

7. Ladle stroganoff into large warmed dinner bowls, and serve immediately.

PRESSURE POINTER

Because of its toughness, top round is a perfect candidate for pressure cooking because the pressure cooker's intense, moist heat tenderizes it and makes it extremely tender.

Swiss Steak

Soy sauce and garlic add pungent undertones to the sweet flavors of bell peppers, onions, and stewed tomatoes.

Yield:	Prep time:	Cook time:	Serving size:
6 cups	15 minutes	15 minutes	1 cup

½ cup all-purpose flour

2 tsp. kosher salt

3 lb. sirloin steak, trimmed of fat and cut into 2-in. cubes

4 TB. unsalted butter, margarine, or vegetable oil

2 medium green bell peppers, ribs and seeds removed, and diced small

3 ribs celery, diced small

2 cloves garlic, minced

1 medium white or yellow sweet onion, diced small

1 (32-oz.) can stewed tomatoes, with juice

1 cup Homemade Beef Stock (recipe in Chapter 8)

1 TB. low-sodium soy sauce

2 TB. cornstarch

½ cup cold water

1. In a large zipper-lock plastic bag, combine all-purpose flour and kosher salt. Add steak, seal the bag, and shake it until steak is coated with flour mixture.

2. In a pressure cooker over medium heat, heat unsalted butter. When hot, add flour-coated beef and brown well on all sides. Using tongs, remove beef from the pressure cooker, and set aside.

3. Return the pressure cooker to high heat, and add green bell peppers, celery, garlic, and onion. Cook for 3 or 4 minutes or until vegetables are slightly brown.

4. Add stewed tomatoes with juice, Homemade Beef Stock, and soy sauce. Using a slotted spoon, return beef to the pressure cooker.

5. Lock the lid in place. Bring to high pressure, and maintain for 15 minutes. Remove from heat, and reduce pressure using the cold water release method.

6. In a small bowl, combine cornstarch and cold water until smooth. Add to the pressure cooker, reduce heat to medium, and cook, stirring frequently, for 1 or 2 minutes or until gravy is thickened.

7. Using a slotted spoon, transfer Swiss steak to warmed dinner plates, and serve immediately.

FOODIE FACT

Swiss steak, also called smothered steak, is a thick cut of beef, either chuck or round, that's been pounded or otherwise tenderized, coated with flour, browned on both sides, and covered with various tomatoes and seasonings.

Green Chile Steak with Tomatoes

Green chiles, chili sauce, cumin, garlic, and chili powder give this sirloin a mouthwatering four-alarm flavor, while the diced tomatoes and onions add sweet undertones.

Yield:	Prep time:	Cook time:	Serving size:
4 cups	10 minutes	15 minutes	1 cup

2 lb. top sirloin, trimmed

¾ tsp. kosher salt

¾ tsp. freshly ground black pepper

1 TB. dried cumin

1 TB. chili powder

3 TB. vegetable or canola oil

2 TB. unsalted butter

2 large white or yellow onions, thinly sliced

2 cloves garlic, peeled and thinly sliced

1 (32-oz.) can diced tomatoes, with juice

1 (12-oz.) can diced green chiles, drained

1 cup water

1 cup bottled chili sauce

1. Season steak with ½ teaspoon kosher salt, ½ teaspoon pepper, cumin, and chili powder.

2. In a pressure cooker over medium-high heat, heat 1 tablespoon vegetable oil. When hot, add steak and brown on all sides. Using tongs, remove meat from the pressure cooker, and set aside.

3. Reduce heat to low. Add remaining 2 tablespoons vegetable oil and unsalted butter to the pressure cooker. When hot, add onions, and cook for about 2 or 3 minutes or until soft. Add garlic, and cook, stirring constantly, for 30 seconds. Do not brown.

4. Using tongs, return steak to the pressure cooker. Add diced tomatoes with juice, green chiles, water, and chili sauce.

5. Lock the lid in place. Bring to high pressure, and maintain for 15 minutes. Remove from heat, and reduce pressure using the natural release method.

6. Add remaining ¼ teaspoon kosher salt and remaining ¼ teaspoon pepper. Ladle chili steak and vegetables into large, warmed soup bowls, and serve immediately.

FOODIE FACT

Green chiles get their hotness from capsaicin, a compound found primarily in the seeds and stems. Cooking and freezing green chiles won't affect their hotness, but you can lower their heat by removing the seeds and stems.

Beef Barbecue Brisket

This sweet-and-sour brisket is infused with the flavors of pungent garlic, spicy chili sauce, and a sugar-spice rub. You don't need an outdoor barbecue to make it, so you can enjoy it any time of year.

Yield:	Prep time:	Cook time:	Serving size:
2 pounds	10 minutes	45 minutes	½ pound

2 TB. vegetable oil	2 lb. beef brisket
1 medium white or yellow onion, diced small	1 tsp. chili powder
3 cloves garlic, minced	½ cup dark brown sugar, firmly packed
2 cups dark beer	1 tsp. kosher salt
1 cup chili sauce	1 tsp. freshly ground black pepper
2 TB. steak sauce	4 hamburger buns

1. In a pressure cooker over medium heat, heat vegetable oil. When hot, add onion and cook for 2 minutes or until onion is soft. Stir in garlic, beer, chili sauce, and steak sauce.

2. Lock the lid in place. Bring to high pressure, and maintain for 2 minutes. Remove from heat, and reduce pressure using the cold water release method.

3. Season brisket with chili powder, dark brown sugar, kosher salt, and pepper. Using tongs, transfer brisket to the pressure cooker.

4. Lock the lid in place. Bring to high pressure, and maintain for 45 minutes. Remove from heat, and reduce pressure using the cold water release method.

5. Using tongs, transfer brisket from the pressure cooker to a cutting board, and let it cool for 5 minutes. Using your hands, shred brisket into fine threads. Stir into the pressure cooker, reduce heat to low, and cook, stirring occasionally, for 2 minutes.

6. Ladle brisket into warmed hamburger buns, and serve immediately.

FOODIE FACT

Although briskets usually require hours of long, slow cooking, with a pressure cooker, you can prepare them in less than an hour.

Korean BBQ Beef

This Asian-style beef combines the sweetness of brown sugar with the pungent flavors of garlic, green onion, and soy. The sesame seeds add a hint of nuts and crunch.

Yield:	Prep time:	Cook time:	Serving size:
6 cups	15 minutes	12 minutes	1 cup

4 (6-oz.) New York strip steaks, fat trimmed	2 cloves garlic, minced
1 tsp. meat tenderizer	¼ cup dark brown sugar, firmly packed
1 tsp. freshly ground black pepper	½ cup water
1 TB. peanut oil	2 large green onions, chopped fine
1 TB. sesame oil	1 tsp. sesame seeds
1 cup low-sodium soy sauce	

1. Season steaks with meat tenderizer and pepper, and set aside.

2. In a pressure cooker over medium heat, add peanut oil and sesame oil. When hot, add steaks and brown on both sides. Using tongs, remove steaks from the pressure cooker, and set aside.

3. Remove the pressure cooker from heat. Using a paper towel, carefully wipe out all traces of fat.

4. In a small bowl, combine soy sauce, garlic, and dark brown sugar until smooth.

5. Return steaks to the pressure cooker, with water and brown sugar mixture, and set over high heat.

6. Lock the lid in place. Bring to high pressure, and maintain for 12 minutes. Remove from heat, and reduce pressure using the cold water release method.

7. Using tongs, transfer steaks from the pressure cooker to warmed dinner plates, top with green onions and sesame seeds, and serve immediately.

FOODIE FACT

Commercial meat tenderizers contain a papaya extract called papain, an enzyme that quickly breaks down tough meat fibers. They're much easier to use than other, more time- and labor-intensive ways to tenderize meat like pounding it with a mallet, or marinating it in a high-acid sauce.

Beef Burgundy

This sophisticated stew gets its complex flavors and depth from a rich sauce that combines red wine, brandy, and savory spices, including parsley and herbes de Provence.

Yield:	Prep time:	Cook time:	Serving size:
6 cups	15 minutes plus over-night marinating	45 minutes	1 cup

2 lb. top round steak, fat removed and cut into cubes

4 large carrots, peeled and thinly sliced into rounds

2 large sweet onions, thinly sliced

3 cups *Burgundy wine*

1 TB. herbes de Provence

4 TB. plus ¼ cup unsalted butter or margarine

2 cloves garlic, minced

1 lb. white button mushrooms, brushed clean of dirt, and thinly sliced

1 TB. fresh parsley, minced

½ cup brandy

4 cups Homemade Beef Stock (recipe in Chapter 8)

¼ cup all-purpose flour

¼ cup port wine

1 tsp. kosher salt

½ tsp. freshly ground black pepper

1. In a large bowl, combine steak, carrots, onions, Burgundy wine, and herbes de Provence. Marinate overnight or for at least 8 hours. Drain in a colander and reserve marinade.

2. In a pressure cooker over medium heat, melt 4 tablespoons unsalted butter. Add marinated steak, and brown well on all sides. Using a slotted spoon or tongs, remove steak from the pressure cooker, and set aside.

3. Add marinated carrots, garlic, mushrooms, and parsley to the pressure cooker, and cook for about 1 or 2 minutes or until soft. Add brandy, and cook for 2 minutes or until liquid has nearly evaporated.

4. Using a slotted spoon, return steak to the pressure cooker. Add reserved marinade and Homemade Beef Stock.

5. Lock the lid in place. Bring to high pressure, and maintain for 45 minutes. Remove from heat, and reduce pressure using the natural release method.

6. In a small bowl, combine all-purpose flour and remaining ¼ cup unsalted butter. Using your hands, roll mixture into small balls to create roux.

7. In the pressure cooker over medium heat, add roux in small batches. Cook, stirring frequently, for 1 minute per batch or until mixture thickens. Reduce heat to low, and stir in port wine.

8. Add kosher salt and pepper, ladle into large dinner bowls, and serve immediately.

STEAM SPEAK

Burgundy wine is a generic name for inexpensive red wines made outside France in Australia, South Africa, and the United States. Don't confuse the term with wines made in Burgundy, a world-famous wine region in France that produces some of the world's best Pinot Noirs and Chardonnays.

Fiesta Beef Tacos

Garlic, chili powder, cumin, and lime gives these beef tacos a spicy, south-of-the-border flavor, while chili beans and grated cheese add a creamy richness and thick texture.

Yield:	Prep time:	Cook time:	Serving size:
6 tacos	10 minutes	15 minutes	2 tacos

2 lb. top round steak

1 tsp. kosher salt

$\frac{1}{2}$ tsp. freshly ground black pepper

2 tsp. chili powder

2 TB. vegetable oil

1 large white onion, diced small

2 cloves garlic, minced

1 tsp. ground cumin

2 (10-oz.) cans diced tomatoes with green chiles

1 cup water

1 (15-oz.) can chili beans, drained and rinsed

6 medium flour *tortillas*, warmed

1 (6-oz.) can black olives, thinly sliced

$\frac{1}{2}$ cup Mexican grated cheese blend

2 large green onions, white and green parts, sliced into thin rounds

2 medium limes, cut into wedges

1. Season steak with kosher salt, pepper, and chili powder, and set aside.

2. In a pressure cooker over medium heat, heat vegetable oil. When hot, add steak and brown on all sides. Using a slotted spoon, remove steak from the pressure cooker, and set aside.

3. Add onion, garlic, cumin, and diced tomatoes with green chiles, and cook, stirring frequently, for 2 minutes. Return steak to the pressure cooker, and add water.

4. Lock the lid in place. Bring to high pressure, and maintain for 15 minutes. Remove from heat, and reduce pressure using the cold water release method.

5. Transfer steak from the pressure cooker to a cutting board, and let cool. Using your hands, shred steak. Return steak to the pressure cooker, and set over low heat. Stir in chili beans, and cook for 5 to 10 minutes or until mixture is warmed through.

6. Ladle beef into warmed tortillas. Top with black olives, grated cheese, and green onions. Garnish with lime wedges, and serve immediately.

STEAM SPEAK

Mexico's daily bread, **tortillas** are made from unleavened corn (masa) or wheat flour. They can be eaten plain or used as the base for tacos, burritos, and many other Mexican dishes.

Orange Spicy Beef Strips

These sweet-and-sour beef strips are infused with a sweet orange flavor and get their spicy kick from chile pepper and garlic.

Yield:	Prep time:	Cook time:	Serving size:
2 pounds	10 minutes	10 minutes	¾ pound

2 lb. stew beef, trimmed and cut into 1-in.-long strips

1 tsp. freshly ground black pepper

2 tsp. peanut oil

6 dried chile peppers

Rind from 3 large oranges, cut into ½-in. strips

3 cloves garlic, minced

4 large carrots, peeled and thinly sliced into rounds

1 cup water

1 cup Homemade Beef Stock (recipe in Chapter 8)

½ cup low-sodium soy sauce

¼ cup Grand Marnier or other orange liqueur, or orange juice

½ cup cornstarch

2 TB. cold water or orange juice

1. Sprinkle beef with pepper, and set aside.

2. In a pressure cooker over medium heat, heat peanut oil. When hot, add chile peppers and orange rind strips, and cook, stirring constantly, for about 3 minutes or until browned. Stir in garlic, and cook for 20 seconds. Do not brown.

3. Increase heat to high. Add beef and carrots, and cook for about 3 minutes or until slightly browned. Stir in water, Homemade Beef Stock, and soy sauce.

4. Lock the lid in place. Bring to high pressure, and maintain for 10 minutes. Remove from heat, and reduce pressure using the natural release method.

5. Reduce heat to medium, stir in Grand Marnier, and cook for 1 minute.

6. In a small bowl, combine cornstarch and cold water, and stir until smooth. Add to the pressure cooker, increase heat to high, and cook, stirring constantly, for 2 or 3 minutes or until mixture has thickened.

7. Ladle beef strips and vegetables into large, warmed bowls, and serve immediately.

FOODIE FACT

Grand Marnier is a cognac-based liqueur that gets its orange flavor from the peels of Haitian bitter oranges. Can't afford it? Gran Gala, a faux-Cointreau/Grand Marnier, costs about half the price.

One-Pot Poultry Pleasers

In This Chapter

- The wonderful world of poultry
- Comparing chickens and turkeys
- No-barby barbecued poultry
- Scrumptious chicken, Cornish game hen, and turkey entrées

A complete protein that's a low-fat and low-calorie alternative to beef, poultry is high in calcium, phosphorous, iron, riboflavin, thiamine, and niacin. Poultry has a mild, delicate flavor that's compatible with a world's worth of herbs, spices, and seasonings. You can prepare it in myriad different ways, from roasts and grilled treats to stews and finger foods. Poultry cooks up so fast, tender, and juicy in the pressure cooker, you can finally retire that turkey baster! (For more information on all the wonderful things you can do with poultry as well as safety and storage tips, see Chapters 9 and 13.)

The most popular poultry birds consumed are chicken, turkey, and Cornish game hen, and you'll find recipes for those in this chapter. But lots more options are available, including quail, duck, goose, pheasant, and guinea fowl.

Whether you're making chicken wings, barbecued chicken, or roasted duck, poultry is a delicious, juicy meat that will appeal to even the pickiest eater in your family!

Checking Out Chickens

Chickens fall into several categories, all of which you can make in your pressure cooker:

- Broiler-fryers weigh up to $3\frac{1}{2}$ pounds and are best broiled or fried.

- Roasters, with a higher fat content, are flavorful and ideal for roasting in your pressure cooker.

- Capons, which are actually roosters castrated at a young age and fed a high-fat diet, range from 4 to 10 pounds and are full-breasted, with tender, juicy, and flavorful meat.

- Rock Cornish hens, also called Cornish game hens, are miniature, $2\frac{1}{2}$-pound chickens that are best broiled, grilled, or roasted. They typically have enough meat for one serving.

The U.S. Department of Agriculture grades chickens A through C. Grade-A chickens contain the most meat and are the chickens you're likely to see in supermarkets. Grade-B chickens are less meaty, and grade-C chickens, which include stewing chickens, are scrawny and contain very little meat.

Talking Turkey

The pilgrims ate wild turkey, a native American bird. Today, the turkey that graces our Thanksgiving Day table is more likely to be a New Holland variety, which has been interbred with other turkeys to produce the most white meat (the American favorite). The female hen generally weighs 8 to 16 pounds, while male toms can weigh as much as 70 pounds (although toms over 20 pounds are harder to find in supermarkets).

BBQ Chicken

A zesty homemade barbecue sauce infuses this chicken with a hot and spicy combo of chili sauce, chili powder, tomato, mustard, and onion.

Yield:	Prep time:	Cook time:	Serving size:
4 to 6 pieces	10 minutes	7 minutes	1 piece

1 small white onion, minced	2 tsp. Worcestershire sauce
½ cup ketchup	1 tsp. dry mustard
½ cup chili sauce	2 lb. chicken thighs, drumsticks, and breasts
1 tsp. chili powder	
¼ cup dark brown sugar, firmly packed	½ tsp. kosher salt
	½ tsp. freshly ground black pepper
½ cup apple cider vinegar	2 TB. peanut oil
½ cup molasses	

1. In a large bowl, combine onion, ketchup, chili sauce, chili powder, dark brown sugar, apple cider vinegar, molasses, Worcestershire sauce, and dry mustard, and mix until smooth.

2. Season chicken with kosher salt and pepper.

3. In a pressure cooker over medium heat, heat peanut oil. When hot, add chicken pieces to the pressure cooker, and cook for 4 to 6 minutes or until brown on all sides. Add barbecue sauce.

4. Lock the lid in place. Bring to high pressure, and maintain for 7 minutes. Remove from heat, and release pressure using the natural release method.

5. Using tongs, transfer chicken pieces to warmed dinner plates, top with sauce, and serve immediately.

Variation: If you want to give your barbecued chicken a distinctive peanut flavor, use Chinese peanut oil. If you prefer a more neutral flavor, use American peanut oil, which has a mild flavor.

FOODIE FACT

With a pressure cooker, you don't have to wait until spring to create fall-off-the-bone barbecued chicken. You can make it any time of year in just one pot, and in far less time than you'd spend barbecuing it on the outdoor grill!

Chicken with Trio of Peppers

Bell peppers, white wine, Worcestershire sauce, hot sauce, and spicy barbecue sauce give this chicken dish its spicy five-alarm flavor.

Yield:	Prep time:	Cook time:	Serving size:
6 cups	15 minutes	10 minutes	1 cup

3 TB. canola or vegetable oil

2 medium yellow onions, sliced into rings

1 large green bell pepper, ribs and seeds removed, and cut into strips

1 large yellow bell pepper, ribs and seeds removed, and cut into strips

1 large red bell pepper, ribs and seeds removed, and cut into strips

1 tsp. kosher salt

½ tsp. freshly ground black pepper

4 (4-oz.) boneless, skinless chicken breasts, cut into 1-in. strips

1 cup dry white wine

2 cups Homemade Chicken Stock (recipe in Chapter 9)

1 tsp. Worcestershire sauce

1 tsp. barbecue sauce

2 tsp. hot sauce

1. In a pressure cooker over medium heat, heat 1 tablespoon canola oil until hot. Add onions, green bell pepper, yellow bell pepper, and red bell pepper, and cook for about 5 minutes or until brown.

2. Add kosher salt and pepper, and cook for 2 minutes. Using a slotted spoon, remove vegetables from the pressure cooker, and set aside.

3. Return the pressure cooker to high heat. Add remaining 2 tablespoons canola oil. When hot, add chicken strips and cook for 5 minutes or until chicken is golden brown.

4. Return vegetables to the pressure cooker, and add white wine, Homemade Chicken Stock, Worcestershire sauce, barbecue sauce, and hot sauce.

5. Lock the lid in place. Bring to high pressure, and maintain for 10 minutes. Remove from heat, and reduce pressure using the cold water release method.

6. Return the pressure cooker to low heat, and stir for 5 minutes or until broth thickens slightly.

7. Ladle chicken and vegetables into warmed bowls, and serve immediately.

FOODIE FACT

Of the hundreds of types of barbecue sauces, most are made with tomatoes, onion, mustard, garlic, brown sugar, and vinegar, although some varieties also include beer and wine. Some have a strong smoky flavor, while others have a sweet molasses flavor. Experiment until you find the barbecue sauces you like best.

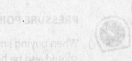

Lemon-Lime Roasted Chicken

This hearty chicken dish is infused with the delicate flavors of lemon and lime and has hints of rosemary and thyme.

Yield:	Prep time:	Cook time:	Serving size:
2 pieces	15 minutes	10 minutes	1 piece

1 (2-lb.) chicken	1 TB. canola or vegetable oil
1 tsp. kosher salt	1 cup dry white wine
½ tsp. freshly ground black pepper	2 cups Homemade Chicken Stock (recipe in Chapter 9)
1 tsp. poultry seasoning	2 sprigs fresh rosemary
2 large fresh lemons, sliced thin	2 sprigs fresh thyme
2 large fresh limes, sliced thin	

1. Rinse chicken inside and out, and pat dry. Remove and discard giblets. Season chicken with kosher salt, pepper, and poultry seasoning. Insert lemon slices and lime slices inside chicken cavity. Using string, tie front legs together.

2. In a pressure cooker over medium heat, heat canola oil. When hot, add chicken and cook for 5 minutes or until chicken is golden brown on all sides. Using tongs, remove chicken from the pressure cooker, and set aside.

3. Stir in white wine, Homemade Chicken Stock, rosemary, and thyme.

4. Spray a rack with nonstick cooking spray, and insert it into the pressure cooker. Place chicken on the rack.

5. Lock the lid in place. Bring to high pressure, and maintain for 10 minutes. Remove from heat, and reduce pressure using the cold water release method.

6. Using tongs, transfer chicken from the pressure cooker to a cutting board. Let cool, and cut into pieces.

7. Transfer chicken to warmed plates, and serve immediately.

PRESSURE POINTER

When buying limes, look for those with a bright color and smooth skin. The limes should also be heavy for their size. Small brown spots on the skin won't affect the flavor or juiciness of limes, but avoid those with hard or shriveled skins.

Garlic and Herb–Roasted Chicken

Garlic, herbs, and onions combined with sage, rosemary, thyme, and oregano give this roasted chicken a savory flavor and delicious aroma.

Yield:	Prep time:	Cook time:	Serving size:
2 pieces	15 minutes	15 minutes	1 piece

1 (2-lb.) chicken

1 tsp. kosher salt

½ tsp. freshly ground black pepper

1 tsp. dried sage

2 sprigs fresh rosemary

2 sprigs fresh thyme

2 sprigs fresh oregano

4 sprigs fresh parsley

4 cloves garlic

1 medium white or yellow onion, sliced

1 TB. canola or vegetable oil

1 cup dry white wine

2 cups Homemade Chicken Stock (recipe in Chapter 9)

1. Rinse chicken inside and out and pat dry. Remove and discard giblets. Sprinkle chicken with kosher salt, pepper, and sage. Insert rosemary, thyme, oregano, parsley, garlic, and onion into chicken cavity. Using string, tie front legs together.

2. In a pressure cooker over medium heat, heat canola oil. When hot, add chicken and cook for 5 minutes or until chicken is golden brown on all sides. Using tongs, remove chicken from the pressure cooker, and set aside.

3. Add white wine and Homemade Chicken Stock to the pressure cooker.

4. Spray a rack with nonstick cooking spray, and insert it into a pressure cooker. Place chicken on the rack.

5. Lock the lid in place. Bring to high pressure, and maintain for 15 minutes. Remove from heat, and reduce pressure using the cold water release method.

6. Using tongs, transfer chicken from the pressure cooker to a cutting board. Let cool, and cut into pieces.

7. Transfer chicken to warmed dinner plates, and serve immediately.

FOODIE FACT

Sage was once revered for its healing powers. Today, the pungent herb is primarily used to impart flavor and fragrance to dishes. Dried sage is sold whole, crumbled, and ground. Store it in a cool, dry place and use it within 6 months of purchase.

Artichoke-Stuffed Chicken Breasts

The fresh and zesty flavors of the Mediterranean shine through in these chicken breasts stuffed with marinated artichokes, onions, and white wine.

Yield:	Prep time:	Cook time:	Serving size:
4 chicken breasts	15 minutes	8 minutes	1 chicken breast

4 (4-oz.) boneless, skinless chicken breasts, trimmed of fat

¾ tsp. kosher salt

½ tsp. freshly ground black pepper

4 tsp. marinated artichokes

1 medium white or yellow onion, diced small

4 thin slices Monterey Jack cheese

¼ cup dry white wine

1 cup Homemade Chicken Stock (recipe in Chapter 9)

1. Using a mallet, pound chicken breasts between 2 sheets of plastic wrap until chicken is ½-inch thick. Sprinkle chicken with kosher salt and pepper.

2. Fold chicken breasts in ½ and stuff each breast with 1 teaspoon marinated artichokes, 1 teaspoon diced onion, and 1 slice Monterey Jack cheese. Use toothpicks to secure chicken.

3. Spray a rack with nonstick cooking spray, and insert it into a pressure cooker. Place chicken on the rack.

4. Set the pressure cooker over high heat, and add white wine and Homemade Chicken Stock.

5. Lock the lid in place. Bring to high pressure, and maintain for 8 minutes. Remove from heat, and reduce pressure using the quick release method.

6. Using a spatula, transfer chicken breasts from the pressure cooker to warmed dinner plates or bowls, and serve immediately.

PRESSURE POINTER

When a recipe calls for dry white wine, use a wine you'd be happy drinking, such as a good Sauvignon Blanc or Chardonnay. If you're on a budget, consider a high-quality generic white wine.

French-Style Chicken in Red Wine

This classic French dish infuses chicken with the rich flavors of red wine, garlic, onion, mushrooms, and bacon, plus a hint of basil, thyme, and parsley.

Yield:	Prep time:	Cook time:	Serving size:
3 pounds	10 minutes	8 minutes	¾ pound

3 lb. chicken, cut into serving pieces

3 TB. all-purpose flour

2 TB. extra-virgin olive oil

4 slices bacon, chopped small

1 large white or yellow onion

2 cloves garlic, minced

1 large carrot, peeled and diced small

1 cup dry red wine

½ tsp. dried thyme

2 TB. fresh parsley, minced

1 tsp. dried basil

1 bay leaf

1 tsp. kosher salt

½ tsp. freshly ground black pepper

1 lb. white mushrooms, brushed clean and sliced

1. Dust chicken pieces with 2 tablespoons all-purpose flour.

2. In a pressure cooker over medium-high heat, heat extra-virgin olive oil. When hot, add chicken pieces, and brown on all sides. Using tongs, transfer chicken pieces to a warm platter, and set aside.

3. Add bacon, onion, garlic, and carrot to the pressure cooker, and cook for about 2 minutes or until onion is soft. Add remaining 1 tablespoon all-purpose flour and red wine, and whisk for about 3 minutes or until mixture is smooth and thickened.

4. Add thyme, parsley, basil, bay leaf, kosher salt, and pepper. Return chicken to the pressure cooker.

5. Lock the lid in place. Bring to high pressure, and maintain for 10 minutes. Remove from heat, and reduce pressure using the quick release method.

6. Return the pressure cooker to medium heat. Add mushrooms, and simmer, uncovered, for 2 minutes. Using tongs, remove bay leaf from the pressure cooker.

7. Ladle chicken onto warmed dinner plates, and serve immediately.

FOODIE FACT

Good red wines to cook with include Cabernet Sauvignon, Pinot Noir, Merlot, Shiraz/Syrah, Zinfandel, and Cabernet Franc.

Herbed Cornish Game Hens

Cornish game hens are infused with the fragrant and savory flavors of basil, thyme, and parsley. The mushrooms and white wine add richness and depth.

Yield:	Prep time:	Cook time:	Serving size:
2 hens	10 minutes	10 minutes	1 hen

2 Cornish game hens

1 tsp. kosher salt

½ tsp. freshly ground black pepper

1 tsp. dried thyme

1 tsp. dried basil

1 TB. fresh parsley, minced

2 TB. extra-virgin olive oil

1 TB. all-purpose flour

1 cup dry white wine

1 cup Homemade Chicken Stock (recipe in Chapter 9)

½ lb. white mushrooms, brushed clean and sliced

1. Rinse Cornish game hens inside and out, and pat dry. Season with kosher salt, pepper, thyme, basil, and parsley. Using string, tie front legs together.

2. In a pressure cooker over high heat, heat extra-virgin olive oil. When hot, add Cornish game hens and brown on all sides. Using a wire whisk, stir in all-purpose flour, white wine, and Homemade Chicken Stock until mixture is smooth.

3. Lock the lid in place. Bring to high pressure, and maintain for 10 minutes. Remove from heat, and reduce pressure using the quick release method.

4. Return the pressure cooker to medium heat. Add mushrooms, and simmer, uncovered, for 2 minutes.

5. Using tongs, transfer Cornish game hens from the pressure cooker to a cutting board. Let cool for 5 minutes, and split in ½ using a sharp boning knife.

6. Transfer Cornish game hens to warmed dinner plates, top with sauce, and serve immediately.

FOODIE FACT

Fresh basil has a pungent flavor that tastes like a combination of licorice and cloves. Dried basil has a much milder flavor and fragrance. Find it in the spice section of most supermarkets, store it in an airtight container in a cool, dark place, and use it within 6 months.

Shredded Turkey Tacos

Garlic, onion, and chile peppers add fire to these shredded turkey tacos, while *Mexican cheese* adds richness and dark beer adds depth and spiciness.

Yield:	Prep time:	Cook time:	Serving size:
12 tacos	10 minutes	15 minutes	2 tacos

2 (1-lb.) turkey drumsticks, skin and fat removed

1 tsp. dried oregano

1 tsp. kosher salt

1 tsp. freshly ground black pepper

4 TB. canola or vegetable oil

4 large cloves garlic, thinly sliced

1 medium white onion, diced small

1 small jalapeño, ribs and seeds removed, and minced

1½ cups dark beer

1 cup water

12 medium flour tortillas

1 large tomato, seeds removed, and chopped small

½ cup shredded Mexican cheese

1. Sprinkle turkey with oregano, kosher salt, and pepper.

2. In a pressure cooker over high heat, heat 2 tablespoons canola oil. When hot, add turkey and brown on all sides. Using tongs, remove turkey from the pressure cooker, and set aside.

3. Add remaining 2 tablespoons canola oil to the pressure cooker, and heat for 2 or 3 minutes or until hot. Add garlic, onion, and jalapeño, and cook for about 5 minutes or until onion is soft. Stir in beer and water.

4. Spray a rack with nonstick cooking spray, and insert it into a pressure cooker. Put turkey on the rack.

5. Lock the lid in place. Bring to high pressure, and maintain for 15 minutes. Remove from heat, and reduce pressure using the natural release method.

6. Using tongs, transfer turkey from the pressure cooker to a cutting board. Cover loosely with aluminum foil. When cool, use your hands to shred turkey.

7. Ladle turkey into flour tortillas, top with tomato and Mexican cheese, and serve immediately.

STEAM SPEAK

Mexican cheese is not actually a cheese produced in Mexico, but a three- or four-cheese blend of cheddar, Monterey Jack, Colby or mozzarella, and pepper Jack. The cheese may have some fine bits of jalapeño in it, or it might contain Mexican seasonings. Find it in the cheese section of most supermarkets.

Turkey Breast Italiano

This moist and tender turkey is enhanced with the flavors of wine and *port* and infused with herbs.

Yield:	Prep time:	Cook time:	Serving size:
6 cups	15 minutes	35 minutes	1 cup

1 (3- or 4-lb.) turkey breast

1 tsp. dried thyme

1 tsp. dried Italian seasoning

1½ tsp. kosher salt

1½ tsp. freshly ground black pepper

2 TB. canola or vegetable oil

1 cup dry white wine

2 cups Homemade Chicken Stock (recipe in Chapter 9)

1 cup port or Madeira wine

2 bay leaves

1 (15-oz.) can diced tomatoes, with juice

1 tsp. dried basil

½ cup shredded mozzarella cheese

1. Sprinkle all sides of turkey breast with thyme, Italian seasoning, 1 teaspoon kosher salt, and 1 teaspoon pepper.

2. In a pressure cooker over medium-high heat, heat canola oil. When hot, add turkey breast and brown. Remove turkey breast from the pressure cooker, and add white wine, Homemade Chicken Stock, port, and bay leaves.

3. Spray a rack with nonstick cooking spray, and insert it into a pressure cooker. Place turkey breast on the rack.

4. Lock the lid in place. Bring to high pressure, and maintain for 35 minutes. Remove from heat, and reduce pressure using the cold water release method.

5. Remove turkey from the pressure cooker, and place on a cutting board. Cover loosely with aluminum foil, and allow to cool. Discard cooking broth.

6. In a small saucepan over low heat, combine tomatoes with juice, basil, remaining ½ teaspoon salt, and remaining ½ teaspoon pepper. Cook for 2 or 3 minutes or until hot.

7. Slice turkey into thick slices and place on large dinner plates. Ladle sauce on top of each slice, sprinkle shredded mozzarella cheese over top, and serve immediately.

STEAM SPEAK

Port is a sweet fortified wine grown in Portugal's Douro Valley and named after Oporto, the city from where it's shipped out to the rest of the world.

Duckling in Orange Sauce

This tender duck breast has deep citrus flavors and just a hint of white wine.

Yield:	Prep time:	Cook time:	Serving size:
3 pounds	10 minutes	15 minutes	⅓ pound

1 (2- or 3-lb.) duck breast, trimmed of fat

½ tsp. kosher salt

½ tsp. freshly ground black pepper

2 TB. vegetable oil

1 cup dry white wine

¾ cup freshly squeezed orange juice

Zest of 1 orange

2 tsp. cornstarch

1. Season duck with kosher salt and pepper.

2. In a pressure cooker over medium heat, heat vegetable oil. When hot, add duck, and brown on all sides. Remove duck from the pressure cooker, and set aside.

3. In a small bowl, mix white wine, ½ cup orange juice, and orange zest. Pour mixture into the pressure cooker.

4. Spray a rack with nonstick cooking spray, and insert it into the pressure cooker. Place duck on the rack.

5. Lock the lid in place. Bring to high pressure, and maintain for 15 minutes. Remove from heat, and allow pressure to release naturally.

6. Remove duck from the pressure cooker, and place on a plate. Cover with aluminum foil to keep warm. Using a heat-safe glove, remove the rack from the pressure cooker.

7. In a small bowl, combine cornstarch with remaining ¼ cup orange juice, and whisk until smooth. Pour mixture into the pressure cooker, and stir into remaining liquid. Cook for about 2 or 3 minutes or until sauce is thickened. Taste sauce and adjust seasoning if necessary.

8. Slice duck into thin slices, and serve on warmed dinner plates with sauce poured on top.

FOODIE FACT

This recipe takes its cue from a popular French dish, Duck in Orange Sauce, a rich dish with complex flavors that's surprisingly easy to make.

Pork, Ham, and Lamb Main Dishes

Chapter

17

In This Chapter

- Lean, mean meats
- A cut for every occasion
- Mouth-watering chops, roasts, and ribs
- Lamb shanks, roasts, and meatballs

High in protein and with less saturated fat than red meats, pork, ham, and lamb are heart-healthy meats that offer a wide variety of cuts to fit any budget. In this chapter, you'll learn more about these meats and get delicious recipes that showcase their rich and savory flavors.

Piggin' Out

Pork is one of the most popular meats in the world and an excellent choice for the pressure cooker. With nearly 20 different cuts—from tenderloin and blade steak to crown roast, pork loin, pork leg, pork shoulder, smoked hocks, and ground pork; to several different kinds of ribs, including back ribs, spare ribs, and country-style ribs; to bacon, ham, and sausage from cured pork—pork offers a wide variety of cuts for any budget.

Pork tenderloin has less fat than skinless chicken breasts and meets the government guidelines for "extra lean," while six other cuts of pork, including pork chops, roasts, legs, and ham, meet federal guidelines for "lean," with less than 10 grams fat, 4.5 grams saturated fat, and 95 milligrams cholesterol per serving. Cured ham, which is extremely lean leg meat, has either been dry-cured with salt and spices (called country-style ham), or wet-cured with a brine solution made up of water, salt, sugar, and spices. At the other extreme is bacon, which is made from the belly of the pig and is extremely fatty. But regardless of the cut, today's pork contains a third less fat than pork sold 50 years ago.

On the Lamb

Lamb refers to the tender and flavorful meat of sheep less than 1 year old. Baby lambs are between 6 and 8 weeks old, and spring lambs are between 3 and 5 months old. Both are milk-fed. Regular lamb is under 1 year old. Mutton, or lamb older than 2 years, is less tender than regular lamb and has a much stronger flavor.

The leanest cuts of lamb, including loin, shank, and leg, are comparable to beef and pork in terms of calories and fat, with about 150 to 170 calories and 2 or 3 grams saturated fat per 3-ounce serving.

Lamb meat comes in many different cuts, including ground, steaks, chops, roasts, riblets, and leg of lamb. Look for baby lamb meat that's pale pink in color and regular lamb meat that's pinkish-red.

One-Pot Pork Roast with Apples and Potatoes

This pot roast combines the sweet flavors of apples and onions with the rich flavors of tenderloin in a savory tomato-wine sauce.

Yield:	Prep time:	Cook time:	Serving size:
3 pounds	15 minutes	25 minutes	¾ pound

3½ lb. pork tenderloin, trimmed of fat	2 cups medium sweet potatoes, peeled and diced into 1-in. cubes
1 tsp. kosher salt	3 cloves garlic, peeled and sliced
1 tsp. freshly ground black pepper	2 medium white or yellow onions, diced small
2 TB. canola or vegetable oil	¼ cup all-purpose flour
3 small Granny Smith (or other tart) apples, skin on, seeds and core removed, and cut into quarters	1 cup dry white wine
	2 cups apple cider or apple juice

1. Season pork with kosher salt and pepper.

2. In a pressure cooker over medium heat, heat canola oil. When hot, add pork and brown on all sides. Using tongs, remove pork from the pressure cooker, and set aside.

3. Add Granny Smith apples, sweet potatoes, garlic, and onions, and cook for about 3 minutes or until vegetables are soft. Add all-purpose flour, white wine, and apple cider, and stir until well blended.

4. Lock the lid in place. Bring to high pressure, and maintain for 25 minutes. Remove from heat, and reduce pressure using the natural release method.

5. Using a spoon, skim excess fat from surface of broth. Using tongs, transfer roast from the pressure cooker to a cutting board. Cover with foil to keep warm. Let sit for 10 minutes before slicing to allow roast to retain its juices. Slice into thick slices, and set aside.

6. Using a slotted spoon, remove apples, sweet potatoes, garlic, and onions from pressure cooker, and set aside.

7. Return the pressure cooker to low heat, and reheat wine-apple roasting juices until hot.

8. Transfer pork slices to warmed dinner plates, top with roasting juices, and serve immediately with apples, sweet potatoes, garlic, and onions.

FOODIE FACT

Granny Smith apples have been cultivated for at least 140 years and were named after Marie Ana Smith, an Australian grandmother who nurtured these apples from the sprouts of French crab apples. Granny Smith apples retain their tart flavor when pressure cooked or baked.

Pulled BBQ Pork Sandwiches

A sweet and tangy sauce makes this tender pork perfect for a delicious barbecue sandwich!

Yield:	Prep time:	Cook time:	Serving size:
16 ounces	10 minutes	25 minutes	4 ounces

1 (1-lb.) pkg. pork tenderloin	2 TB. Worcestershire sauce
1 cup ketchup	1 TB. coarse-grain mustard
1 small sweet onion, diced medium	1½ cups apple cider
3 TB. dark brown sugar	4 rolls or buns
¼ cup cider vinegar	

1. In a pressure cooker over medium-high heat, add pork tenderloin, ketchup, onion, dark brown sugar, cider vinegar, Worcestershire sauce, mustard, and apple cider.

2. Lock the lid in place. Bring to high pressure, and maintain for 10 minutes. Remove from heat, and reduce pressure using the natural release method.

3. Reduce heat to low, and let pork simmer for about 10 minutes or until liquid has evaporated.

4. Using a slotted spoon, transfer pork from the pressure cooker to a cutting board and let cool. When pork is cool, shred it with your hands and return it to the pressure cooker. Set the pressure cooker over medium heat, and cook for about 5 minutes or until hot.

5. Ladle pork into rolls or buns, and serve immediately.

FOODIE FACT

Pulled pork usually requires cooking over slow heat for several hours so the meat can be easily pulled apart. With a pressure cooker, you can make delicious pulled pork in about a half hour.

BBQ-Style Pork Chops

A rich and spicy sauce, along with hints of molasses and Worcestershire sauce, make these pork chops a sweet and savory standout.

Yield:	Prep time:	Cook time:	Serving size:
4 pork chops	10 minutes	7 minutes	1 pork chop

½ tsp. kosher salt	1 cup ketchup
½ tsp. freshly ground black pepper	¼ cup apple cider vinegar
2 TB. dark brown sugar	¼ cup molasses
1 TB. chili powder	2 tsp. Worcestershire sauce
4 (5-oz.) boneless pork chops	1 tsp. dry mustard
4 TB. extra-virgin olive oil	1 cup water
1 small white onion, diced small	1 cup apple cider
1 clove garlic, finely chopped	

1. In a small bowl, combine kosher salt, pepper, dark brown sugar, and chili powder until well blended. Sprinkle mixture on both sides of pork chops, and rub into meat using your fingers.

2. In a pressure cooker over medium-high heat, heat 2 tablespoons extra-virgin olive oil. When hot, add pork chops, and cook for about 2 minutes per side or until both sides are brown. Using tongs, transfer pork chops from the pressure cooker to a cutting board, and set aside.

3. In the pressure cooker over medium heat, add remaining 2 tablespoons extra-virgin olive oil. When hot, add onion and garlic, and cook for 2 minutes.

4. Using tongs, return pork chops to the pressure cooker. Add ketchup, apple cider vinegar, molasses, Worcestershire sauce, dry mustard, water, and apple cider.

5. Lock the lid in place. Bring to high pressure, and maintain for 7 minutes. Remove from heat, and reduce pressure using the natural release method.

6. Using tongs, transfer pork chops to warmed dinner plates, top with sauce, and serve immediately.

UNDER PRESSURE

Never substitute regular cider for hard cider or cider vinegar in a recipe. The results may make you pucker! Apple cider, which does not contain alcohol, is made by pressing the juice and drinking it straight or diluting it with water, while hard cider is apple cider that's been fermented so it contains alcohol.

Ham and Yams

Onions and yams give baked ham a rich, sweet flavor, while cloves and mustard add depth and kick.

Yield:	Prep time:	Cook time:	Serving size:
3 pounds	10 minutes	20 minutes	⅓ pound

3 lb. cooked ham	1 TB. Dijon mustard
1 TB. whole cloves	1 large white onion, cut into thin slices
1½ cups water	
½ cup dark brown sugar, firmly packed	4 medium yams, skin on, scrubbed clean, and cut in ½

1. Using a sharp knife, score ham into a diamond pattern. Insert cloves in the middle of the diamonds.

2. Spray a rack with nonstick cooking spray, and insert it into a pressure cooker.

3. In a small bowl, whisk together water, dark brown sugar, and Dijon mustard until smooth. Place ham on the insert rack, and cover with mustard mixture, onion, and yams.

4. Lock the lid in place. Bring to high pressure, and maintain for 20 minutes. Remove from heat, and reduce pressure using the natural release method.

5. Transfer ham from the pressure cooker to a cutting board, and slice. Remove yams from the pressure cooker, and cut into quarters.

6. Place ham and yams on warmed dinner plates, and serve immediately.

FOODIE FACT

Nonstick cooking spray prevents food from sticking to the pan without adding extra calories or fat. Made of vegetable oil and lecithin, it comes in several flavors, including butter, olive oil, and canola oil.

Lamb Shank Provençal

Lamb goes Italian in this zesty dish flavored with garlic, herbs, and a rich tomato sauce.

Yield:	Prep time:	Cook time:	Serving size:
2 shanks	10 minutes	25 minutes	1 shank

2 lamb shanks	½ tsp. dried thyme
1 tsp. kosher salt	¼ tsp. dried rosemary
1 tsp. freshly ground black pepper	1 cup dry red wine
2 TB. vegetable oil	1 cup Homemade Chicken Stock (recipe in Chapter 9)
1 large carrot, peeled and diced small	1 cup Homemade Beef Stock (recipe in Chapter 8)
1 large white or yellow onion, diced small	1 large tomato, seeded and diced
1 medium shallot, diced small	1 tsp. canned tomato paste
3 cloves garlic, cut in ½	

1. Season lamb shanks with kosher salt and pepper.

2. In a pressure cooker over medium heat, heat vegetable oil. When hot, add lamb shanks to the pressure cooker and brown on all sides. Using tongs, remove shanks from the pressure cooker, and set aside.

3. Add carrot, onion, shallot, and garlic to the pressure cooker, and cook for about 2 minutes or until vegetables are soft. Stir in thyme and rosemary.

4. Using tongs, return lamb shanks to the pressure cooker. Add red wine, Homemade Chicken Stock, and Homemade Beef Stock.

5. Lock the lid in place. Bring to high pressure, and maintain for 25 minutes. Remove from heat, and reduce pressure using the natural release method.

6. Using tongs, transfer shank from the pressure cooker to a cutting board, and set aside.

7. Skim excess fat from broth with a spoon.

8. Return the pressure cooker to low heat. Add tomato and tomato paste, and cook, stirring constantly, for 2 minutes.

9. Using tongs, transfer lamb shanks from the cutting board to warmed deep bowls, top with tomato sauce, and serve immediately.

PRESSURE POINTER

To warm dinner plates, simply put them in a conventional oven on low heat (about 170°F or less) for about 5 minutes.

Elegant Lamb Roast

This juicy roast is infused with the flavors of lemon, garlic, and oregano for a Mediterranean take on lamb.

Yield:	Prep time:	Cook time:	Serving size:
5 pounds	15 minutes	35 minutes	¾ pound

5 lb. boneless leg of lamb

2 large lemons, cut in ½

¼ cup chopped fresh oregano or 1 TB. dried

1 tsp. kosher salt

1 tsp. freshly ground black pepper

1 whole bulb garlic, cloves separated and peeled

¼ cup extra-virgin olive oil

1 cup Homemade Chicken Stock (recipe in Chapter 9)

1. Rub entire surface of leg of lamb with lemons.

2. In a small bowl, combine oregano, kosher salt, and pepper. Rub mixture into leg of lamb.

3. In a pressure cooker over high heat, add leg of lamb and surround with garlic cloves. Pour extra-virgin olive oil over lamb and garlic cloves.

4. Squeeze remaining lemon juice into a small bowl and combine with Homemade Chicken Stock. Pour mixture over lamb.

5. Lock the lid in place. Bring to high pressure, and maintain for 35 minutes. Remove from heat, and reduce pressure using the quick release method.

6. Using tongs, transfer leg of lamb from the pressure cooker to a cutting board. Cover with aluminum foil, and let cool for 10 minutes.

7. Return the pressure cooker to low heat, and reheat roasting juices for 2 or 3 minutes or until hot.

8. Slice lamb, and transfer to warmed dinner plates. Ladle juice over lamb, and serve immediately.

FOODIE FACT

If you're buying fresh oregano, choose bright green bunches that have no yellowing or wilting. Refrigerate in a plastic bag, and use within 3 days. Store dried oregano in a cool, dark place, and use within 6 months.

BBQ Lamb Shank

This spicy barbecued lamb is infused with the savory flavors of tomato and red wine, and has undertones of garlic, shallots, rosemary, and thyme.

Yield:	Prep time:	Cook time:	Serving size:
2 shanks	15 minutes	25 minutes	1 shank

2 lb. lamb shank	3 cloves garlic, cut in $\frac{1}{2}$
$\frac{1}{2}$ tsp. kosher salt	$\frac{1}{2}$ tsp. dried thyme
1 tsp. freshly ground black pepper	$\frac{1}{4}$ tsp. dried rosemary
2 TB. vegetable oil	1 cup dry red wine
1 large carrot, peeled and diced small	2 cups Homemade Beef Stock (recipe in Chapter 8)
1 large white or yellow onion, diced small	1 large tomato, seeded and diced
1 medium shallot, diced small	2 tsp. tomato paste

1. Season lamb shank with kosher salt and pepper.

2. In a pressure cooker over medium heat, heat vegetable oil. When hot, add lamb shank, and brown on all sides. Using tongs, remove shank from the pressure cooker, and set aside.

3. Add carrot, onion, shallot, and garlic to the pressure cooker, and cook for about 2 minutes or until soft. Stir in thyme and rosemary. Stir in red wine and Homemade Beef Stock.

4. Lock the lid in place. Bring to high pressure, and maintain for 25 minutes. Remove from heat, and reduce pressure using the natural release method.

5. Using tongs, transfer shank from the pressure cooker to a cutting board.

6. Skim excess fat from sauce using a spoon.

7. Return the pressure cooker to low heat. Add tomato and tomato paste, and stir until blended.

8. Using tongs, transfer lamb shanks to warmed deep bowls, top with tomato sauce, and serve immediately.

FOODIE FACT

Rosemary, a native to the Mediterranean, has been cultivated since 500 B.C.E. The highly aromatic herb has pine and lemon undertones and was originally used to treat nervous disorders. Today, rosemary is used to season meats (and in particular, lamb), vegetables, soups, and fruits.

Lamb Meatballs

These Mediterranean-style meatballs are spiced with mint, oregano, garlic, and parsley, and served in a rich tomato sauce.

Yield:	Prep time:	Cook time:	Serving size:
24 meatballs	15 minutes	5 minutes	6 meatballs

2 lb. ground lamb

1 tsp. kosher salt

1 tsp. freshly ground black pepper

2 TB. minced white or yellow onion

2 cloves garlic, minced

2 tsp. dried mint

½ cup feta cheese

1 large egg

½ cup dried breadcrumbs

2 TB. extra-virgin olive oil

1 small white or yellow onion, diced small

1 TB. dried oregano

1 (28-oz.) can crushed tomato purée

1½ cups water

4 cups cooked angel hair pasta

¼ cup fresh parsley, minced

1. In a medium bowl, combine ground lamb, kosher salt, pepper, minced onion, garlic, mint, feta cheese, egg, and breadcrumbs. Shape mixture into 24 (2-inch) meatballs, and set aside.

2. In a pressure cooker over medium heat, heat extra-virgin olive oil. When hot, stir in diced onion, and cook for about 3 minutes or until soft.

3. Stir in oregano, tomato purée, and water. Using a ladle, add meatballs to the pressure cooker.

4. Lock the lid in place. Bring to high pressure, and maintain for 5 minutes. Remove from heat, and release pressure using the cold water release method.

5. Ladle meatballs onto plates of hot pasta, top with sauce, garnish with fresh parsley, and serve immediately.

UNDER PRESSURE

Don't substitute canned tomato paste for tomato purée in recipes. Tomato purée is made from tomatoes that have been cooked briefly and strained, and has a slightly thicker consistency than tomato sauce, which is made from tomatoes cooked for several hours, strained, and reduced to a thick, concentrated paste.

Spicy and Sweet Pork Ribs

Sweet flavors of cider and brown sugar make for melt-in-your-mouth tender pork ribs.

Yield:	Prep time:	Cook time:	Serving size:
1 rack	20 minutes	15 minutes	¼ rack

1 rack baby back ribs

1 tsp. kosher salt

1 tsp. freshly ground black pepper

2 TB. extra-virgin olive oil

1 medium white onion, diced small

1 large carrot, diced small

1 large celery rib, diced small

1 cup ketchup

¼ cup apple cider vinegar

¼ cup molasses

¼ cup dark brown sugar, firmly packed

½ tsp. dry mustard

1 cup water

1 cup apple cider or apple juice

1. Rub ribs with kosher salt and pepper.

2. In a pressure cooker over medium heat, heat extra-virgin olive oil. When hot, add onion, carrot, and celery, and cook for about 3 minutes or until soft.

3. Add ketchup, apple cider vinegar, molasses, dark brown sugar, and dry mustard.

4. Lock the lid in place. Bring to high pressure, and maintain for 5 minutes. Remove from heat, and reduce pressure using the quick release method.

5. Remove sauce from the pressure cooker, and set aside.

6. In the clean pressure cooker, add water and apple cider. Place an insert rack on the bottom of the pressure cooker. Cut ribs apart into sections so they'll fit on the rack. Add ribs, and set the pressure cooker over high heat.

7. Lock the lid into place. Bring to high pressure, and maintain for 20 minutes. Turn heat off and allow pressure to release naturally. Carefully open the lid and, using tongs, remove ribs.

8. Transfer ribs to a medium-hot grill or place on a baking sheet and place in a 400°F oven. Cook, brushing both sides of the ribs with sauce until well coated, for about 8 to 10 minutes per side. Serve immediately.

FOODIE FACT

With a pressure cooker, you can make delicious pork barbecued ribs any time of year.

1 tsp. dry mustard

½ cup water

On the Side

Side dishes can make or break a meal. In Part 6, companion dishes play a star role. You'll find delicious recipes for grains, rice, pasta, and vegetables that complement a wide range of entrées, from meat and fish to vegetarian meals.

One chapter focuses on great grains that give any meal extra nutrition, flavor, and heartiness. From barley and rice to risotto and pasta, you learn how to use your pressure cooker to prepare grains in record time and even use it to quick-soak grains that normally take 24 hours to soak.

Another chapter shows you how to use your pressure cooker to prepare vegetables that come out of the pressure cooker as nutritious, crispy, flavorful, and colorful as they went in.

Part 6 ends with a chapter that shows you how to make sassy sauces that ignite the flavor of everything from entrées and side dishes to appetizers and dips. If you've been looking for the perfect homemade barbecue sauce, marinara sauce, chutney, or horseradish, you'll find a recipe for it here.

Amazing Grains

In This Chapter

- The secret world of rice
- A grain for every occasion
- Prepping and soaking grains
- Perfect pressure cooker pasta

A pressure cooker lets you easily quick-soak grains with no overnight wait, and also dramatically slashes the cooking time.

All About Rice

Rice is a staple that feeds half the world's population. The more than 7,000 varieties of rice are divided into two categories. Aquatic rice is grown in rice paddies, while hill-grown rice is grown in tropical or subtropical terrain. If the only rice you've ever eaten is Minute Rice, you're in for a taste sensation that's packed with nutrients.

Because white rice has the husk, bran, and germ removed, it's not as nutritious as brown rice, which does not have the vitamin-packed outer husk removed. Unlike white rice, which has a bland flavor and soft consistency, brown rice is chewy and has a nutlike flavor. White rice cooks quickly in the pressure cooker and doesn't require presoaking. Brown rice should be soaked for about 4 hours before pressure cooking. If the rice isn't presoaked, increase the cooking time by 15 minutes.

Rice is classified and sold according to the size of its grain. Long-grain rice is the most popular type of rice, and comes in white and brown varieties. The elongated grains remain fluffy, firm, and separate when cooked and can be enjoyed alone or combined in rice dishes such as rice pilaf. The fragrant basmati rice is among the more exotic types of long-grain rice.

Short-grain rice is fat and round and has the highest starch content of all rice. When cooked, it's moist and sticky. This rice is popular in Chinese and Asian cuisine because it clumps, making it easy to handle with chopsticks. Italian Arborio rice, which is used to make risotto, is another type of short-grain rice.

Medium-grain rice is shorter and moister than long-grain rice. Although medium-grain rice is fluffy right after it's cooked, it gets sticky and begins to clump together as it cools.

Grains of Truth

Your pressure cooker also makes quick work of a variety of grains, each with its own distinctive flavor and texture. Here are just a few grains that work well in your pressure cooker:

- Amaranth, an ancient grain with a nutty, spicy taste and sticky texture
- Barley, a chewy, hearty grain that's great in soup and stews
- Buckwheat, a nutritious seed with a roasted flavor
- Bulgur, a hearty grain used in Middle Eastern cuisine
- Spelt, a healthy alternative to wheat with a light nutty flavor
- Quinoa, super-high in protein with a nutty flavor

Perfect Pasta

Today's pressure cooker makes it faster and easier than ever to make casseroles and other one-pot meals that contain noodles, macaroni, and pasta.

For the best results, use large, fat types of pasta in your pressure cooker rather than small, thin types. Good choices include egg noodles, ziti, elbow macaroni, bow-ties, spirals, and penne pasta.

When choosing pasta for your pressure cooker, avoid American brands, which are usually thin and flimsy; instead, use imported Italian brands, which are thicker and more substantial. Never use fresh or refrigerated pastas in your pressure cooker because they cook much faster than dried pasta. Be sure your pasta is made from 100 percent semolina durum wheat, which retains its shape and firmness during cooking.

Best Barley Greek Salad

This Italian-style salad combines the hearty flavors of barley with the tangy flavors of feta, olives, and balsamic dressing.

Yield:	Prep time:	Cook time:	Serving size:
3 cups	5 minutes	17 minutes	½ cup

2 TB. unsalted butter or margarine

1 TB. extra-virgin olive oil

2 large shallots, minced

2 cloves garlic, minced

1½ cups pearl barley, rinsed

2½ cups water

1 cup bottled balsamic salad dressing

1 cup feta cheese, crumbled

1 cup cherry tomatoes, cut in ½

¾ cup kalamata olives, pitted and cut in ½

3 TB. fresh Italian parsley, minced

1 tsp. kosher salt

1 tsp. freshly ground black pepper

1. In a pressure cooker over medium heat, melt unsalted butter and extra-virgin olive oil. Add shallots, and cook for 1 or 2 minutes or until soft. Add garlic, and cook for 20 seconds or until garlic is fragrant. Do not brown.

2. Add pearl barley, and stir until coated with butter and oil mixture. Add water.

3. Lock the lid in place. Bring to high pressure, and maintain for 17 minutes. Remove from heat, and reduce pressure using the quick release method.

4. Drain pearl barley in a colander, and rinse with cold water. Let cool for 10 minutes.

5. Transfer pearl barley to a large bowl. Stir in balsamic dressing, feta cheese, cherry tomatoes, kalamata olives, Italian parsley, kosher salt, and pepper.

6. Cover the bowl with a kitchen towel, and refrigerate for at least 2 hours.

7. Serve salad hot or cold as a side dish or hearty lunch.

FOODIE FACT

Balsamic vinegar is Italian vinegar made from white grapes that grow in the Reggio Emilia and neighboring Modena regions of Italy. The grapes are cooked and concentrated until dark and rich and then aged in wood barrels for several years—from 3 years for young vinegars to more than 100 years for expensive gourmet vinegars.

Corn Pudding

This old-fashioned corn pudding combines the sweet flavors of corn and red bell peppers with the hearty flavor of cornmeal and the rich creaminess of half-and-half and eggs.

Yield:	Prep time:	Cook time:	Serving size:
4 cups	5 minutes	10 minutes	½ cup

1 medium red bell pepper, ribs and seeds removed, and diced small	2 large eggs, beaten
1 cup frozen corn, defrosted	½ cup cornmeal
1 (15-oz.) can cream of corn	1 tsp. kosher salt
½ cup half-and-half or evaporated milk	½ tsp. freshly ground black pepper
	1½ cups water

1. Coat a 2-quart casserole with nonstick cooking spray.

2. In a large bowl, combine red bell pepper, corn, cream of corn, half-and-half, eggs, cornmeal, kosher salt, and pepper. Cover casserole dish tightly with aluminum foil.

3. Place a rack in the pressure cooker. Add water, and place casserole on rack. Set the pressure cooker over high heat.

4. Lock the lid in place. Bring to high pressure, and maintain for 10 minutes. Remove from heat, and reduce pressure using the quick release method.

5. Serve hot as a side dish.

FOODIE FACT

Cornmeal is made from dried corn kernels that have been ground using water, stone, or steel methods. Depending on the type of corn used, cornmeal can be white, yellow, or blue.

Lemon Rice

The delicate flavors of lemon and butter dominate this chewy and satisfying white rice dish.

Yield:	Prep time:	Cook time:	Serving size:
3 cups	15 minutes	20 minutes	1 cup

1 cup long-grain white rice	½ stick (4 TB.) unsalted butter, melted
2 TB. canola or vegetable oil	
3 cups water	1 tsp. kosher salt
Zest of 1 large lemon	¼ tsp. freshly ground black pepper
Juice of 1 large lemon	

1. In a pressure cooker over high heat, add white rice and canola oil, and stir until rice is coated with oil. Add water.

2. Lock the lid in place. Bring to high pressure, and maintain for 3 minutes. Remove from heat, and reduce pressure using the natural release method.

3. Stir in lemon zest, lemon juice, melted unsalted butter, kosher salt, and pepper.

4. Serve hot as a side dish.

PRESSURE POINTER

When a recipe calls for long-grain rice, be sure to use long-grain and not sure-grain rice. Long-grain rice is five times as long as wide. When cooked, it becomes light and fluffy and separates easily.

Black Forbidden Rice

This rice appears black when uncooked, but purple when cooked. It has a very chewy texture with a nice, nutty flavor.

Yield:	Prep time:	Cook time:	Serving size:
3 cups	15 minutes	13 minutes	¾ cup

1 cup black rice

3 cups water

2 TB. canola or vegetable oil

1 tsp. kosher salt

1 tsp. freshly ground black pepper

1. In a pressure cooker over high heat, add black rice, water, canola oil, kosher salt, and pepper.

2. Lock the lid in place. Bring to high pressure, and maintain for 12 minutes. Remove from heat, and reduce pressure using the natural release method.

3. Serve hot as a side dish.

FOODIE FACT

According to Chinese legend, black rice was so delicious, nutritious, and rare that only emperors were permitted to eat it, which is why it was called forbidden rice.

Coconut Jasmine Rice

The sweet flavors of sweet coconut and sugar combine with aromatic jasmine rice for a dish that's a perfect compliment to Asian cuisine.

Yield:	Prep time:	Cook time:	Serving size:
3 cups	5 minutes	3 minutes	¾ cup

1 cup jasmine rice, rinsed

4 cups water

½ cup unsweetened coconut milk

1 TB. sugar

1 tsp. kosher salt

1. In a pressure cooker over medium heat, add jasmine rice, water, coconut milk, sugar, and kosher salt.

2. Lock the lid in place. Bring to high pressure, and maintain for 3 minutes. Remove from heat, and reduce pressure using the natural release method.

3. Serve hot as a side dish.

PRESSURE POINTER

If a recipe calls for basmati rice, feel free to substitute jasmine rice, which has a similar flavor and fragrance to basmati rice and is much less expensive.

Wild Rice Pilaf

This chewy rich dish combines the nutty flavor of wild rice with hints of onion and parsley.

Yield:	Prep time:	Cook time:	Serving size:
2 cups	15 minutes	20 minutes	¾ cup

2 TB. unsalted butter or margarine	1 cup water
2 TB. white or yellow onion, minced	1 TB. vegetable or canola oil
1 cup wild rice	1 tsp. kosher salt
2 cups Homemade Chicken Stock (recipe in Chapter 9)	1 tsp. freshly ground black pepper
	1 TB. Italian parsley, minced

1. In a pressure cooker over medium heat, melt unsalted butter. Add onion, and cook for 1 minute or until soft. Add wild rice, and stir until coated with butter. Add Homemade Chicken Stock, water, vegetable oil, kosher salt, and pepper.

2. Lock the lid in place. Bring to high pressure. Reduce heat to low, and maintain low pressure for 20 minutes. Remove from heat, and reduce pressure using the natural release method.

3. Fluff rice with a fork, and stir in Italian parsley. Serve hot as a side dish.

PRESSURE POINTER

Before pressure cooking wild rice, clean it thoroughly by soaking it in a bowl of cold water so any debris can float to the surface. Be careful not to overcook it, or the rice will become mushy.

Classic Risotto

The creaminess of Arborio rice combines with the rich flavors of Parmesan cheese, butter, white wine, and just a hint of onion in this savory risotto.

Yield:	Prep time:	Cook time:	Serving size:
4 cups	15 minutes	15 minutes	½ cup

2 TB. extra-virgin olive oil	4 cups Homemade Chicken Stock (recipe in Chapter 9)
3 TB. unsalted butter	1 tsp. kosher salt
1 small white onion, diced fine	¾ tsp. freshly ground black pepper
2 cups Arborio rice	½ cup freshly grated Parmesan cheese
⅓ cup dry white wine	

1. In a pressure cooker over medium-high heat, heat extra-virgin olive oil and 1 tablespoon unsalted butter. When hot, add onion and cook for 2 minutes or until onion is soft.

2. Add Arborio rice, and stir for 30 seconds to coat with butter and olive oil. Add white wine, Homemade Chicken Stock, kosher salt, and pepper, and bring to a boil.

3. Lock the lid in place. Bring to high pressure, and maintain for 7 minutes. Remove from heat, and reduce pressure using the quick release method.

4. Return the pressure cooker to low heat, and cook, uncovered, stirring constantly, for 3 to 5 minutes or until all liquid is absorbed. Stir in remaining 2 tablespoons unsalted butter and Parmesan cheese.

5. Serve immediately as a main or side dish.

FOODIE FACT

Although Parmesan cheese is made in the United States, Argentina, and Australia, the queen of Parmesan cheese is Italy's Parmigiano-Reggiano, which is aged much longer than the others and features a deliciously sharp flavor and a melt-in-your-mouth texture.

Pasta Primavera

This thick and chunky pasta dish combines the fresh flavors of asparagus, broccoli, zucchini, tomatoes, and peas with just a hint of garlic and leek.

Yield:	Prep time:	Cook time:	Serving size:
16 ounces	15 minutes	5 minutes	4 ounces

1 (12-oz.) pkg. angel hair pasta

1 TB. vegetable oil

1½ tsp. kosher salt

1 TB. extra-virgin olive oil

2 leeks, green and white parts, chopped fine

2 cloves garlic, minced

½ lb. asparagus, cut into 1-in. pieces

½ lb. broccoli, separated into florets

2 large zucchini, cut into 1-in. cubes (skin on)

1 cup frozen peas, defrosted

1 pt. cherry or grape tomatoes, cut in ½

¼ cup fresh flat-leaf parsley, minced

1 tsp. freshly ground black pepper

⅓ cup freshly grated Parmesan cheese

1. In a pressure cooker over high heat, add water and bring to a boil. Add angel hair pasta, vegetable oil, and 1 teaspoon kosher salt. Stir to separate pasta.

2. Lock the lid in place. Bring to high pressure, and maintain for 5 minutes. Remove from heat, and reduce pressure using the cold water release method.

3. Strain pasta in a colander, and rinse with cold water. Transfer to a large mixing bowl.

4. Return the pressure cooker to medium heat. Add extra-virgin olive oil, leeks, and garlic, and cook for 30 seconds. Add asparagus, broccoli, zucchini, and peas, and cook for 2 minutes or until coated with olive oil.

5. Ladle vegetable mixture on top of pasta. Stir in cherry tomatoes, parsley, remaining ½ teaspoon kosher salt, and pepper, and top with Parmesan cheese.

6. Serve as a side dish or main dish.

 FOODIE FACT

Primavera is Italian for "spring style" and refers to dishes in which fresh vegetables are tossed or diced with pasta or other foods.

Old-Fashioned Macaroni and Cheese

Extra-sharp cheddar cheese, sour cream, and butter give this hearty dish extra creaminess, richness, and tang, while cayenne, Worcestershire sauce, and nutmeg lend just a touch of fire.

Yield:	Prep time:	Cook time:	Serving size:
8 cups	20 minutes	45 minutes	¾ cup

3 cups water

1 (16-oz.) pkg. macaroni

1½ tsp. kosher salt

1¼ cups grated extra-sharp white cheddar cheese

1 tsp. dry mustard

½ tsp. ground nutmeg

¼ tsp. cayenne

½ cup sour cream

2 large eggs, beaten

1½ cups half-and-half

1½ cups milk

1 small white or yellow sweet onion, grated

1 tsp. Worcestershire sauce

½ tsp. freshly ground black pepper

1. Preheat the oven to 350°F. Coat a 9×13-inch glass baking dish with nonstick cooking spray.

2. In a pressure cooker over high heat, add water and bring to a boil. Add macaroni and 1 teaspoon kosher salt, and stir to separate macaroni.

3. Lock the lid in place. Bring to high pressure, and maintain for 5 minutes. Remove from heat, and reduce pressure using the cold water release method. Strain macaroni in a colander and transfer to a large mixing bowl.

4. Add 1 cup extra-sharp white cheddar cheese, and mix well. Add dry mustard, nutmeg, and cayenne, and mix until thoroughly combined.

5. In a separate bowl, combine sour cream, eggs, half-and-half, milk, onion, Worcestershire sauce, remaining ½ teaspoon kosher salt, and pepper. Add to macaroni mixture and stir until combined.

6. Pour macaroni mixture into the prepared baking dish, and top with remaining ¼ cup extra-sharp white cheddar cheese.

7. Bake, uncovered, for 30 to 40 minutes or until cheese is brown and casserole is hot and bubbly.

8. Remove casserole from the oven and let cool for 10 minutes before serving. Serve hot as a side dish or main meal.

FOODIE FACT

Cheddar cheese was once named after the English village in which it was produced at the end of the sixteenth century. Today, it refers to a process called "cheddaring" during which slabs of partially drained curd are stacked, turned, and restacked to give the cheese the same smooth, tight texture of the original cheddar cheese.

Eat Your Veggies

Chapter
19

In This Chapter

- The importance of eating your greens
- Cruciferous veggies to the rescue
- Getting to the root of things
- Versatile vine veggies

Veggies are loaded with disease-fighting antioxidants. Make them in a pressure cooker, and they come out the way they went in: nutritious, crisp, and colorful. Steaming veggies in your pressure cooker is not only one of the easiest ways to cook vegetables, it's also the healthiest. Because they cook faster in steam than in water, they absorb less water and retain more nutrients as well as their natural color, texture, and flavor.

Whether you're looking for a hearty vegetable dish that can double as a vegetarian entrée or a flavorful side dish that adds color and texture to a meal, the recipes in this chapter represent the entire vegetable kingdom, from leafy greens and sturdy root vegetables to nutrient-packed cruciferous and vine veggies.

A-to-Z Greens

If you've never ventured beyond lettuce in the greens department, you're in for a treat. Your pressure cooker can open a world of leafy greens that steam to perfection and pack a nutritional wallop.

Steamed spinach is a super food that's one of the highest-ranking vegetables in terms of providing complete nutrition. High in fiber, it also packs in every other nutrient needed for health except vitamins D and B$_{12}$.

Other nutrient-rich leafy greens that steam up in a jiffy include Swiss chard, which tastes a bit like spinach; collard greens, a Southern staple that's great with ham hocks or black-eyed peas; kale, a hearty green that has a strong cabbage flavor; its close cousin, turnip greens; beet greens, which have a fresh flavor similar to chard; and dandelion greens, which can be steamed, sautéed, or added to soups to pump up flavor. Once you taste dandelion greens, you'll never call them a weed again!

Splendiferous Cruciferous

Cruciferous vegetables include broccoli, Brussels sprouts, cabbage, cauliflower, chard, kale, mustard greens, turnips, and rutabagas, and are high in fiber, vitamins, and minerals. They're delicious steamed alone or with other vegetables or meat.

Cruciferous veggies contain cancer-fighting antioxidants, including beta-carotene and sulforaphane, which is responsible for the sulfurous smell produced during cooking. To reduce the smell during pressure cooking, add 1 tablespoon vinegar and 1 table-spoon sugar to the water, or place a slice of crust-free bread on top of the pressure cooker so it can absorb the smell.

Getting Back to Your Roots

Root vegetables—carrots, potatoes, turnips, beets, garlic, onions, parsnips, rutabaga, and sweet potatoes—are high in potassium, beta-carotene, and other essential vita-mins and minerals.

There are a few stars among root vegetables. The carrot is a powerhouse of vitamin A that helps improve eye health and night vision. Sweet potatoes are also high in vitamin A. Garlic is a super food packed with disease-fighting antioxidants. Studies show garlic may help lower high cholesterol and reduce the risk of heart disease and many types of cancer.

Fresh from the Vine and Stem

From peas and green beans to peppers, tomatoes, and corn, vine and stem veggies provide a host of nutrients and a wealth of pressure cooking opportunities. Tomatoes are extremely high in vitamin C and lycopene, a valuable substance that helps decrease bad cholesterol and helps reduce the risk of prostate cancer in men. Green peas help maintain bone health; green beans are loaded with vitamin K; and red peppers are loaded with vitamin C as well as beta-carotene, essential for eye health. Corn is another nutritional powerhouse, with high levels of fiber, which helps lower cholesterol levels and reduce the risk of colon cancer.

Maple Whipped Sweet Potatoes

Maple syrup gives sweet potatoes a rich, sweet, and buttery flavor. For best results, use pure maple syrup made in New England or Canada.

Yield:	Prep time:	Cook time:	Serving size:
2 cups	5 minutes	15 minutes	½ cup

4 large sweet potatoes, skin on and scrubbed	¼ tsp. freshly ground black pepper
1½ cups water	½ cup pure maple syrup
1 tsp. kosher salt	¼ cup unsalted butter or margarine

1. Place a rack in a pressure cooker. Place sweet potatoes on the rack, add water, and set the pressure cooker over high heat.

2. Lock the lid in place. Bring to high pressure, and maintain for 15 minutes. Remove from heat, and reduce pressure using the cold water release method.

3. Using a slotted spoon, transfer potatoes from the pressure cooker to a colander, drain, and let cool.

4. Transfer potatoes to a large bowl, and using an electric mixer on medium speed, blend potatoes with kosher salt, pepper, maple syrup, and unsalted butter.

5. Serve hot as a side dish.

FOODIE FACT

We have the American Indians to thank for maple syrup. They taught the colonists how to tap trees by inserting a spout into the tree, catching the sap in a bucket, and boiling down the sap into syrup.

Old-Fashioned Potato Salad
with Green Beans

Red potatoes and green beans give this traditional potato salad extra zest and crunch.

Yield:	Prep time:	Cook time:	Serving size:
1 pound	5 minutes	12 minutes	½ pound

1½ cups water

8 small new red potatoes, skin on
and scrubbed well

1 lb. fresh green beans, trimmed

1½ cups mayonnaise

1 tsp. kosher salt

½ tsp. freshly ground black pepper

1. Pour water into a pressure cooker. Insert a rack in the pressure cooker, and place potatoes on the rack. Set the pressure cooker over high heat.

2. Lock the lid in place. Bring to high pressure, and maintain for 10 minutes. Remove from heat, and reduce pressure using the quick release method.

3. Return the pressure cooker to high heat, and add green beans.

4. Lock the lid in place. Bring to high pressure, and maintain for 3 minutes. Remove from heat, and reduce pressure using the cold water release method.

5. Transfer potatoes and green beans to a colander, and drain. Rinse with cold water, and let cool.

6. Cut potatoes into quarters, and place in a large bowl. Add mayonnaise, kosher salt, and pepper, and mix well.

7. Serve potato salad hot or cold as a side dish.

PRESSURE POINTER

Regular mayonnaise contains 65 percent oil by weight. To reduce the fat content of potato salad, substitute reduced- or fat-free mayonnaise for regular mayonnaise. Reduced-fat versions contain 25 to 50 percent less fat than regular mayonnaise.

Carrot Mashed Potatoes

Fresh carrots give these mashed potatoes a sweet flavor, beautiful orange color, and extra nutrients.

Yield:	Prep time:	Cook time:	Serving size:
2 cups	5 minutes	8 minutes	½ cup

2 cups water	½ tsp. freshly ground black pepper
4 large carrots, peeled, cut into quarters	¾ cup unsalted butter or margarine
2 lb. russet potatoes, peeled and quartered	½ cup whole milk or low-fat buttermilk
1 tsp. kosher salt	

1. Add water to a pressure cooker. Insert a rack in the pressure cooker, and place carrots and potatoes on the rack. Set the pressure cooker over high heat.

2. Lock the lid in place. Bring to high pressure, and maintain for 8 minutes. Remove from heat, and reduce pressure using the cold water release method.

3. Transfer carrots and potatoes to a colander, and drain. Let cool for 5 minutes.

4. Place carrots and potatoes in a large bowl. Add kosher salt, pepper, unsalted butter, and whole milk, and beat with an electric mixer on medium speed until creamy.

5. Serve hot as a side dish.

FOODIE FACT

A rack has many holes in it, so it doesn't matter what you put in the pressure cooker first, the rack or the water. Do whatever is easiest for you.

Tarragon Vegetable Medley

The flavors of zucchini, onion, carrot, and asparagus combine in a zesty medley spiced with tomatoes, parsley, and an undertone of tarragon, which has a mild licorice flavor.

Yield:	Prep time:	Cook time:	Serving size:
2 cups	10 minutes	5 minutes	½ cup

½ cup canola or vegetable oil

1 large white onion, cut into large cubes

2 medium zucchini, cut into large chunks

1 large carrot, peeled and cut into ½-in. slices

1 lb. asparagus, trimmed

¼ cup fresh parsley, minced

½ cup fresh tarragon

1 tsp. kosher salt

1 tsp. freshly ground black pepper

1 cup Homemade Chicken Stock (recipe in Chapter 9)

3 large tomatoes, cut into small chunks, seeds removed

1. In a pressure cooker over high heat, heat canola oil. When hot, add onion, zucchini, carrot, asparagus, and parsley, and cook for 1 minute. Stir in ¼ cup tarragon, kosher salt, pepper, and Homemade Chicken Stock.

2. Lock the lid in place. Bring to high pressure, and maintain for 5 minutes. Remove from heat, and reduce pressure using the quick release method.

3. Stir in tomatoes and remaining ¼ cup tarragon.

4. Serve hot as a side dish.

UNDER PRESSURE

Never use more tarragon than a recipe calls for. The herb has a strong, aniselike flavor that can easily dominate the flavor of a dish if used in excess.

Grandma's Green Beans

Coarse-grain mustard and horseradish give these green beans a spicy bite.

Yield:	Prep time:	Cook time:	Serving size:
1 pound	10 minutes	4 minutes	¼ pound

½ cup water

1 lb. fresh green beans, trimmed

2 TB. unsalted butter or margarine

1 large white or yellow onion, minced

1 TB. coarse-grain mustard

1 TB. cream-style horseradish

½ tsp. kosher salt

½ tsp. freshly ground black pepper

1. Add water to a pressure cooker. Insert a steamer basket in the pressure cooker, and place green beans in the steamer basket. Set the pressure cooker over high heat.

2. Lock the lid in place. Bring to high pressure, and maintain for 4 minutes. Remove from heat, and reduce pressure using the cold water release method.

3. Using a slotted spoon, transfer beans from the pressure cooker to a large bowl.

4. In a frying pan over medium heat, heat unsalted butter. When hot, add onion, and cook for about 10 minutes or until brown.

5. Stir in mustard and horseradish. Pour mixture over beans, and add kosher salt and pepper.

6. Serve hot as a side dish.

FOODIE FACT

Horseradish is grown primarily for its large, white, spicy roots, which are ground and combined with vinegar or beet juice to make white or red horseradish.

Mushrooms and Peas

This simple dish features mushrooms and peas in a light butter sauce with parsley undertones.

Yield:	Prep time:	Cook time:	Serving size:
2½ cups	5 minutes	2 minutes	½ cup

2 cups fresh peas	2½ tsp. kosher salt
1 lb. fresh white or brown button mushrooms, sliced	1 tsp. freshly ground black pepper
1 cup water	2 tsp. fresh parsley, minced
2 TB. unsalted butter or margarine, melted	

1. In a pressure cooker over high heat, add peas, mushrooms, and water.

2. Lock the lid in place. Bring to high pressure, and maintain for 2 minutes. Remove from heat, and reduce pressure using the cold water release method.

3. Transfer peas and mushrooms to a large bowl, and stir in melted unsalted butter, kosher salt, pepper, and parsley.

4. Serve hot as a side dish.

PRESSURE POINTER

When buying mushrooms, choose those that are evenly colored and have tightly closed caps. If the gills are showing, the mushrooms are too old to use. Also avoid mushrooms with soft spots or damaged skins or those that are broken.

Swiss Chard with Cranberries and Pine Nuts

Dried sweet cranberries add sweetness to chard, while pine nuts add nuttiness and crunch.

Yield:	Prep time:	Cook time:	Serving size:
2 cups	5 minutes	2 minutes	½ cup

1½ cups water

1 medium white onion, cut into medium cubes

1 large bunch Swiss chard, stems removed, washed, and coarsely chopped

¼ cup extra-virgin olive oil

¼ cup dried cranberries

1 tsp. kosher salt

1 tsp. freshly ground black pepper

½ cup pine nuts

1. Place water and onion in a pressure cooker. Insert a steamer basket in the pressure cooker, and place Swiss chard in the basket. Set the pressure cooker over high heat.

2. Lock the lid in place. Bring to high pressure, and maintain for 2 minutes. Remove from heat, and reduce pressure using the natural release method.

3. Using tongs, transfer Swiss chard to a large bowl. Stir in extra-virgin olive oil, dried cranberries, kosher salt, pepper, and pine nuts.

4. Serve hot as a side dish.

FOODIE FACT

Swiss chard is a member of the beet family but tastes similar to spinach. Packed with vitamins A and C and iron, Swiss chard has green, crinkly leaves, and silvery, celerylike stalks. Look for chard with tender leaves and crisp stalks.

Cauliflower with Breadcrumbs

Breadcrumbs and butter give crisp cauliflower a rich flavor and crunchy texture.

Yield:	Prep time:	Cook time:	Serving size:
2 cups	5 minutes	2 minutes	½ cup

1 cup water	½ cup fresh breadcrumbs
1 large head cauliflower, separated into florets	2 tsp. fresh parsley, finely chopped
2½ tsp. kosher salt	½ stick (4 TB.) unsalted butter or margarine, melted
1 tsp. freshly ground black pepper	

1. Pour water into a pressure cooker. Insert a steamer basket in the pressure cooker, and place cauliflower florets in the basket. Set the pressure cooker over high heat.

2. Lock the lid in place. Bring to high pressure, and maintain for 2 minutes. Remove from heat, and reduce pressure using the cold water release method.

3. Using tongs, transfer cauliflower to a colander, and drain. Transfer to a large bowl, and stir in kosher salt, pepper, breadcrumbs, parsley, and unsalted butter.

4. Serve hot as a side dish.

PRESSURE POINTER

If a recipe calls for fresh breadcrumbs, do not substitute dried breadcrumbs. To make fresh breadcrumbs, place bread slices trimmed of their crust in a food processor or blender, and process until the bread is in crumbs.

Brussels Sprouts with Balsamic Glaze

Balsamic vinegar gives Brussels sprouts a sweet and tangy flavor.

Yield:	Prep time:	Cook time:	Serving size:
1 pound	15 minutes	3 minutes	½ pound

1 TB. extra-virgin olive oil	1 cup water
1 lb. Brussels sprouts, outside leaves removed	1 large shallot, minced
1 tsp. kosher salt	½ cup balsamic vinegar
1 tsp. freshly ground black pepper	¼ cup extra-virgin olive oil

1. In a pressure cooker over medium heat, add extra-virgin olive oil, Brussels sprouts, kosher salt, and pepper, and cook, stirring constantly, for 4 minutes or until Brussels sprouts are slightly browned. Add water.

2. Lock the lid in place. Bring to high pressure, and maintain for 2 minutes. Remove from heat, and reduce pressure using the cold water release method.

3. Using a slotted spoon, transfer Brussels sprouts to a large bowl. Add shallot, balsamic vinegar, and extra-virgin olive oil, and toss until well blended.

4. Serve hot as a side dish.

FOODIE FACT

Cultivated since the sixteenth century, Brussels sprouts are a member of the cabbage family and resemble tiny cabbages. Buy Brussels sprouts with bright green sprouts and compact heads.

Braised Cabbage and Apples

Cinnamon and apples combine to give cabbage a sweet and tangy flavor and a savory fragrance.

Yield:	Prep time:	Cook time:	Serving size:
4 wedges	15 minutes	7 minutes	1 wedge

1 medium head red cabbage, cut into 4 wedges

1 TB. minced onion

1 large red Gala apple, cored and sliced into wedges

1 tsp. kosher salt

1 bay leaf

1 (3-in.) cinnamon stick

½ cup water

2 TB. unsalted butter or margarine

2 TB. cider vinegar

1 TB. light brown sugar

½ tsp. ground cinnamon

1. Place red cabbage into a pressure cooker. Add onion, apple, kosher salt, bay leaf, cinnamon stick, and water.

2. Lock the lid in place. Bring to high pressure, and maintain for 2 minutes. Remove from heat, and reduce pressure using the cold water release method.

3. Using tongs, remove and discard bay leaf and cinnamon stick. Stir in unsalted butter, cider vinegar, light brown sugar, and cinnamon. Cook over low heat, stirring constantly, for 5 minutes.

4. Serve hot as a side dish.

FOODIE FACT

Brown sugar is white sugar combined with molasses, which gives it a soft texture, brown color, and slightly spicy flavor. Brown sugar comes in light and dark varieties. The lighter the color, the more delicate the flavor. If a recipe calls for light brown sugar, don't substitute dark brown sugar.

Corn on the Cob with Lime Compound Butter

Lime juice and zest give sweet, crunchy corn a fresh and tangy flavor and fragrance.

Yield:	Prep time:	Cook time:	Serving size:
4 ears	15 minutes	2 minutes	1 ear

1 stick (8 TB.) unsalted butter, soft-ened to room temperature

2 shallots, minced

2 tsp. fresh Italian parsley, minced

2 tsp. kosher salt

Zest of 1 large lime

Juice of 1 large lime

2 cups water

4 ears fresh corn, husks and silks removed

1. In a large bowl, combine unsalted butter, shallots, Italian parsley, kosher salt, lime zest, and lime juice. Roll mixture into a log, wrap in waxed paper and plastic wrap, and refrigerate for at least 4 hours.

2. Add water to a pressure cooker. Insert a steamer basket in the pressure cooker, and place corn in the steamer basket. Set the pressure cooker over high heat.

3. Lock the lid in place. Bring to high pressure, and maintain for 2 minutes. Remove from heat, and reduce pressure using the cold water release method.

4. Using tongs, remove corn from the pressure cooker and transfer to a serving platter.

5. Serve corn hot with a 1-inch slice chilled lime butter.

FOODIE FACT

Before the colonists came to the New World, they'd never seen corn on the cob, or Indian corn. The plant is so versatile that you can use every part of it. Eat the kernels, use the husks to make tamales, use the corn silk to make medicinal tea, and feed the corn stalks to livestock.

Asian-Style Broccoli

Ginger, garlic, sesame oil, and soy sauce give broccoli a sweet and spicy Asian twist, while sesame seeds add a light crunch.

Yield:	Prep time:	Cook time:	Serving size:
1 pound	10 minutes	2 minutes	½ pound

2 TB. sesame oil

1 TB. extra-virgin olive oil

1 clove garlic, minced

1 slice ginger, peeled and sliced
  into ¼-in. pieces

1 lb. fresh broccoli, stems trimmed
  and cut into florets

1 tsp. kosher salt

½ tsp. freshly ground black pepper

⅓ cup water

2 TB. low-sodium soy sauce

2 green onions, green and white
  parts, sliced thin

1 TB. toasted sesame seeds

1. In a pressure cooker over medium heat, add sesame oil, extra-virgin olive oil, garlic, and ginger, and cook for 1 or 2 minutes or until garlic is golden brown. Add broccoli, and cook, stirring constantly, for 20 seconds or until broccoli turns bright green. Add kosher salt and pepper.

2. Remove broccoli mixture from the pressure cooker, and set aside.

3. Insert a steamer basket in the pressure cooker. Place broccoli mixture in the steamer basket, and add water and soy sauce to the pressure cooker.

4. Lock the lid in place. Bring to high pressure, and maintain for 2 minutes. Remove from heat, and reduce pressure using the cold water release method.

5. Transfer broccoli to a large bowl. Top with soy sauce mixture, green onions, and sesame seeds.

6. Serve hot as a side dish.

UNDER PRESSURE

Fresh ginger has a peppery, slightly sweet flavor and a pungent aroma. If a recipe calls for fresh ginger, do not substitute dried ginger, which has a completely different flavor and is more commonly used for making cakes, pies, soups, and curries.

Saucy Sauces and Toppers

In This Chapter

- Presto pressure cooker sauces
- Easy homemade condiments
- All aboard the pressure cooker gravy train!

Whether it's a rich tomato sauce or a spicy barbecue sauce, a sprightly sauce or condiment is a sure way to bring all the elements of a dish together. It could be a feisty homemade horseradish that adds pizzazz to hotdogs and sauerkraut, savory chutney that kicks up the flavor of curry, a rich and meaty sauce that turns pasta into a memorable meal, or a tangy cranberry sauce that gives any holiday meal a special flourish. In this chapter, you'll find savory sauces for topping all sorts of side dishes and entrées. You'll want to try them all!

Making homemade sauces can be complicated and time-consuming using conventional cooking methods, but with a pressure cooker, you can create sensational no-stir sauces in a fraction of the time. Simply add the ingredients to the pressure cooker, and let it do the rest!

DIY Pasta and Meat Sauces

At one time, to make *bellissimo* pasta sauce you almost had to have an Italian grand-mother who was willing to relinquish her secret recipe for it. Even then, mastering Grandma's pasta sauce required some culinary expertise, not to mention hours of slaving over a hot stove to ensure the sauce didn't boil over or burn. Today, even if you don't have a drop of Italian blood in your extended family, if you have a pressure cooker, you can make perfecto pasta sauce in the same time it takes to boil pasta.

A pot of pasta is the ideal meal for hectic workdays when you need to get dinner on the table presto. Add homemade pasta sauce, and you turn a plate of naked noodles into a labor of love. Just don't tell anyone how fast and easy it was to make that sauce!

Making Gravy Is Gravy!

If you've been resorting to packaged or canned gravies because you think it's too difficult to make homemade gravy, you can stop that practice right now. Your pressure cooker excels at making rich, thick gravies—hold the lumps! Simply remove the meat and vegetables from the pressure cooker, add cornstarch and water to the juices, stir until the mixture thickens, and you've got savory gravy.

Homemade Condiments and Sauces

Homemade condiments have a fresh, zesty flavor you just can't get from a can, jar, or squeeze bottle. After making the delicious and economical recipes in this chapter, you may never want to waste your money on store-bought gourmet mustard or horseradish again.

You can also make homemade barbecue sauce in your pressure cooker and create mouth-watering ribs and steaks without hassling with an outdoor grill. Just brush a little homemade barbecue sauce on the meat, place it in the pressure cooker, and in less than 20 minutes you're ready to sink your teeth into juicy, flavorful meat.

Finally, for a sure way to wow your family, serve homemade cranberry sauce with that holiday turkey dinner. You'll find a fast and easy recipe for it in this chapter, plus much more.

Bolognese Pasta Sauce

This zesty pasta sauce combines the flavors of beef, pork, and *veal* in a velvety-rich tomato base.

Yield:	Prep time:	Cook time:	Serving size:
3½ cups	10 minutes	10 minutes	1 cup

2 TB. extra-virgin olive oil

1 lb. lean ground beef

1 lb. ground pork

1 lb. ground veal

2 TB. white or yellow onion, finely diced

1 medium carrot, peeled and chopped small

1 medium rib celery, chopped small

1 clove garlic, minced

1 (28-oz.) can crushed tomatoes, with juice

3 TB. tomato paste

1 tsp. dried oregano

2 tsp. dried basil

1 TB. fresh parsley, minced

1 bay leaf

½ cup dry red wine

2 cups Homemade Beef Stock (recipe in Chapter 8)

1 tsp. kosher salt

½ tsp. freshly ground black pepper

1. In a pressure cooker over medium heat, heat 1 tablespoon extra-virgin olive oil. When hot, add beef, pork, and veal, and brown for 3 or 4 minutes. Transfer meat to a colander, drain to remove excess fat, and set aside.

2. In the pressure cooker over high heat, heat remaining 1 tablespoon extra-virgin olive oil. When hot, add onion, carrot, celery, and garlic, and cook for about 2 minutes or until soft.

3. Stir in crushed tomatoes with juice, tomato paste, oregano, basil, parsley, bay leaf, red wine, and Homemade Beef Stock. Return beef, pork, and veal to the pressure cooker.

4. Lock the lid in place. Bring to high pressure, and maintain for 10 minutes. Remove from heat, and reduce pressure using the natural release method.

5. Remove bay leaf. Season with kosher salt and pepper, and serve over your choice of pasta. Or freeze sauce and use within 6 months. (For details on storing and freezing sauces and other leftovers, see Chapter 2.)

STEAM SPEAK

Veal is the term used for a young calf between 1 and 3 months old. It has a delicate taste and texture and a creamy white color.

Italian Sausage and Beef Sauce

Italian sausage and beef add richness and depth to this zesty meat sauce, while tomatoes and onions add sweetness and garlic adds a hint of fire.

Yield:	Prep time:	Cook time:	Serving size:
3½ cups	10 minutes	10 minutes	1 cup

3 TB. extra-virgin olive oil

1 lb. lean ground beef

1 lb. Italian sausage, casings removed

½ small white or yellow onion, finely diced

1 medium carrot, peeled and diced fine

1 rib celery, finely chopped

1 clove garlic, minced

1 (28-oz.) can crushed tomatoes, with juice

3 TB. tomato paste

1 tsp. dried oregano

2 tsp. dried basil

1 TB. fresh parsley, minced

1 bay leaf

½ cup dry red wine

1 cup Homemade Beef Stock (recipe in Chapter 8)

1 tsp. kosher salt

1 tsp. freshly ground black pepper

1. In a pressure cooker over medium heat, heat 2 tablespoons extra-virgin olive oil. When hot, add beef and Italian sausage, and cook for 3 or 4 minutes or until browned. Transfer meat to a colander, drain excess fat, and set aside.

2. Add remaining 1 tablespoon extra-virgin olive oil to the pressure cooker. When hot, add onion, carrot, celery, and garlic, and cook for about 3 minutes or until soft.

3. Add crushed tomatoes with juice, tomato paste, oregano, basil, parsley, bay leaf, red wine, and Homemade Beef Stock. Return beef and Italian sausage to the pressure cooker.

4. Lock the lid in place. Bring to high pressure, and maintain for 10 minutes. Remove from heat, and reduce pressure using the natural release method.

5. Season sauce with kosher salt and pepper, and serve over your choice of pasta. Or freeze sauce and use within 6 months.

PRESSURE POINTER

If a recipe calls for Italian sausage, don't substitute regular sausage or your sauce will taste flat. Italian sausage has an extra flavor kick, thanks to the garlic and fennel or anise seed. If you want your sauce to be extra spicy, use hot Italian sausage, which is flavored with hot peppers. If you prefer a sweeter, milder sauce, use sweet Italian sausage, which does not contain peppers.

Mushroom, Tomato, and Black Olive Sauce

Kalamata olives, mushrooms, and tomatoes marry the sunny flavors of Greece is this rich and savory sauce.

Yield:	Prep time:	Cook time:	Serving size:
3 cups	10 minutes	10 minutes	1 cup

3 TB. extra-virgin olive oil

1 lb. white or brown mushrooms, brushed clean and sliced thin

½ small white or yellow onion, finely diced

4 cloves garlic, minced

1 tsp. dried basil

1 tsp. Italian seasoning

5 or 6 medium Roma tomatoes (2 lb.), seeds removed and diced small

1 cup dry red wine

1 cup kalamata olives, pitted and cut in ½

1 tsp. kosher salt

¾ tsp. freshly ground black pepper

1. In a pressure cooker over medium heat, heat 2 tablespoons extra-virgin olive oil. When hot, add mushrooms, and cook for 2 or 3 minutes or until well browned. Using a slotted spoon, remove mushrooms and set aside.

2. Add remaining 1 tablespoon extra-virgin olive oil to the pressure cooker. Stir in onion, garlic, basil, and Italian seasoning, and cook for 3 minutes.

3. Return mushrooms to the pressure cooker, and stir until combined with sauce. Stir in Roma tomatoes, red wine, and kalamata olives until well combined.

4. Lock the lid in place. Bring to high pressure, and maintain for 10 minutes. Remove from heat, and reduce pressure using the natural release method.

5. Season sauce with kosher salt and pepper, and serve over your choice of pasta or chicken. Or freeze sauce and use within 6 months.

UNDER PRESSURE

Wild mushrooms have a more exciting flavor than commercial white or brown ones, but many wild mushrooms are highly poisonous. Before picking mushrooms to eat, it's important to know which species are edible and which are not. It can be difficult to tell the difference between some edible and poisonous mushrooms, so your best bet is to "pick" your mushrooms in the produce aisle, or go mushroom-picking with a certified expert.

Classic Marinara Sauce

This full-bodied *marinara sauce* is spiced with oregano, basil, and red wine, and gets a kiss of sweetness from the carrot and onion.

Yield:	Prep time:	Cook time:	Serving size:
3½ cups	10 minutes	10 minutes	1 cup

2 TB. extra-virgin olive oil

2 TB. white onion, finely diced

1 medium carrot, peeled and diced fine

1 rib celery, finely chopped

1 clove garlic, minced

1 (28-oz.) can crushed tomatoes, with juice

3 TB. tomato paste

1 tsp. dried oregano

2 tsp. dried basil

1 TB. fresh parsley, minced

1 bay leaf

¼ cup dry red wine

1 tsp. kosher salt

1 tsp. freshly ground black pepper

1. In a pressure cooker over medium heat, heat extra-virgin olive oil. When hot, add onion, carrot, celery, and garlic, and cook for about 2 minutes or until soft.

2. Add crushed tomatoes with juice, tomato paste, oregano, basil, parsley, bay leaf, and red wine.

3. Lock the lid in place. Bring to high pressure, and maintain for 10 minutes. Remove from heat, and reduce pressure using the natural release method.

4. Season with kosher salt and pepper, and serve over your choice of pasta or chicken. Or freeze sauce and use within 6 months.

STEAM SPEAK

Marinara sauce is a very spicy tomato sauce made with garlic, onions, and oregano and traditionally used on pasta, pizza, and meats. The term *alla marinara* refers to a dish served with marinara sauce.

BBQ Sauce

This rich and spicy barbecue sauce gets its sweetness from apple cider vinegar, *molasses*, and brown sugar, and its zest from mustard, Worcestershire sauce, and cider vinegar.

Yield:	Prep time:	Cook time:	Serving size:
4 cups	10 minutes	7 minutes	¼ cup

1 TB. extra-virgin olive oil	1 tsp. dry mustard
1 small red onion, diced small	2 tsp. Worcestershire sauce
2 cloves garlic, finely chopped	1 TB. chili powder
1 cup ketchup	1 cup water
¼ cup apple cider vinegar	1 tsp. kosher salt
¼ cup molasses	1 tsp. freshly ground black pepper
2 TB. dark brown sugar, firmly packed	

1. In a pressure cooker over medium-high heat, heat extra-virgin olive oil. When hot, add onion, and cook for 2 minutes. Add garlic, and cook for 20 seconds. Do not brown.

2. Stir in ketchup, apple cider vinegar, molasses, dark brown sugar, dry mustard, Worcestershire sauce, chili powder, water, kosher salt, and pepper.

3. Lock the lid in place. Bring to high pressure, and maintain for 7 minutes. Remove from heat, and reduce pressure using the natural release method.

4. Serve with barbecued chicken, beef, pork, or fish. Or freeze sauce and use within 6 months.

STEAM SPEAK

Molasses is made from the syrupy, brownish-black mixture that remains after sugar cane is refined and the sugar crystals are extracted. Light molasses is made from the first boiling of the sugar syrup, while dark molasses comes from the second boiling and is dark in color.

Mushroom Beef Gravy

Sautéed mushrooms, garlic, butter, and sherry add richness and depth to this savory beef gravy.

Yield:	Prep time:	Cook time:	Serving size:
2 cups	10 minutes	15 minutes	1 cup

3 TB. unsalted butter or margarine

1 medium white or yellow onion, diced small

2 cloves garlic, minced

1 lb. brown button mushrooms, brushed free of dirt and sliced thin

1 TB. fresh parsley, minced

2 tsp. freshly ground black pepper

2⅛ cups Homemade Beef Stock (recipe in Chapter 8)

½ cup *cornstarch*

⅛ cup dry sherry or dry white wine

1. In a pressure cooker over medium heat, melt unsalted butter. Add onion, garlic, mushrooms, parsley, pepper, and 2 cups Homemade Beef Stock, and cook for about 3 minutes or until onions are soft.

2. Lock the lid in place. Bring to high pressure, and maintain for 15 minutes. Remove from heat, and reduce pressure using the natural release method.

3. In a small bowl, whisk together cornstarch, sherry, and remaining ⅛ cup Homemade Beef Stock until smooth.

4. Return the pressure cooker to high heat. Add cornstarch mixture, stirring constantly with a wooden spoon until smooth.

5. Serve with your choice of meat, vegetable, or pasta dishes. Or freeze gravy and use within 6 months.

STEAM SPEAK

Cornstarch is a powdery, flourlike substance made from the kernel of corn and is used to thicken puddings, soups, and sauces. Because it tends to clump, it's best mixed with a small amount of cold water before being added to a recipe.

Beet Horseradish Sauce

This spicy, all-purpose horseradish combines the zesty flavors of horseradish and vinegar with the sweetness of beets and sugar.

Yield:	Prep time:	Cook time:	Serving size:
½ quart	5 minutes	5 minutes	⅛ cup

1 lb. fresh beets, rinsed and scrubbed	1 tsp. sugar
	1 tsp. kosher salt
⅓ cup raw horseradish, peeled and grated	⅛ tsp. freshly ground black pepper
	1 cup water
2 TB. white vinegar	

1. In a pressure cooker over high heat, add beets, horseradish, white vinegar, sugar, kosher salt, pepper, and water.

2. Lock the lid in place. Bring to high pressure, and maintain for 5 minutes. Remove from heat, and reduce pressure using the natural release method.

3. When horseradish mixture is cool, transfer to a food processor fitted with a metal blade, and purée for 1 minute, or until smooth.

4. Serve horseradish with your choice of meat, vegetables, or pasta. Or refrigerate horseradish in a glass jar with a tight lid and use within 6 weeks.

PRESSURE POINTER

When buying raw horseradish, look for roots that aren't blemished or withered. Refrigerate it wrapped in a plastic bag, and peel before using.

Pineapple Chutney

This flavor-packed chutney marries the sweetness of pineapple, raisins, and onion with the zest of gingerroot.

Yield:	Prep time:	Cook time:	Serving size:
3 cups	10 minutes	5 minutes	¼ cup

1 large pineapple, core and peel removed, and cut into 2-in. cubes	⅓ cup sugar
1 medium sweet onion, diced small	1 (¼-in.) piece fresh gingerroot, peeled and grated
1 cup golden raisins	1½ cups water

1. In a pressure cooker over high heat, add pineapple, onion, golden raisins, sugar, gingerroot, and water.

2. Lock the lid in place. Bring to high pressure, and maintain for 5 minutes. Remove from heat, and reduce pressure using the natural release method.

3. When chutney is cool, serve with your choice of curries and stews. Or refrigerate chutney in a glass jar with a tight lid and use within 6 weeks.

FOODIE FACT

You can tell a pineapple is ripe if it's slightly soft to the touch, has a strong color, and has no signs of greening. Overripe pineapples have soft or dark areas on the skin. You can ripen an unripe pineapple by storing it at room temperature for several days.

Sweet Surrender

Can't stand the heat? Don't get out of kitchen! Instead, just turn off the oven and turn on your pressure cooker for a wide array of luscious desserts. Even some longtime pressure cooker veterans don't realize their cookers are capable of turning out a wide variety of sweet treats in a fraction of the time required by conventional methods. If you're still skeptical, you'll find a bevy of tempting, calories-be-damned delights in Part 7 that will make a believer out of you.

We give you an entire chapter on creamy desserts you can make in your pressure cooker, from scrumptious cheesecakes and delicate, light-as-air custards and flans to rich and creamy puddings. There's even a no-fail recipe for luscious chocolate fudge.

In another chapter, you learn how to use your pressure cooker to transform fresh and canned fruits—from peaches and pears to bananas and pineapples—into delectable and nutritious desserts that give any meal a sweet ending. If you thought desserts like Pineapple Holiday Cake, Peach Crunch, and Red Wine–Poached Pears were too complicated for you to master, your pressure cooker will turn you into a four-star dessert chef in no time flat!

Maybe you've always wanted to get into canning but feared it was too complicated, risky, and time-consuming. Your pressure cooker can make no-hassle blue-ribbon jams and fruit butters in a jiffy, as well as quick and easy applesauce that would take you hours to make on the stove.

Crème de la Crème

In This Chapter

- Rich and creamy cheesecakes
- Light and airy custards
- Proof is in the pudding
- Sweet treats for sweet teeth

Believe it or not, your humble pressure cooker can make delicate, luscious desserts with the same precision as your oven—but without drying out any of the sweet treats. And with a pressure cooker, you can make delectable desserts in the middle of the summer without turning your kitchen into a sauna!

Before getting started, you'll want to invest in a few insert pans such as a 7-inch springform pan for cheesecakes, a 1½-quart soufflé dish for puddings, and some 4-ounce ramekins or custard cups for custards. You can find them in kitchenware stores, or order them from online outlets such as Adventures in Cooking at adventuresincooking.com. (For more information on the various types of insert pans used in pressure cooking, see Chapter 2.)

Be sure to cover insert pans with heavy-duty aluminum foil instead of regular foil to keep out extra moisture.

Creamy Cheesecakes and Custards, Decadent Puddings, and More

If you don't believe you can make delicious cheesecake in a pressure cooker, this chapter has three recipes to prove you wrong. Because the pressure cooker uses moist heat, your cheesecakes will come out creamier and moister than those baked in the oven. And because it only takes about 25 minutes to make a cheesecake in a pressure cooker compared to 90 minutes in your oven, you'll save time, money, and energy, too.

There's a very good reason why pressure cookers make such silky-smooth custards. Eggs break down into solids and liquids at temperatures exceeding 325°F, and the pressure cooker's internal temperature is only 250°F. Because a pressure cooker has a moderate temperature and moist steam environment, you'll create creamy custards that don't get a skin on top.

Love fudge but hate all that stirring, not to mention the hassles and guesswork of using a candy thermometer? Making fudge in a pressure cooker eliminates all that, plus the risk that your fudge will come out grainy, crystallized, hard, lumpy, or scorched. With a pressure cooker, your fudge will come out rich, creamy, and smooth every single time—regardless of the weather or the type of pan you use.

Lemon Cheesecake

This creamy-rich cheesecake has just a hint of lemon.

Yield:	Prep time:	Cook time:	Serving size:
1 (7-inch) cheesecake	15 minutes	15 minutes	1 slice

1 cup graham cracker crumbs	1 tsp. pure vanilla extract
½ cup margarine or unsalted butter, melted	Zest of 1 large lemon
	Juice of 1 large lemon
1 (8-oz.) pkg. cream cheese, at room temperature	2 large eggs
½ cup sugar	2 cups water

1. In a small bowl, combine graham cracker crumbs with melted margarine. Set aside.

2. Line a 7-inch springform pan with parchment paper. Spray both the bottom of the pan and the parchment paper with nonstick cooking spray.

3. Place graham cracker crust mixture on top of the parchment paper, and press firmly to set on the bottom of the pan. Line the outside of the pan with heavy-duty aluminum foil, and extend the foil up beyond the height of the springform pan.

4. In a large bowl, and using an electric mixer on medium-high speed, blend cream cheese and sugar for 5 minutes or until very smooth. Add vanilla extract, lemon zest, and lemon juice. Add eggs, and mix just until eggs are combined. Do not overmix. Pour mixture into crust. Using a spatula, carefully smooth top of cheesecake.

5. Add water to a pressure cooker. Insert a rack in the bottom of the pressure cooker, and place the springform pan on the rack. Set the pressure cooker over medium-high heat.

6. Lock the lid in place. Bring to high pressure, and maintain for 15 minutes. Remove from heat, and reduce pressure using the natural release method.

7. Using heat-safe gloves, transfer the springform pan to a cooling rack. Let cheesecake cool for 30 to 45 minutes. Cover with aluminum foil, and refrigerate overnight.

8. To remove cheesecake from the pan, gently loosen the springform pan release lever until cheesecake comes out of the pan. Place a paper towel on top of cheesecake, and flip it over onto a platter. Remove the bottom of the springform pan, peel off the parchment paper, and flip cheesecake back over using a plate.

9. Cut cheesecake using a sharp knife dipped in hot water. Transfer slices to dessert plates, and serve immediately.

PRESSURE POINTER

The easiest way to get a springform pan into and out of your pressure cooker is to use an aluminum foil cradle. Fold a 24-inch length of foil lengthwise and then fold in half twice. You'll end up with a cradle about 3 inches wide. To use, position the pan in the center of the strip, pull up the ends, and use the ends as handles to lift the pan into or out of the pressure cooker. Fold the handles over the dessert before closing the lid, and cook the dessert with the cradle inside the pressure cooker.

White Chocolate Amaretto Cheesecake

White chocolate and amaretto add sweetness and spice to this decadent cheesecake.

Yield:	Prep time:	Cook time:	Serving size:
1 (7-inch) cheesecake	15 minutes	15 minutes	1 slice

1 cup graham cracker crumbs	1 tsp. pure vanilla extract
½ cup margarine or unsalted butter, melted	¼ cup amaretto liquor
	2 large eggs
1 (8-oz.) pkg. cream cheese, at room temperature	½ cup white chocolate chips
	2 cups water
½ cup sugar	

1. In a small bowl, combine graham cracker crumbs with melted margarine. Set aside.

2. Line a 7-inch springform pan with parchment paper. Spray both the bottom of the pan and the parchment paper with nonstick cooking spray.

3. Place graham cracker crust mixture on top of the parchment paper, and press firmly to set on the bottom of the pan. Line the outside of the pan with heavy-duty aluminum foil, and extend the foil up beyond the height of the springform pan.

4. In a large bowl, and using an electric mixer on medium speed, blend cream cheese and sugar for 5 minutes or until very smooth. Add vanilla extract and amaretto liquor. Add eggs, and mix just until eggs are combined. Do not overmix. Fold in white chocolate chips. Pour mixture into crust. Using a spatula, carefully smooth top of cheesecake.

5. Add water to a pressure cooker. Insert a rack in the bottom of the pressure cooker, and place the springform pan on the rack. Set the pressure cooker over high heat.

6. Lock the lid in place. Bring to high pressure, and maintain for 10 minutes. Remove the pressure cooker from heat, and reduce pressure using the natural release method.

7. Using heat-safe gloves, transfer the springform pan to a cooling rack. Let cheesecake cool for 30 to 45 minutes. Cover with aluminum foil, and refrigerate overnight.

8. To remove cheesecake from the pan, gently loosen the springform pan release lever until cheesecake comes out of pan. Place a paper towel on top of cheesecake, and flip it over onto a platter. Remove the bottom of the springform pan, peel off the parchment paper, and flip cheesecake back over using a plate.

9. Cut cheesecake using a sharp knife dipped in hot water. Transfer slices to dessert plates, and serve immediately.

PRESSURE POINTER

If a puddle of water forms on the top of a cheesecake, custard, or pudding, don't sweat it! Just blot it carefully with a paper towel, and no one will know the difference!

Ricotta Cheesecake

Lighter and less dense than traditional cheesecakes, this scrumptious dessert is laced with the soft flavors of vanilla and lemon.

Yield:	Prep time:	Cook time:	Serving size:
1 (7-inch) cheesecake	15 minutes	15 minutes	1 slice

1 cup graham cracker crumbs

½ cup margarine or unsalted butter, melted

½ cup cream cheese, at room temperature

½ cup *ricotta cheese*

½ cup sugar

2 tsp. pure vanilla extract

Zest of 1 large lemon

Juice of 1 large lemon

2 large eggs

2 cups water

1. In a small bowl, combine graham cracker crumbs with melted margarine. Set aside.

2. Line a 7-inch springform pan with parchment paper. Spray both the bottom of the pan and the parchment paper with nonstick cooking spray.

3. Place graham cracker crust mixture on top of the parchment paper, and press firmly to set on the bottom of the pan. Line the outside of the pan with heavy-duty aluminum foil, and extend the foil up beyond the height of the springform pan.

4. In a large bowl, and using an electric mixer on medium speed, blend cream cheese, ricotta cheese, and sugar for 5 minutes or until very smooth. Add vanilla extract, lemon zest, and lemon juice. Add eggs, and mix just until eggs are combined. Do not overmix. Pour mixture into crust. Using a spatula, carefully smooth top of cheesecake.

5. Add water to a pressure cooker. Place a rack in the bottom of the pressure cooker, and place the springform pan on the rack. Set the pressure cooker over high heat.

6. Lock the lid in place. Bring to high pressure, and maintain for 15 minutes. Remove the pressure cooker from heat, and release pressure using the natural release method.

7. Using heat-safe gloves, transfer the springform pan to a cooling rack. Let cheesecake cool for 30 to 45 minutes. Cover with aluminum foil, and refrigerate overnight.

8. To remove cheesecake from the pan, gently loosen the springform pan release lever until cheesecake comes out of the pan. Place a paper towel on top of cheesecake, and flip it over onto a platter. Remove the bottom of the springform pan, peel off the parchment paper, and flip cheesecake back over using a plate.

9. Cut cheesecake using a sharp knife dipped in hot water. Transfer slices to dessert plates, and serve immediately.

STEAM SPEAK

Ricotta cheese really isn't cheese at all but a dairy product made from reheated whey. Rich, fresh, and slightly grainy but smoother than cottage cheese, ricotta cheese makes a deliciously light and fluffy cheesecake.

Lemon Custard Cups

These silky and creamy custard cups have a rich lemony flavor that melts in your mouth.

Yield:	Prep time:	Cook time:	Serving size:
6 cups	15 minutes	12 minutes	1 cup

½ cup sugar	1 cup heavy cream or half-and-half
1 TB. cornstarch	Zest of 2 large lemons
2 large eggs	Juice of 2 large lemons
2 large egg yolks	2 cups water
2 cups whole milk	

1. In a large bowl, combine sugar and cornstarch. Whisk in eggs and egg yolks. Stir in whole milk, heavy cream, lemon zest, and lemon juice.

2. Pour lemon mixture into 6 heat-safe glass custard cups. Cover the top of each cup with a piece of aluminum foil, pressing the foil firmly against the cup to secure.

3. Add water to a pressure cooker. Insert a rack in the bottom of the pressure cooker, and place cups on the rack. (If there's not enough room for all the cups, stack them alternately on top of each other on the rack.) Set the pressure cooker over high heat.

4. Lock the lid in place. Bring to high pressure, and maintain for 12 minutes. Remove the pressure cooker from heat, and reduce pressure using the quick release method.

5. Using a heat-safe glove, transfer the cups to a cooling rack. Remove the aluminum foil, and let cool.

6. Serve warm, or cover custard cups with aluminum foil, refrigerate, and serve cold.

PRESSURE POINTER

Watching your waistline? To reduce the fat content, use half-and-half instead of heavy cream. Half-and-half, which is equal parts milk and cream, has 10 to 12 percent fat, while heavy cream—also called whipping cream—has nearly four times the fat, or a whopping 36 to 40 percent.

Vanilla Custard

If you love vanilla, you'll love this rich and fluffy custard.

Yield:	Prep time:	Cook time:	Serving size:
6 cups	10 minutes	4 minutes	1 cup

2 cups whole milk	¼ tsp. kosher salt
2 large eggs	1 tsp. pure vanilla extract
¼ cup granulated sugar	½ cup boiling water

1. Coat 6 heat-safe glass custard cups with nonstick cooking spray.

2. In a pressure cooker over high heat, *scald* whole milk.

3. In a large bowl, beat eggs. Add sugar and kosher salt, and stir until well blended. Add scalded milk to egg mixture, and blend well. Stir in vanilla extract.

4. Pour custard into the prepared cups. Cover each cup with a piece of aluminum foil, pressing the foil firmly against each cup to secure.

5. Add boiling water to the pressure cooker. Insert a rack in the pressure cooker, and place the custard cups on the rack, stacking them alternately if necessary. Set the pressure cooker over high heat.

6. Lock the lid in place. Bring to high pressure, and maintain for 4 minutes. Remove from heat, and reduce pressure using the natural release method. After 5 minutes, reduce any remaining pressure using the cold water release method.

7. Using a heat-safe glove, carefully transfer the cups to a cooling rack. Remove the foil from the cups, and let cool for 5 to 10 minutes. Serve immediately.

Variations: For **Caramel Custard Cups,** melt ¼ cup sugar in a skillet over low heat for 4 or 5 minutes or until it caramelizes, stirring constantly. Pour some of the caramel syrup into each of the custard cups. Pour vanilla custard into the cups, and proceed as directed. Chill and unmold. For **Chocolate Custard Cups,** use chocolate milk instead of regular milk. For **Maple Custard Cups,** omit the sugar and vanilla, and use ⅓ cup maple syrup instead.

STEAM SPEAK

When you **scald** milk, you heat it just until it's about to boil and then remove it from heat. Scalding milk helps prevent it from souring.

Indian Pudding

Molasses and cornmeal add sweetness and texture to this delicious bread pudding.

Yield:	Prep time:	Cook time:	Serving size:
6 slices	10 minutes	55 minutes	1 slice

½ cup whole-wheat flour

½ cup all-purpose flour

⅓ cup cornmeal

½ tsp. baking soda

½ tsp. baking powder

¼ tsp. kosher salt

½ cup molasses

1 large egg

½ cup half-and-half

2 cups water

1. Coat a 6-quart baking dish with nonstick cooking spray.

2. In a large bowl, combine whole-wheat flour, all-purpose flour, cornmeal, baking soda, baking powder, and kosher salt.

3. In a separate large bowl, combine molasses, egg, and half-and-half. Using a wooden spoon, stir egg mixture into flour mixture, mixing until smooth.

4. Pour batter into the prepared baking dish. Cover the dish with heavy-duty aluminum foil, pressing foil firmly against the edge of the dish to secure.

5. Add water to a pressure cooker. Insert a rack in the pressure cooker, and place custard cups on the rack. (If there's not enough room for all the cups, stack them alternately on top of each other on the rack.) Set the pressure cooker over high heat.

6. Lock the lid in place, and cook over low heat for 30 minutes. Increase heat to high. Bring to low pressure, and maintain for 55 minutes. Remove the pressure cooker from heat, and reduce pressure using the natural release method.

7. Using heat-safe gloves, transfer the baking dish to a cooling rack. Remove the aluminum foil, and let pudding cool for 10 minutes. Scoop pudding into 6 custard cups, and serve warm.

STEAM SPEAK

Indian pudding dates to Colonial times and refers to a baked pudding that contains milk, butter, molasses, eggs, spices, and cornmeal. It's named after the cornmeal, which was once called Indian meal.

Rice Pudding

This rich and chewy rice pudding stars hints of butter and vanilla.

Yield:	Prep time:	Cook time:	Serving size:
6 cups	30 minutes	40 minutes	1 cup

1 cup short-grain white rice, uncooked

2 cups sugar

5 cups whole milk

1 TB. unsalted butter

1 TB. pure vanilla extract

1. In a pressure cooker over high heat, combine white rice, sugar, and whole milk, and cook for 5 minutes or until mixture comes to a boil.

2. Lock the lid in place. Bring to low pressure, and maintain for 25 minutes. Remove the pressure cooker from heat, and reduce pressure using the natural release method.

3. Stir in unsalted butter and vanilla extract.

4. Ladle pudding into custard cups and serve warm, or cover custard cups with aluminum foil, refrigerate, and serve cold.

FOODIE FACT

Rice pudding may qualify as a delicious dessert today, but it began life as an ancient "restorative" for the young and infirm. Formulas for rice pudding appeared in medical texts before recipes ever showed up in cookbooks.

Date Pudding

Chewy dates give this silky pudding extra sweetness and texture.

Yield:	Prep time:	Cook time:	Serving size:
6 cups	10 minutes	80 minutes	1 cup

2½ cups fresh breadcrumbs, toasted

¾ cup brown sugar, firmly packed

½ tsp. baking soda

½ tsp. baking powder

½ tsp. ground cinnamon

⅛ tsp. ground nutmeg

1 cup dried dates, diced small

1 large egg, beaten

¾ cup whole milk

3 cups water

1. Coat 6 heat-safe custard cups with nonstick cooking spray.

2. In a large mixing bowl, combine breadcrumbs, brown sugar, baking soda, baking powder, cinnamon, nutmeg, and dates.

3. In a small bowl, combine egg and whole milk. Add to breadcrumb mixture, and mix until thoroughly combined.

4. Pour pudding into cups. Cover the top of each cup with a piece of heavy-duty aluminum foil, pressing the foil firmly against each cup to secure.

5. Add water to a pressure cooker. Place a rack in the pressure cooker, and place the custard cups on the rack.

6. Lock the lid in place, and cook over low heat for 30 minutes. Increase heat to high. Bring to high pressure, and maintain for 50 minutes. Remove the pressure cooker from heat, and reduce pressure using the cold water release method.

7. Using heat-safe gloves, transfer the custard cups to a cooling rack. Let cool for 10 minutes, and serve warm. Or cover custard cups with plastic wrap, refrigerate, and serve cold.

FOODIE FACT

Dates are green when they're unripe and turn into a golden brown or red as they ripen. They are picked green and dried. When buying dried dates, look for plump, soft dates with a shiny, smooth skin, and avoid shriveled dates with mold or sugar crystals on the skin.

Chocolate Brownie Pudding

A chocolate lover's delight, this rich pudding features the flavors of cocoa in a warm, sweet pudding.

Yield:	Prep time:	Cook time:	Serving size:
6 cups	15 minutes	65 minutes	1 cup

¼ cup unsalted butter or marga- rine, at room temperature	⅓ cup self-rising flour
¼ cup sugar	1 TB. *cocoa powder*
1 large egg	3 TB. whole milk, or as needed
	2 cups water

1. Coat a cake mold with nonstick cooking spray.

2. In a large bowl, combine unsalted butter and sugar. Add egg, and beat with a wooden spoon for 2 minutes or until smooth.

3. Mix in self-rising flour, cocoa powder, and 1 to 3 tablespoons whole milk, or enough that batter is thin and consistency of cake mix.

4. Pour mixture into the prepared cake mold, and cover tightly with aluminum foil.

5. Add water to a pressure cooker. Insert a rack in the pressure cooker, and place the cake mold on the rack. Place the lid on the pressure cooker, set over low heat, and cook for 25 minutes.

6. Lock the lid in place. Bring to low pressure, and maintain for 20 minutes. Remove the pressure cooker from heat, and reduce pressure using the quick release method.

7. Scoop pudding into small custard cups, and serve warm. Or cover custard cups with plastic wrap, refrigerate, and serve cold.

STEAM SPEAK

If a recipe calls for **cocoa powder,** don't substitute hot chocolate or hot cocoa, which contain powdered milk and sugar. Cocoa powder is an unsweetened powder derived from cocoa butter and has a more concentrated cocoa flavor than hot chocolate powders.

Chocolate Fudge Cake

The pressure cooker makes this rich, fudgelike cake moist and mouthwatering.

Yield:	Prep time:	Cook time:	Serving size:
6 slices	15 minutes	40 minutes	1 slice

1 (18.25-oz.) box devil's food cake mix with pudding	¼ cup canola or vegetable oil
4 medium eggs	5 cups water
1 TB. cocoa powder	1 (13.4-oz.) can chocolate fudge frosting

1. Coat a 1-quart round baking dish or a 6-cup cake pan with nonstick cooking spray.

2. In a large bowl, combine cake mix, eggs, cocoa powder, canola oil, and 1 cup water. Using an electric mixer on medium speed, beat for 3 minutes or until well blended. Scrape down the sides of the bowl, and pour mixture into the prepared cake pan. Cover the pan with two layers of aluminum foil.

3. Add remaining 4 cups water to a pressure cooker. Insert a rack in the bottom of the pressure cooker, and place the baking dish on the rack. Set the pressure cooker over medium-high heat.

4. Lock the lid in place. Bring to high pressure, and maintain for 40 minutes. Remove the pressure cooker from heat, and reduce pressure using the quick release method.

5. Using heat-safe gloves, transfer baking dish to a cooling rack. Let cake cool completely and then carefully flip cake onto a cake platter.

6. Frost with chocolate fudge frosting, cut into 6 slices, and serve immediately on dessert plates.

FOODIE FACT

It took Betty Crocker nearly a decade to develop the first cake mix. Beginning in 1943, the Betty Crocker labs and kitchens began to develop an easy cake mix. But the scientists soon discovered consumers didn't want Betty doing all the work. Consumers told scientists they preferred to add their own eggs, so the powdered eggs were removed from the mix, and the directions were changed to call for two fresh eggs.

Chocolate Fudge

Creamy-rich and chock-full of nuts, this fudge will satisfy the most discriminating sweet tooth.

Yield:	Prep time:	Cook time:	Serving size:
16 pieces	5 minutes	10 minutes	2 pieces

1 (14-oz.) can sweetened condensed milk

1 (12-oz.) pkg. semisweet chocolate
chips

2 cups water

½ cup walnuts or pecans, chopped

1 tsp. pure vanilla extract

1. In a metal or heat-proof baking dish, combine condensed milk and semisweet chocolate chips. Cover with waxed paper, and place a sheet of aluminum foil over the waxed paper to secure.

2. Add water to a pressure cooker. Insert a rack in the pressure cooker, and place the baking dish on the rack. Set the pressure cooker over high heat.

3. Lock the lid in place. Bring to high pressure, and maintain for 10 minutes. Remove the pressure cooker from heat, and reduce pressure using the cold water release method.

4. Remove the waxed paper and aluminum foil from the baking dish, and stir fudge mixture thoroughly. Add walnuts and vanilla extract, and stir until well blended.

5. Drop fudge mixture onto waxed or parchment paper, and let set until firm. When cool, cut into 16 pieces and serve.

FOODIE FACT

We have a kitchen blooper to thank for fudge, which is an American invention that resulted from an accidental "fudged" batch of caramels. Fudge was sold for the first time in 1886 at a local Baltimore grocery store. The cost: 40¢ a pound.

Fruity Favorites

In This Chapter

- Moist and fruity cakes
- Fantastic fruit desserts
- Hearty applesauce
- Homemade jams and compotes

From cakes to compotes, your pressure cooker can transform fresh and canned fruits into sweet, nutritious desserts and treats. No time for canning? Let your pressure cooker churn out homemade jams and preserves in a jiffy, or use it to make sweet and spicy homemade applesauce better than anything you could ever find in a jar.

Your pressure cooker also makes light work of fruity desserts, cooking them in just a fraction of the time required by conventional cooking methods. Whole or halved plums, prunes, raisins, sliced or dried apples, and whole or halved apricots take 2 or 3 minutes to cook. Dried apricots, peach halves, and pear halves take 3 or 4 minutes. Apples cut into chunks and dried pears take about 4 or 5 minutes in the pressure cooker.

Keep reading for delicious fruitful desserts just a few minutes away!

Yummy Fruit Desserts

Making moist cakes revolving around fruit is a piece of cake (pun intended) in your pressure cooker, which steams fruits to tender perfection and preserves far more of their natural flavors, colors, and nutrients than traditional cooking methods. Once you taste the homemade Pineapple Holiday Cake, Banana Walnut Cake, and Peach Crunch recipes in this chapter, you'll never settle for store-bought fruit desserts again.

Although it's easy enough to open a can, nothing comes close to the intense flavor of homemade poached fruits made in your pressure cooker. Whether you eat them as is, or spoon them over cake, ice cream, pancakes, French toast, or bread pudding, poached fruits are delicious and nutritious. Plus, you can serve them warm in the winter, chilled in the summer, or whenever the craving hits.

Your pressure cooker also makes scrumptious applesauce minus the hours of cooking and stirring. Just bring the apples to high pressure, and you've got homemade apple-sauce in minutes!

Any type of apple works with homemade applesauce (with the exception of Red Delicious apples, which come out too mealy), but for the best flavor, combine a vari-ety of apples with different characteristics. For instance, the tart flavor of Empires or Pippins moderates the sweetness of Golden Delicious apples and results in a sophis-ticated applesauce that's not too sweet. Or combine sweet Macintosh apples and juicy Jonathan apples for a sweeter applesauce.

> **PRESSURE POINTER**
>
> Apples vary widely in terms of moisture content, so if you're making applesauce with juicy apples, you may have to simmer the applesauce a few minutes to boil away excess liquid and boost the apple flavor.

Fruity Jams and Compotes

Years ago, it was common for housewives to "put up" jars of fruit jams, preserves, and purées to take advantage of the bounty of the harvest and so the family would have fresh fruit in the winter when it was no longer available on the tree. Today, although fresh fruit and jams are available year-round, nothing beats the flavor, texture, and nutrients of homemade preserves.

Your pressure cooker wasn't designed to can fresh fruits and vegetables, but it excels at making homemade jams, preserves, and butters. If you're interested in canning fruits and vegetables, you may want to invest in a pressure canner, which eliminates the hassles and guesswork of traditional canning.

Pineapple Holiday Cake

This modern take on fruitcake is moist, sweet, and studded with pineapples, raisins, cherries, and dates.

Yield:	Prep time:	Cook time:	Serving size:
6 slices	15 minutes	40 minutes	1 slice

1 (15-oz.) can crushed pineapple, with juice

½ cup unsalted butter or margarine

½ cup brown sugar, firmly packed

1 cup golden raisins

½ cup dried cherries, chopped

½ cup dried dates, chopped

1 tsp. baking soda

2 eggs, beaten

½ cup self-rising flour, sifted

½ cup all-purpose flour, sifted

⅛ tsp. kosher salt

2 cups water

1 pt. heavy whipping cream, whipped and sweetened with ⅓ cup confectioners' sugar

1. Coat a 6-quart baking dish with nonstick cooking spray.

2. In a pressure cooker over low heat, combine crushed pineapple with juice, unsalted butter, brown sugar, golden raisins, dried cherries, and dried dates. Simmer for 3 minutes or until brown sugar dissolves.

3. Stir in baking soda, and remove the pressure cooker from heat. Let cool for 30 minutes.

4. Pour cake batter into a large bowl, and add eggs. Using a spatula, fold in self-rising flour, all-purpose flour, and kosher salt.

5. Pour cake batter into the prepared dish, and cover with heavy-duty aluminum foil, pressing foil firmly against the edge of the dish to secure.

6. Add water to the pressure cooker. Insert a rack in the pressure cooker, and place the baking dish on the rack. Set the pressure cooker over medium-high heat.

7. Lock the lid in place. Bring to high pressure, and maintain for 40 minutes. Remove from heat, and reduce pressure using the natural release method.

8. Using heat-safe gloves, transfer the baking dish to a cooling rack. Let cake cool slightly, and then invert it onto a serving platter.

9. Cut cake into 6 slices, and serve with sweetened whipped cream.

FOODIE FACT

Fruitcake dates to Roman times and was made with pomegranate seeds, pine nuts, and raisins mixed into barley mash. In the Middle Ages, honey, spices, and preserved fruits were added. Because fruitcakes supplied a dense and compact form of nutrition and kept for months, they were a popular food among crusaders and hunters, who carried them during long journeys away from home.

Banana Walnut Cake

This banana cake is moist and rich, chock-full of walnuts, and spiced with cinnamon and *nutmeg*. The cream cheese frosting adds extra creaminess and sweetness.

Yield:	Prep time:	Cook time:	Serving size:
6 slices	15 minutes	20 minutes	1 slice

1 (18.25-oz.) box vanilla cake mix with pudding	5 cups water
4 medium eggs	1 large banana, peeled and mashed
1 tsp. ground cinnamon	½ cup walnuts, chopped
¼ tsp. ground nutmeg	1 (13.4-oz.) can cream cheese frosting
¼ cup canola oil	

1. Coat a 1-quart round baking dish or a 6-quart cake pan with nonstick cooking spray. Cover with two layers of aluminum foil.

2. In a large mixing bowl, combine cake mix, eggs, cinnamon, nutmeg, canola oil, and 1 cup water. Using an electric mixer on medium speed, beat for 2 or 3 minutes or until well blended.

3. Scrape down the sides of the bowl, and fold in banana and walnuts. Pour batter into the prepared baking dish or cake pan.

4. Add remaining 4 cups water to a pressure cooker. Insert a rack in bottom of the pressure cooker, and place the baking dish or cake pan on the rack. Set the pressure cooker over high heat.

5. Lock the lid in place. Bring to high pressure, and maintain for 35 minutes. Remove from heat, and reduce pressure using the quick release method.

6. Using heat-safe gloves, transfer the baking dish or cake pan to a cooling rack. Let cake cool completely, and then invert it onto a cake platter.

7. Frost cake with cream cheese frosting, cut into 6 slices, and serve immediately.

STEAM SPEAK

Nutmeg is the fruit of a tropical evergreen and was one of the spices Columbus was searching for during his expedition to the East Indies. Nutmeg is sold ground or whole and gives a variety of foods a warm, sweet, and spicy flavor and fragrance.

Peach Crunch

Sugar, cinnamon, and breadcrumbs give these peaches a sweet flavor and crunchy texture. Serve with vanilla ice cream for a special treat.

Yield:	Prep time:	Cook time:	Serving size:
4 squares	10 minutes	14 minutes	1 square

1 cup dried breadcrumbs

¼ cup sugar

½ tsp. ground cinnamon

Zest of 1 large lemon

Juice of 1 large lemon

3 large peaches, peeled, seeded, and sliced

¼ cup unsalted butter or margarine, melted

2 cups water

2 cups vanilla ice cream

1. Coat a 6-inch baking dish with nonstick cooking spray.

2. In a large bowl, combine breadcrumbs, sugar, cinnamon, lemon zest, and lemon juice.

3. Alternate adding layers of peaches and breadcrumb mixture in the prepared baking dish until all ingredients are used up. Pour melted unsalted butter over top. Cover the baking dish with heavy-duty aluminum foil.

4. Add water to a pressure cooker. Insert a rack in the pressure cooker, and place the baking dish on the rack. Set the pressure cooker over medium-high heat.

5. Lock the lid in place. Bring to high pressure, and maintain for 14 minutes. Remove from heat, and reduce pressure using the quick release method.

6. Using heat-safe gloves, transfer the baking dish to a cooling rack. Remove the aluminum foil, and transfer the baking dish to an oven broiler and broil for 30 seconds, or until top of peach crunch is golden brown.

7. Ladle into dessert bowls, and serve hot, topped with a scoop of vanilla ice cream.

 PRESSURE POINTER

If you buy unripe peaches, place them in a paper bag pierced with several holes and let them set at room temperature for a few days to ripen.

Red Wine-Poached Pears

This simple but elegant recipe infuses pears with the flavors of nutmeg, cinnamon, and red wine.

Yield:	Prep time:	Cook time:	Serving size:
4 pears	10 minutes	4 minutes	1 pear

2 cups water	¼ tsp. ground nutmeg
½ cup sugar	4 large pears, peeled but with core and stems intact
2 fresh lemon slices	
2 (3-in.) cinnamon sticks, broken in ½	2 cups dry red wine

1. In a pressure cooker over medium heat, add water, sugar, lemon slices, cinnamon sticks, and nutmeg. Simmer for 2 or 3 minutes or until sugar dissolves.

2. Insert a steamer basket in the pressure cooker. Trim bottom of pears so they sit flat, and place pears in the basket so they stand upright. Set the pressure cooker over high heat.

3. Lock the lid in place. Bring to high pressure, and maintain for 2 minutes. Remove from heat, and reduce pressure using the quick release method.

4. Add red wine.

5. Lock the lid in place. Bring to high pressure, and maintain for 2 minutes. Remove from heat, and reduce pressure using the quick release method.

6. Using heat-safe gloves, remove the steamer basket from the pressure cooker. Using a slotted spoon, transfer pears from the basket to a deep bowl. Leave juices in the pressure cooker.

7. Return the pressure cooker to high heat, and boil juices for 10 minutes or until they're the consistency of syrup. Let syrup cool, and pour over pears. Store pears in syrup overnight at room temperature.

8. Remove lemon slices and cinnamon sticks. To serve, stand pears upright in deep dessert bowls, and top with syrup.

PRESSURE POINTER

Unlike most fruits, pears should be picked or purchased when they're still hard and then ripened at room temperature. If you buy ripe pears, refrigerate them and eat or use them within a few days.

Cinnamon Apple Wedges

Brown sugar and cinnamon give these hot apples a sweet, spicy twist. Serve with a dollop of heavy whipped cream for extra richness.

Yield:	Prep time:	Cook time:	Serving size:
3 cups	5 minutes	4 minutes	1 cup

1 cup dry red wine

1 cup apple juice

¾ cup dark brown sugar, firmly packed

1 (3-in.) cinnamon stick

2 lemon slices

4 large red Gala apples, peeled, cored, and cut into wedges

1 pt. heavy whipping cream, whipped

1. In a pressure cooker over low heat, combine red wine, apple juice, dark brown sugar, cinnamon stick, and lemon slices. Simmer for 2 or 3 minutes or until sugar dissolves.

2. Insert a steamer basket in the pressure cooker. Place apples wedges in the basket.

3. Lock the lid in place. Bring to high pressure, and maintain for 4 minutes. Remove from heat, and reduce pressure using the quick release method.

4. Transfer apple wedges to dessert bowls, top with whipped cream, and serve warm or at room temperature.

FOODIE FACT

An apple a day may not necessarily keep the doctor away, but it will provide many nutrients, including fiber, vitamins A and C, and quercetin, an antioxidant that may help prevent cancers and heart disease.

Homemade Applesauce

With hints of cinnamon, nutmeg, and cloves, this applesauce has a fresh, spicy flavor and fragrance you'll never find in a jar or can.

Yield:	Prep time:	Cook time:	Serving size:
3 pints	15 minutes	5 minutes	¼ cup

4 or 5 medium Jonathan apples (3 lb.), peeled, cored, and quartered

2 (3-in.) cinnamon sticks, broken in ½

½ cup light brown sugar, firmly packed

1 cup apple juice

¼ tsp. ground nutmeg

¼ tsp. ground cloves

1. In a pressure cooker over high heat, combine apples, cinnamon sticks, light brown sugar, apple juice, nutmeg, and cloves.

2. Lock the lid in place. Bring to high pressure, and maintain for 5 minutes. Remove from heat, and reduce pressure using the quick release method.

3. Let cool for 10 minutes. Using tongs, remove and discard cinnamon sticks.

4. Transfer applesauce mixture to a blender or a food processor fitted with a metal blade, and purée for 2 or 3 minutes or until smooth.

5. Ladle applesauce into dessert dishes, and serve hot, cold, or at room temperature. Store applesauce in an airtight container in the refrigerator and use within 1 week.

PRESSURE POINTER

The flavor of your applesauce will vary depending on the apples you use. If you find this recipe too sweet or too tart, mix and match different types of cooking apples until you find a combination that delights your taste buds!

Ginger Cranberry Applesauce

The sweetness of this sophisticated applesauce is tempered with hints of ginger and cranberries. It's not too sweet but just right for enjoying alone or scooped over oatmeal or cake.

Yield:	Prep time:	Cook time:	Serving size:
3 cups	10 minutes	7 minutes	½ cup

1 (12-oz.) pkg. fresh cranberries

2 large red *Gala apples*, peeled, cored, and cut into quarters

⅓ cup sugar

½ cup apple juice

1 (½-in.) piece fresh gingerroot, peeled

1½ cups water

1 tsp. ground cinnamon

1. In a pressure cooker over high heat, add cranberries, apples, sugar, apple juice, gingerroot, and water.

2. Lock the lid in place. Bring to high pressure, and maintain for 7 minutes. Remove from heat, and reduce pressure using the natural release method.

3. When mixture is cool, transfer to a food processor fitted with a metal blade and purée for 2 or 3 minutes or until smooth. Add cinnamon, and mix well.

4. Eat applesauce hot or cold or ladled over cake, pancakes, oatmeal, and other foods. Or refrigerate applesauce in a glass jar with a tight lid and use within 2 weeks.

STEAM SPEAK

Gala apples are a mild, sweet, and versatile apple. They're delicious to eat, and they're ideal for pressure cooking and baking. If you can't find Gala apples, you can substitute another type of baking apple, such as Braeburn, Gravenstein, or York Imperial apples.

Spiced Apple Butter

This sweet and silky apple butter has hints of cinnamon, allspice, and cloves, and turns ordinary toast into a sweet flavor sensation.

Yield:	Prep time:	Cook time:	Serving size:
2 cups	15 minutes	5 minutes	½ cup

2 cups port wine	1 (3-in.) cinnamon stick, broken in ½
1 cup water	
4 or 5 medium red Gala apples (3 lb.), peeled and cored	1 tsp. ground allspice
	¼ tsp. ground cloves
2 tsp. ground cinnamon	2 cups sugar

1. In a pressure cooker over high heat, add port wine, water, and apples.

2. Lock the lid in place, and bring to high pressure. When pressure is reached, remove the pressure cooker from heat, and reduce pressure using the natural release method. Let mixture cool for 15 minutes.

3. Place apples in a food processor fitted with a metal blade, and process for 2 or 3 minutes or until smooth.

4. In the pressure cooker over low heat, add processed apples, cinnamon, cinnamon stick, allspice, cloves, and sugar, and simmer, uncovered and stirring frequently, for about 45 minutes or until sugar dissolves.

5. Let apple butter cool, and remove and discard cinnamon stick. Ladle butter into glass jars, leaving at least 1 inch between the top of the jar and the lid. Store apple butter in the refrigerator, and use within 4 weeks.

FOODIE FACT

Grand Rapids, Ohio, has turned apple butter into an art form. Every October, the historic canal town sponsors its annual Applebutterfest, during which 2,300 pints of apple butter are made in three 50-gallon copper kettles and sold in pint jars. Learn more at applebutterfest.org.

Spiced Peach Jam

This savory jam combines the flavors of fresh peaches with hints of lemon, cinnamon, and nutmeg. Spread it on bread or toast, or add a dollop to oatmeal, pancakes, and French toast.

Yield:	Prep time:	Cook time:	Serving size:
2 pints	15 minutes	5 minutes	¼ cup

1 cup sugar	¼ tsp. ground nutmeg
½ large lemon, cut into slices	6 to 8 large peaches (2 lb.), peeled and cored
2 (3-in.) cinnamon sticks, broken in ½	1 (2-oz.) package dry pectin

1. In a pressure cooker over medium heat, combine sugar, lemon slices, cinnamon sticks, and nutmeg. Reduce heat to low, and simmer just until sugar dissolves.

2. Insert a steamer basket in the pressure cooker. Place peaches in the basket.

3. Lock the lid in place. Bring to high pressure, and maintain for 5 minutes. Remove from heat, and reduce pressure using the natural release method.

4. Return the pressure cooker to medium heat, and stir in pectin. Increase heat to high, bring to a boil, and boil for 1 minute. Skim foam from surface using a ladle or spoon. Remove and discard cinnamon sticks.

5. Ladle jam into clean glass jars, leaving at least 1 inch between the top of the jar and the lid, and let cool. Jam can be refrigerated for up to 4 weeks and frozen for up to 6 months.

FOODIE FACT

What's the difference between jam, jelly, and preserves? Jam is a thick mixture of fruit, sugar, and usually pectin that's puréed until the fruit is soft. Jelly is a clear, bright mixture made from fruit juice, sugar, and pectin that's tender but firm enough to hold its shape. Preserves are similar to jam but contain chunks or pieces of fruit.

Dried Fruit Compote

This hearty medley of chewy apricots, peaches, prunes, pears, and raisins is spiced with hints of citrus and cinnamon and is a savory compliment to chicken and pork dishes.

Yield:	Prep time:	Cook time:	Serving size:
2 cups	5 minutes	15 minutes	¼ cup

2 cups water	¼ cup golden raisins
1 TB. cornstarch	½ cup sugar
½ cup dried apricots, diced	⅛ tsp. kosher salt
½ cup dried peaches, diced	Zest of ¼ large orange, sliced thin
½ cup dried prunes, diced	Zest of ¼ large lemon, sliced thin
½ cup dried pears, diced	2 TB. red hot cinnamon candies

1. In a small bowl, combine water and cornstarch until smooth.

2. In a pressure cooker over high heat, combine cornstarch mixture, dried apricots, dried peaches, dried prunes, dried pears, golden raisins, sugar, kosher salt, orange zest, lemon zest, and cinnamon candies.

3. Lock the lid in place. Bring to high pressure, and maintain for 15 minutes. Remove from heat, and reduce pressure using the natural release method.

4. Using a slotted spoon, transfer fruit to a cutting board and let cool.

5. Serve compote with chicken or pork. Store compote in an airtight container in the refrigerator and use it within 4 weeks.

FOODIE FACT

Compote is a chilled dish of fresh or dried fruit slowly cooked in sugary syrup made of liquor and spices. Because pressure cooking preserves the shape, texture, flavors, colors, and nutrients of fruit, it's a foolproof way to make compote.

al dente   Italian for "against the teeth." Refers to pasta or rice that's neither soft nor hard but just slightly firm against the teeth.

all-purpose flour   Flour that contains only the inner part of the wheat grain. Usable for all purposes, from cakes to gravies.

allspice   Named for its flavor echoes of several spices (cinnamon, cloves, nutmeg), allspice is used in many desserts and in rich marinades and stews.

almonds   Mild, sweet, and crunchy nuts that combine nicely with creamy and sweet food items.

amaranth   An ancient Aztec grain with a nutty, spicy flavor and a sticky texture.

Arborio rice   A plump Italian rice used, among other purposes, for risotto.

artichoke hearts   The center part of the artichoke flower, often found canned in grocery stores.

arugula   A spicy-peppery garden plant with leaves that resemble a dandelion and have a distinctive—and very sharp—flavor.

balsamic vinegar   Vinegar produced primarily in Italy from a specific type of grape and aged in wood barrels. It's heavier, darker, and sweeter than most vinegars.

basil   A flavorful, almost sweet, resinous herb delicious with tomatoes and used in all kinds of Italian or Mediterranean-style dishes.

beat   To quickly mix substances.

black pepper   A biting and pungent seasoning, freshly ground pepper is a must for many dishes and adds an extra level of flavor and taste.

blanch   To place a food in boiling water for about 1 minute (or less) to partially cook the exterior and then submerge in or rinse with cool water to halt the cooking.

blend   To completely mix something, usually with a blender or food processor, slower than beating.

blue cheese   A blue-veined cheese that crumbles easily and has a somewhat soft texture, usually sold in a block. The color is from a flavorful, edible mold often added or injected into the cheese.

boil   To heat a liquid to a point where water is forced to turn into steam, causing the liquid to bubble. To boil something is to insert it into boiling water. A rapid boil is when a lot of bubbles form on the surface of the liquid.

borscht   A rich soup originating in Russia and Poland made with beets, sour cream, and other ingredients, and served hot or cold.

bouillabaisse   A seafood stew.

bouillon   Dried essence of stock from chicken, beef, vegetable, or other ingredients. This is a popular starting ingredient for soups as it adds flavor (and often a lot of salt).

breadcrumbs   Tiny pieces of crumbled dry bread, often used for topping or coating.

Brie   A creamy cow's milk cheese from France with a soft, edible rind and a mild flavor.

brine   A highly salted, often seasoned, liquid used to flavor and preserve foods. To brine a food is to soak, or preserve, it by submerging it in brine. The salt in the brine penetrates the fibers of the meat and makes it moist and tender.

broil   To cook in a dry oven under the overhead high-heat element.

broth   *See* stock.

brown   To cook in a skillet, turning, until the food's surface is seared and brown in color, to lock in the juices.

brown rice   Whole-grain rice including the germ with a characteristic pale brown or tan color. It's more nutritious and flavorful than white rice.

bulgur   A wheat kernel that's been steamed, dried, and crushed and is sold in fine and coarse textures.

cacciatore   An Italian-style dish prepared with tomatoes, onions, mushrooms, herbs, and wine.

Cajun cooking   A style of cooking that combines French and Southern characteristics and includes many highly seasoned stews and meats.

canapés   Bite-size hors d'oeuvres usually served on a small piece of bread or toast.

capers   Flavorful buds of a Mediterranean plant, ranging in size from *nonpareil* (about the size of a small pea) to larger, grape-size caper berries produced in Spain.

caponata   A Sicilian dish made with eggplant, tomatoes, olives, pine nuts, capers, anchovies, and vinegar cooked together in olive oil and served as a salad, side dish, or dip.

capons   Roosters castrated at a young age and fed a high-fat diet to yield tender, juicy, and flavorful meat.

caramelize   To cook sugar over low heat until it develops a sweet caramel flavor. The term is increasingly gaining use to describe cooking vegetables (especially onions) or meat in butter or oil over low heat until they soften, sweeten, and develop a caramel color.

caraway   A distinctive, spicy seed used for bread, pork, cheese, and cabbage dishes. It's known to reduce stomach upset, which is why it's often paired with, for example, sauerkraut.

cayenne   A fiery spice made from (hot) chile peppers, especially the cayenne chile, a slender, red, and very hot pepper.

cheddar   The ubiquitous hard cow's milk cheese with a rich, buttery flavor that ranges from mellow to sharp.

chickpeas (or **garbanzo beans**)   Yellow-gold, roundish beans used as the base ingredient in hummus. Chickpeas are high in fiber and low in fat.

chiles (or **chilies**)   Any one of many different "hot" peppers, ranging in intensity from the relatively mild ancho pepper to the blisteringly hot habanero.

chili powder   A seasoning blend that includes chile pepper, cumin, garlic, and oregano. Proportions vary among different versions, but they all offer a warm, rich flavor.

Chinese five-spice powder   This staple of Chinese cooking is a pungent mixture of equal parts cinnamon, cloves, fennel seed, anise, and Szechuan peppercorns.

chives   A member of the onion family, chives grow in bunches of long leaves that resemble tall grass or the green tops of onions and offer a light onion flavor.

chop To cut into pieces, usually qualified by an adverb such as "*coarsely* chopped," or by a size measurement such as "chopped into $\frac{1}{2}$-inch pieces." "Finely chopped" is much closer to mince.

chorizo A spiced pork sausage eaten alone and as a component in many recipes.

chutney A thick condiment often served with Indian curries made with fruits and/or vegetables with vinegar, sugar, and spices.

cider vinegar A vinegar produced from apple cider, popular in North America.

cilantro A member of the parsley family and used in Mexican dishes (especially salsa) and some Asian dishes. Use in moderation, as the flavor can overwhelm. The seed of the cilantro is the spice coriander.

cinnamon A rich, aromatic spice commonly used in baking or desserts. Cinnamon can also be used for delicious and interesting entrées.

cioppino A savory fish stew inspired by Italian cuisine that includes tomatoes and a variety of seafood.

clove A sweet, strong, almost wintergreen-flavor spice used in baking and with meats such as ham.

cold water release method A technique used in pressure cooking that rapidly lowers the pressure and temperature inside the pressure cooker.

compote A chilled dish of fresh or dried fruit slowly cooked in a sugary syrup made of liquid and spices.

coriander A rich, warm, spicy seed used in all types of recipes, from African to South American, from entrées to desserts.

Cornish game hens Miniature chickens weighing less than 3 pounds that have enough meat for one serving.

count In terms of seafood or other foods that come in small sizes, the number of that item that compose 1 pound. For example, 31 to 40 count shrimp are large appetizer shrimp often served with cocktail sauce; 51 to 60 are much smaller.

couscous Granular semolina (durum wheat) cooked and used in many Mediterranean and North African dishes.

crudités Fresh vegetables served as an appetizer, often all together on one tray.

cumin   A fiery, smoky-tasting spice popular in Middle Eastern and Indian dishes. Cumin is a seed; ground cumin seed is the most common form used in cooking.

curd   A gelatinous substance resulting from coagulated milk used to make cheese. Curd also refers to dishes of similar texture, such as dishes made with egg (lemon curd).

curing   A method of preserving uncooked foods, usually meats or fish, by either salting and smoking or pickling.

curry   Rich, spicy, Indian-style sauces and the dishes prepared with them. A curry uses curry powder as its base seasoning.

curry powder   A ground blend of rich and flavorful spices used as a basis for curry and many other Indian-influenced dishes. Common ingredients include hot pepper, nutmeg, cumin, cinnamon, pepper, and turmeric. Some curry can also be found in paste form.

custard   A cooked mixture of eggs and milk popular as a base for desserts.

dash   A few drops, usually of a liquid, released by a quick shake of, for example, a bottle of hot sauce.

deglaze   To scrape up the bits of meat and seasoning left in a pan or skillet after cooking. Usually this is done by adding a liquid such as wine or broth and creating a flavorful stock that can be used to create sauces.

devein   To remove the dark vein from the back of a large shrimp with a sharp knife.

dice   To cut into small cubes about ¼-inch square.

Dijon mustard   Hearty, spicy mustard made in the style of the Dijon region of France.

dill   A herb perfect for eggs, salmon, cheese dishes, and of course, vegetables (pickles!).

dredge   To cover a piece of food with a dry substance such as flour or cornmeal.

entrée   The main dish in a meal. In France, however, the entrée is considered the first course.

extra-virgin olive oil   *See* olive oil.

extracts   Concentrated flavorings derived from foods or plants through evaporation or distillation that impart a powerful flavor without altering the volume or texture of a dish.

fennel   In seed form, a fragrant, licorice-tasting herb. The bulbs have a mild flavor and a celerylike crunch and are used as a vegetable in salads or cooked recipes.

feta   A white, crumbly, sharp, and salty cheese popular in Greek cooking and on salads. Traditional feta is usually made with sheep's milk, but feta-style cheese can be made from sheep's, cow's, or goat's milk.

filé powder   A popular spice in Southern cuisine, filé powder is made from dried sassafras leaves and imparts a woodsy flavor to foods.

fillet   A piece of meat or seafood with the bones removed.

flake   To break into thin sections, as with fish.

floret   The flower or bud end of broccoli or cauliflower.

flour   Grains ground into a meal. Wheat is perhaps the most common flour. Flour is also made from oats, rye, buckwheat, soybeans, etc. *See also* all-purpose flour; whole-wheat flour.

fold   To combine a dense and light mixture with a circular action from the middle of the bowl.

fricassee   A dish, usually chicken, cut into pieces and cooked in a liquid or sauce.

frittata   A skillet-cooked mixture of eggs and other ingredients that's not stirred but is cooked slowly and then either flipped or finished under the broiler.

fry   *See* sauté.

garlic   A member of the onion family, a pungent and flavorful element in many savory dishes. A garlic bulb contains multiple cloves. Each clove, when chopped, provides about 1 teaspoon garlic. Most recipes call for cloves or chopped garlic by the teaspoon.

garnish   An embellishment not vital to the dish but added to enhance visual appeal.

gasket   The rubber seal in the lid of a pressure cooker that traps steam inside the pressure cooker, which then builds into pressure and cooks the food.

gazpacho   A cold, uncooked soup originating in Spain that's a puréed mixture of tomatoes, bell peppers, onions, celery, and cucumber.

ginger Available in fresh root or dried, ground form, ginger adds a pungent, sweet, and spicy quality to a dish.

Gorgonzola A creamy and rich Italian blue cheese. "Dolce" is sweet, and that's the kind you want.

goulash A stew of Hungarian origin made with beef and vegetables and flavored with paprika.

grate To shave into tiny pieces using a sharp rasp or grater.

grits Coarsely ground grains, usually corn.

Gruyère A rich, sharp cow's milk cheese made in Switzerland that has a nutty flavor.

handful An unscientific measurement; the amount of an ingredient you can hold in your hand.

Havarti A creamy, Danish, mild cow's milk cheese perhaps most enjoyed in its herbed versions such as Havarti with dill.

hazelnuts (also **filberts**) A sweet nut popular in desserts and, to a lesser degree, in savory dishes.

herbes de Provence A seasoning mix including basil, fennel, marjoram, rosemary, sage, and thyme, common in the south of France.

hoisin sauce A sweet Asian condiment similar to ketchup made with soybeans, sesame, chile peppers, and sugar.

horseradish A sharp, spicy root that forms the flavor base in many condiments from cocktail sauce to sharp mustards. Prepared horseradish contains vinegar and oil, among other ingredients. Use pure horseradish much more sparingly than the prepared version, or try cutting it with sour cream.

hummus A thick, Middle Eastern spread made of puréed chickpeas, lemon juice, olive oil, garlic, and often tahini (sesame seed paste).

infusion A liquid in which flavorful ingredients such as herbs have been soaked or steeped to extract that flavor into the liquid.

insert pans A variety of dishes and pans placed inside a pressure cooker that enable you to cook many different foods at once. *See also* interrupted cooking.

interrupted cooking   A pressure cooking technique used to prepare dishes with ingredients that take varying times to cook. *See also* insert pans; rack.

Italian seasoning   A blend of dried herbs, including basil, oregano, rosemary, and thyme.

jicama   A juicy, crunchy, sweet, large, round Central American vegetable. If you can't find jicama, try substituting sliced water chestnuts.

julienne   A French word meaning "to slice into very thin pieces."

kalamata olives   Traditionally from Greece, these medium-small long black olives have a smoky rich flavor.

kasha   Also called buckwheat, kasha is a brown fruit seed with a roasted flavor.

Key limes   Very small limes grown primarily in Florida known for their tart taste.

knockwurst   A short link of beef or pork sausage flavored with garlic.

kosher salt   A coarse-grained salt made without any additives or iodine.

lentils   Tiny lens-shape pulses used in European, Middle Eastern, and Indian cuisines.

liquid smoke   A liquid that adds a smoky flavor to food so it tastes like it was grilled over a wood fire.

macerate   To mix sugar or another sweetener with fruit. The fruit softens, and its juice is released to mix with the sweetener.

marinate   To soak meat, seafood, or other food in a seasoned sauce, called a marinade, which is high in acid content. The acids break down the muscle of the meat, making it tender and adding flavor.

marjoram   A sweet herb, a cousin of and similar to oregano popular in Greek, Spanish, and Italian dishes.

meld   To allow flavors to blend and spread over time. Melding is often why recipes call for overnight refrigeration and is also why some dishes taste better as leftovers.

mince   To cut into pieces smaller than diced pieces, about $\frac{1}{8}$ inch or smaller.

mirin   A sweet, golden, low-alcohol wine made from glutinous rice that can be substituted for regular white wine in recipes.

miso   A fermented, flavorful soybean paste, key in many Japanese dishes.

natural release method   A technique used in pressure cooking that allows the pressure and temperature inside the cooker to decrease naturally.

Niçoise   A garnish made of garlic, tomatoes, anchovies, black olives, capers, and lemon juice that originated in Nice, France, and is used in salads, stews, and other dishes.

nutmeg   A sweet, fragrant, musky spice used primarily in baking.

olive oil   A fragrant liquid produced by crushing or pressing olives. Extra-virgin olive oil—the most flavorful and highest quality—is produced from the first pressing of a batch of olives; oil is also produced from later pressings.

olives   The fruit of the olive tree commonly grown on all sides of the Mediterranean. Black olives are also called ripe olives. Green olives are immature, although they're also widely eaten. *See also* kalamata olives.

oregano   A fragrant, slightly astringent herb used in Greek, Spanish, and Italian dishes.

orzo   A rice-shape pasta used in Greek cooking.

paella   A grand Spanish dish of rice, shellfish, onion, meats, rich broth, and herbs.

pan-in-pot cooking   A pressure cooking technique in which foods are cooked in insert pans. *See also* insert pans.

paprika   A rich, red, warm, earthy spice that also lends a rich red color to many dishes.

Parmesan   A hard, dry, flavorful cheese primarily used grated or shredded as a seasoning for Italian-style dishes.

parsley   A fresh-tasting green leafy herb, often used as a garnish.

pâté   A savory loaf that contains spices; often a lot of fat; and meats, poultry, or seafood. Served cold and spread or sliced on crusty bread or crackers.

pecans   Rich, buttery nuts, native to North America, that have a high unsaturated fat content.

peppercorns   Large, round, dried berries ground to produce pepper.

pesto   A thick spread or sauce made with fresh basil leaves, garlic, olive oil, pine nuts, and Parmesan cheese. Some newer versions are made with other herbs.

pickle   A food, usually a vegetable such as a cucumber, that's been pickled in brine.

pilaf   A rice dish in which the rice is browned in butter or oil and then cooked in a flavorful liquid such as a broth, often with the addition of meats or vegetables. The rice absorbs the broth, resulting in a savory dish.

pinch   An unscientific measurement term indicating the amount of an ingredient you can hold between your finger and thumb. Typically, this measurement applies to a dry, granular substance such as an herb or seasoning.

pine nuts (also **pignoli** or **piñon**)   Nuts grown on pine trees that are rich (read: high fat), flavorful, and a bit pine-y. Pine nuts are a traditional component of pesto and add a wonderful hearty crunch to many other recipes.

pita bread   A flat, hollow wheat bread often used for sandwiches or sliced, pizza style, into slices. It's terrific soft with dips or baked or broiled as a vehicle for other ingredients.

poach   To cook a food in simmering liquid, such as water, wine, or broth.

polenta   A mush made from cornmeal that can be eaten hot with butter or cooked until firm and cut into squares.

porcini mushrooms   Rich and flavorful mushrooms used in rice and Italian-style dishes.

porcupine   A term referring to a type of meatball or meatloaf made with ground beef, rice, onion, tomato soup, and seasonings.

port   A sweet fortified wine grown in Portugal's Douro Valley and named after Oporto, the city from where it's shipped out to the rest of the world.

portobello mushrooms   A mature and larger form of the smaller crimini mushroom, portobellos are brown, chewy, and flavorful. Often served as whole caps, grilled, or as thin sautéed slices.

preheat   To turn on an oven, broiler, or other cooking appliance in advance of cooking so the temperature will be at the desired level when the assembled dish is ready for cooking.

pressure regulator valve   A fixture on a pressure cooker that lets you control the amount of pressure in the cooker.

prosciutto   A dry, salt-cured ham that originated in Italy.

purée   To reduce a food to a thick, creamy texture, usually using a blender or food processor.

quick release method   A pressure cooking technique used during interrupted cooking that allows the cooker to return to pressure very quickly. *See also* interrupted cooking.

quinoa   A grain with a nutty flavor that's extremely high in protein and calcium.

rack   A pressure cooking accessory that raises food above the water or liquid in the pressure cooker so food steams more efficiently. *See also* insert pans.

ragout   A thick, rich stew originating in France that contains meat, poultry, or fish and that's often used as a rich sauce for noodles.

ramekin   A small dish that can be used as an insert in pressure cooking to make custards, puddings, and individual servings of casseroles and vegetables.

ratatouille   A French stew that's a mélange of summer vegetables cooked together and served as a side dish or entrée or used as a filling for stuffed crepes and omelets.

reduce   To boil or simmer a broth or sauce to remove some of the water content, resulting in more concentrated flavor and color.

render   To cook a meat to the point where its fat melts and can be removed.

reserve   To hold a specified ingredient for another use later in the recipe.

rice vinegar   Vinegar produced from fermented rice or rice wine, popular in Asian-style dishes. Different from rice wine vinegar.

ricotta   A fresh Italian cheese smoother than cottage cheese with a slightly sweet flavor.

risotto   A popular Italian rice dish made by browning Arborio rice in butter or oil and then slowly adding liquid to cook the rice, resulting in a creamy texture. *See also* Arborio rice.

Rock Cornish hens   *See* Cornish game hens.

roast   To cook something uncovered in an oven, usually without additional liquid.

Roquefort   A world-famous (French) creamy but sharp sheep's milk cheese containing blue lines of mold.

rosemary   A pungent, sweet herb used with chicken, pork, fish, and especially lamb. A little of it goes a long way.

roux   A mixture of butter or another fat and flour used to thicken sauces and soups.

safety handles   Heat-resistant handles on a pressure cooker that make it easier to lift. Handles line up to indicate the pressure cooker is properly closed.

saffron   A spice made from the stamens of crocus flowers, saffron lends a dramatic yellow color and distinctive flavor to a dish. Use only tiny amounts of this expensive herb.

sage   An herb with a musty yet fruity, lemon-rind scent and "sunny" flavor.

salt pork   Pork cured with salt.

sauté   To pan-cook over lower heat than used for frying.

savory   A popular herb with a fresh, woody taste.

scald   To heat milk just until it's about to boil and then remove it from heat. Scalding milk helps prevent it from souring.

sear   To quickly brown the exterior of a food, especially meat, over high heat to preserve interior moisture.

sesame oil   An oil, made from pressing sesame seeds, that's tasteless if clear and aromatic and flavorful if brown.

shallot   A member of the onion family that grows in a bulb somewhat like garlic and has a milder onion flavor. When a recipe calls for shallot, use the entire bulb.

shellfish   A broad range of seafood, including clams, mussels, oysters, crabs, shrimp, and lobster. Some people are allergic to shellfish, so take care with its inclusion in recipes.

shiitake mushrooms   Large, dark brown mushrooms with a hearty, meaty flavor. Can be used either fresh or dried, grilled or as a component in other recipes, and as a flavoring source for broth.

shred   To cut into many long, thin slices.

short-grain rice   A starchy rice popular in Asian-style dishes because it readily clumps, making it perfect for eating with chopsticks.

simmer   To boil gently so the liquid barely bubbles.

skillet (also **frying pan**)   A generally heavy, flat-bottomed metal pan with a handle designed to cook food over heat on a stovetop or campfire.

skim   To remove fat or other material from the top of liquid.

slice To cut into thin pieces.

steam To suspend a food over boiling water and allow the heat of the steam (water vapor) to cook the food. A quick-cooking method, steaming preserves a food's flavor and texture.

steep To let sit in hot water, as in steeping tea in hot water for 10 minutes.

stew To slowly cook pieces of food submerged in a liquid. Also, a dish prepared by this method.

sticky rice (or **glutinous rice**) *See* short-grain rice.

stir-fry To cook small pieces of food in a wok or skillet over high heat, moving and turning the food quickly to cook all sides.

stock A flavorful broth made by cooking meats and/or vegetables with seasonings until the liquid absorbs these flavors. This liquid is then strained and the solids are discarded. Stock can be eaten alone or used as a base for soups, stews, etc.

stroganoff A dish consisting of thin slices of beef, onions, and mushrooms sautéed in butter and combined with a sour cream sauce.

tahini A paste made from sesame seeds used to flavor many Middle Eastern recipes.

tapenade A thick, chunky spread made from savory ingredients such as olives, lemon juice, and anchovies.

tarragon A sweet, rich-smelling herb perfect with seafood, vegetables (especially asparagus), chicken, and pork.

teriyaki A Japanese-style sauce composed of soy sauce, rice wine, ginger, and sugar that works well with seafood as well as most meats.

thyme A minty, zesty herb.

tiered cooking A pressure cooking technique in which two or more layers of racks are placed inside the pressure cooker for preparing foods that cook at varying times. *See also* rack; interrupted cooking.

toast To heat something, usually bread, so it's browned and crisp.

tofu A cheeselike substance made from soybeans and soy milk.

tomatillo A small, round fruit with a distinctive spicy flavor, often found in south-of-the-border dishes. To use, remove the papery outer skin, rinse off any sticky residue, and chop like a tomato.

turmeric   A spicy, pungent yellow root used in many dishes, especially Indian cuisine, for color and flavor. Turmeric is the source of the yellow color in many prepared mustards.

veal   Meat from a calf, generally characterized by mild flavor and tenderness.

vegetable steamer   An insert for a pressure cooker with tiny holes in the bottom designed to fit inside the cooker to hold food to be steamed above boiling water. *See also* steam.

venison   Deer meat.

vinegar   An acidic liquid widely used as dressing and seasoning, often made from fermented grapes, apples, or rice. *See also* balsamic vinegar; cider vinegar; rice vinegar; white vinegar; wine vinegar.

walnuts   A rich, slightly woody flavored nut.

wasabi   Japanese horseradish, a fiery, pungent condiment used with many Japanese-style dishes. It's most often sold as a powder, so you add water to create a paste.

water chestnuts   A tuber, popular in many types of Asian-style cooking. The flesh is white, crunchy, and juicy, and the vegetable holds its texture whether cool or hot.

whisk   To rapidly mix, introducing air to the mixture.

white mushrooms   Button mushrooms. When fresh, they have an earthy smell and an appealing "soft crunch."

white vinegar   The most common type of vinegar, produced from grain.

whole-wheat flour   Wheat flour that contains the entire grain.

wild rice   Actually a grass with a rich, nutty flavor, popular as an unusual and nutritious side dish.

wine vinegar   Vinegar produced from red or white wine.

Worcestershire sauce   Originally developed in India and containing tamarind, this spicy sauce is used as a seasoning for many meats and other dishes.

zest   Small slivers of peel, usually from a citrus fruit such as a lemon, lime, or orange.

zester   A kitchen tool used to scrape zest off a fruit. A small grater also works well.

Troubleshooting Common Problems

Modern-day pressure cookers are virtually goof-proof, but accidents can happen. Here are some of the most common problems that occur with pressure cookers, along with probable causes and foolproof fixes. If you run into a problem not addressed here, contact your pressure cooker's customer service representative for help or advice. (For contact information for the major pressure cooker manufacturers in the United States, see Appendix C.)

I Can't Get the Lid to Close

Probable causes:

- The cover isn't centered on top of the pressure cooker.
- The rubber gasket isn't in the right position in the lid.

Foolproof fixes:

- Remove the lid, and be sure it's sitting squarely on top of the pot before trying to close it again. You should hear a click when the cover closes properly.
- Check the gasket, and be sure it's laying flat inside the groove of the lid.

My Pressure Cooker Lost Pressure

Probable causes:

- The burner or heat source isn't hot enough.
- There's not enough liquid in the pot to create steam.
- The rubber gasket is damaged or improperly placed and is breaking the seal between the lid and pot.

- The pressure regulator valve is dirty or has food particles lodged in it.

- The pressure cooker was dropped or damaged, which activated the safety valve, which in turn alerted the pressure cooker not to build pressure.

Foolproof fixes:

- Turn up the heat!

- Be sure there's at least 1 or 2 cups liquid in the pressure cooker, depending on the model.

- Double-check the gasket to be sure it's in the proper position and that it doesn't have any cracks or tears.

- Clean the pressure regulator valve according to the manufacturer's specifications.

- If the safety valve has been activated, it means your pressure cooker is damaged and needs repairs. Call the manufacturer for details on how to proceed.

My Pressure Cooker Is Leaking Steam

Probable causes:

- The cover isn't completely closed.

- The gasket is damaged or out of position.

- There's too much food and/or liquid in the pressure cooker. (Your pressure cooker should never be more than two-thirds full.)

Foolproof fixes:

- Use the quick release method to release any pressure that may have accumulated in the pressure cooker and then open and close the lid so it's properly positioned on top of the pot.

- Use the quick release method to release any pressure that may have accumulated in the pressure cooker. Then, open the lid and check to see if the gasket is properly positioned. Some gaskets have small holes or openings that must be lined up for the pressure cooker to operate properly. If the gasket has a crack or tear, replace it before using the pressure cooker again.

- Remove enough food or liquid from the pressure cooker so it's half full of food or two-thirds full of liquid.

- If the gasket has melted or bonded to pressure cooker, you can safely remove it using WD-40 or a similar solvent found in auto supply stores. Never use abrasive cleansers or solvents on your pressure cooker because they'll scratch and damage the finish.

The Lid Won't Budge

Probable causes:

- There's still some pressure remaining in the pot.

- A vacuum has formed.

- The lid wasn't properly positioned before you started cooking.

Foolproof fixes:

- Release any remaining pressure in the pressure cooker using the cold water release method and then try to open the lid again. Remember, safety features on modern-day pressure cookers make it impossible to open the lid if the pressure has not been released completely.

- If the lid still won't budge after releasing all the pressure, you're probably dealing with a vacuum. Over high heat, bring the food inside the pot to pressure again and then re-release the pressure using the quick release method.

- If the lid still won't budge, don't force it. Try applying a thin film of Vaseline to the gasket and the rim of the pressure cooker bottom to eliminate any resistance. Don't worry about the Vaseline burning—it can withstand higher heats than cooking oil.

Everything Came Out Mushy

Probable causes:

- The food was cooked too long under pressure.

Foolproof fixes:

- Be sure you start the cooking time when the pressure cooker reaches pressure, rather than when you put the pressure cooker on the burner.

- If you followed the recipe directions correctly, make a note that the cooking time is too long, and reduce it the next time you make that recipe.

- To eliminate guesswork, always use a digital timer that measures cooking time to the second.

PRESSURE POINTER

While most people wouldn't willingly turn string beans or pasta into mush, if you have a baby in the family, your pressure cooker could be your new best friend. You can create fast, easy, nutritious, and delicious baby food in your pressure cooker your infant will go goo-goo gaga over.

I Cracked a Filling on My Pressure-Cooked Beans

Probable causes:

- The heat is too low, so the pressure cooker didn't reach pressure.
- The pressure cooker didn't maintain pressure long enough.
- The beans weren't cooked long enough.

Foolproof fixes:

- Always bring the pressure cooker to pressure over high heat, unless otherwise specified in the recipe.

- Don't lower the heat until the pressure indicator valve indicates the pressure cooker has come to pressure, or the jiggler valve is jiggling and turning.

- To continue cooking food that's not quite done, remove the pressure cooker from heat, release the pressure using the quick release method, carefully remove the lid and reposition it so it sets squarely on top of the pressure cooker, and cook the food for another minute or two or until it's done.

The Food Burned and Is Stuck to the Bottom of the Pot

Probable causes:

- There isn't enough liquid in the dish to cook it properly.

- The heat was too high, so liquid evaporated and food burned and stuck to the bottom of the pressure cooker.

Foolproof fixes:

- Double-check the recipe to be sure you added enough liquid. If you followed the recipe, make a note to add more liquid the next time you make it.

- Electric burners can take a while to cool off. If you're using an electric stove, consider setting a second burner on low and moving the pressure cooker to the second burner after it has reached pressure.

- To remove burned or scorched food from the pressure cooker, follow cleaning and maintenance instructions in Chapter 1.

The Pressure Is Building, but the Pressure Indicator Isn't Rising

Probable cause:

- Food or dirt particles are lodged in the indicator and are causing it to stick.

Foolproof fix:

- Clean the pressure indicator following the manufacturer's directions.

My Pressure Cooker Has Lost Its Shine and Looks Old

Probable causes:

- High-acid foods, such as tomatoes and tomato sauce, can interact with aluminum and dull the finish.

- Hard water that contains lots of minerals can dull the finish and make it look cloudy.

- Dried beans can leave a cloudy deposit on the bottom of your pressure cooker.

- The heat was too high, or there wasn't enough liquid in the pressure cooker, so the food burned and scorched the finish.

- The pressure cooker was cleaned with abrasive cleansers that dulled the finish.

Foolproof fixes:

- To prevent acidic foods from dulling the finish of your pot, remove them from the pressure cooker as soon as they're done.

- Be sure you use enough liquid and oil to prevent food from burning and scorching. To remove scorch and burn marks from your pressure cooker, see cleaning directions in Chapter 1.

- To keep the outside of your pressure cooker mirror-shiny, clean it with non-abrasive cleansers.

Help! The Safety Valves Have Been Activated

Probable causes:

- You didn't lower the heat or remove the pressure cooker from the heat after it reached pressure.

Foolproof fixes:

- Reduce the heat to the lowest possible setting to maintain pressure.

- Always remove the pressure cooker from heat when it reaches the pressure specified in the recipe.

- Never exceed the pressure specified in the recipe. If you followed the directions and the food still didn't cook thoroughly, follow the fixes in the earlier "I Cracked a Filling on My Pressure-Cooked Beans" section.

Resources

Appendix

C

Whether you need repairs or parts, sometimes the best place to get help and advice is directly from your pressure cooker's manufacturer. The following list provides the addresses, phone numbers, and e-mail or website addresses for the customer service departments of today's most popular pressure cooker brands in the United States.

Because warranties and return policies differ from one manufacturer to the next, be sure to talk to a customer service representative before packing up your pressure cooker and sending it away for repairs, exchanges, or refunds. If you send your cooker to the wrong place, you may never see it again!

Fagor (Cook's Essentials Pressure Cookers)
Fagor America, Inc.
Box 94
Lyndhurst, NJ 07071
1-800-207-0806
info@fagoramerica.com
www.fagoramerica.com

Hawkins Futura
Bay City International
Box 11706
Green Bay, WI 54307
920-339-0510
baycitygb@aol.com
www.baycityintl.com

Innova
Innova, Inc.
409 West 76th Street
Davenport, IA 52806
1-800-767-5160
www.innova.com

Kuhn Rikon (Duromatic Pressure Cookers)
Kuhn Rikon Corporation
350 Bon Air Center #240
Greenbrae, CA 94904
415-461-3927
kuhnrikon@kuhnrikon.com
www.kuhnrikon.com

Magefesa
North American Promotions, Ltd.
1232 West NW Highway
Palatine, IL 60067
1-888-787-9991
napl@interaccess.com
www.magefesausa.com

Manttra
Manttra, Inc.
5721 Bayside Road, Suite J
Virginia Beach, VA 23455
877-962-6887
fax: 757-318-7604
www.manttra.com

Mirro
Mirro Company
1512 Washington Street
Manitowoc, WI 54220
1-800-527-7727
moreinfo@mirro.com
www.mirro.com

Presto
National Presto Industries, Inc.
3925 North Hastings Way
Eau Claire, WI 55703
1-800-877-0441
contact@GoPresto.com
www.presto-net.com

T-Fal
T-Fal Corporation
25 Riverside Drive
Pine Brook, NJ 07058
1-800-395-8325
askt-fal@t-fal.com
www.t-falusa.com

Index

G

W-X-Y-Z